Communications in Computer and Information Science **2809**

Rationale

The CCIS series is devoted to the publication of proceedings of computer science conferences. Its aim is to efficiently disseminate original research results in informatics in printed and electronic form. While the focus is on publication of peer-reviewed full papers presenting mature work, inclusion of reviewed short papers reporting on work in progress is welcome, too. Besides globally relevant meetings with internationally representative program committees guaranteeing a strict peer-reviewing and paper selection process, conferences run by societies or of high regional or national relevance are also considered for publication.

Topics

The topical scope of CCIS spans the entire spectrum of informatics ranging from foundational topics in the theory of computing to information and communications science and technology and a broad variety of interdisciplinary application fields.

Information for Volume Editors and Authors

Publication in CCIS is free of charge. No royalties are paid, however, we offer registered conference participants temporary free access to the online version of the conference proceedings on SpringerLink (http://link.springer.com) by means of an http referrer from the conference website and/or a number of complimentary printed copies, as specified in the official acceptance email of the event.

CCIS proceedings can be published in time for distribution at conferences or as post-proceedings, and delivered in the form of printed books and/or electronically as USBs and/or e-content licenses for accessing proceedings at SpringerLink. Furthermore, CCIS proceedings are included in the CCIS electronic book series hosted in the SpringerLink digital library at http://link.springer.com/bookseries/7899. Conferences publishing in CCIS are allowed to use our online conference service (Meteor) for managing the whole proceedings lifecycle (from submission and reviewing to preparing for publication) free of charge.

Publication process

The language of publication is exclusively English. Authors publishing in CCIS have to sign the Springer CCIS copyright transfer form, however, they are free to use their material published in CCIS for substantially changed, more elaborate subsequent publications elsewhere. For the preparation of the camera-ready papers/files, authors have to strictly adhere to the Springer CCIS Authors' Instructions and are strongly encouraged to use the CCIS LaTeX style files or templates.

Abstracting/Indexing

CCIS is abstracted/indexed in DBLP, Google Scholar, EI-Compendex, Mathematical Reviews, SCImago, Scopus. CCIS volumes are also submitted for the inclusion in ISI Proceedings.

How to start

To start the evaluation of your proposal for inclusion in the CCIS series, please send an e-mail to ccis@springer.com

Jiancheng Chi · Hong Yu · Lei Wang ·
Zichuan Xu
Editors

CCF Computer Network Teaching and Computer Network Engineering Discipline Construction

16th CCF Symposium, CNETCNED 2025
Dalian, China, August 18–20, 2025
Proceedings

Springer

Editors
Jiancheng Chi
Dalian University of Technology
Dalian City, China

Hong Yu
Dalian University of Technology
Dalian City, China

Lei Wang
Dalian University of Technology
Dalian City, China

Zichuan Xu
Dalian University of Technology
Dalian City, China

ISSN 1865-0929 ISSN 1865-0937 (electronic)
Communications in Computer and Information Science
ISBN 978-981-95-7123-9 ISBN 978-981-95-7124-6 (eBook)
https://doi.org/10.1007/978-981-95-7124-6

This Springer imprint is published by the registered company Springer Nature Singapore Pte Ltd.
The registered company address is: 152 Beach Road, #21-01/04 Gateway East, Singapore 189721, Singapore

Preface

This volume contains the fourteen papers presented at the 16th CCF Symposium on Computer Network Teaching and Network Engineering Discipline Construction (CNETC-NED 2025), which was an event devoted to exploring emerging teaching methodologies, intelligent educational technologies, and novel pedagogical practices in the rapidly evolving field of computing. The contributions included in this volume stem from teaching reform initiatives, research-oriented coursework, laboratory innovation projects, and collaborative educational experiments conducted by instructors and students across multiple institutions.

In recent years, artificial intelligence—especially AIGC technologies and large language models—has profoundly reshaped the landscape of computer science education. Intelligent development assistants, automated code generation, adaptive learning platforms, virtual experimentation frameworks, and data-driven evaluation systems have brought new opportunities for enhancing the effectiveness of instruction. These developments enable more personalized, interactive, and efficient learning experiences, while challenging educators to rethink course design, assessment structures, and competency cultivation strategies. The works presented in this volume reflect the diverse ways in which instructors and students have begun to integrate these capabilities into practical teaching environments.

The topics addressed by the papers span a broad and interdisciplinary range of themes. Several contributions propose AIGC-empowered teaching modes for comprehensive course design, demonstrating how intelligent programming assistants and automated evaluation tools can support students' development of algorithmic thinking and engineering practice. Other works introduce LLM-assisted laboratory methodologies that improve experimental efficiency and promote deeper conceptual understanding. A number of papers focus on the redesign of computer network curricula, including SPOC+BOPPPS-based teaching frameworks, outcome-oriented assessment systems, and innovative mechanisms for course content organization in the era of intelligence.

Additional contributions explore data-driven approaches to educational management, communication technologies applied in instructional scenarios, UAV-related course frameworks, and machine-learning-based techniques for analyzing and enhancing security education. Together, these papers present a holistic perspective on the future direction of computer science education, highlighting the growing need for intelligent support tools, practice-oriented models, interdisciplinary integration, and continuous curricular innovation.

A total of 14 papers were selected for inclusion in this volume. Each paper underwent review and discussion by the organizing committee and invited domain experts. The selected works were chosen based on their originality, practical relevance, methodological rigor, and contribution to advancing adhere to the traditional structure of a formal academic conference, the quality of the submissions reflects significant effort and innovation on the part of the authors, as well as the increasing interest in intelligent, data-driven approaches to computer science pedagogy.

We would like to express our sincere appreciation to all authors for their valuable contributions, insightful ideas, and dedication to improving computing education. We also extend our gratitude to the educators and researchers who provided constructive feedback during the review and discussion process, as well as to the project teams and institutions whose support and coordination made the preparation of this volume possible. Their collective efforts have been instrumental in ensuring the high quality and cohesive vision presented throughout this collection.

We hope that the papers included in this volume will inspire further exploration of innovative teaching models, encourage the adoption of intelligent educational technologies, and support ongoing efforts toward improving the learning experience of students in computer science and related fields. It is our hope that this compilation will serve as both a reference and a catalyst for educators, researchers, and practitioners committed to advancing the future of computing education.

August 2025

Jiancheng Chi
Hong Yu
Lei Wang
Zichuan Xu

Organization

General Co-chairs

Zhongxuan Luo	Dalian University of Technology, China
Zongli Jiang	Beijing University of Technology, China
Xingwei Wang	Northeastern University, China
Li Zhang	Beihang University, China
Keqiu Li	Tianjin University, China

Program Committee Co-chairs

Mingwei Xu	Tsinghua University, China
Guang Cheng	Southeast University, China
Wei Li	Southeast University, China
Xin Fan	Dalian University of Technology, China
Na Lei	Dalian University of Technology, China

Program Committee Members

Guangwei Bai	Nanjing Tech University, China
Jiangtao Cui	Xidian University, China
Xiaolin Gui	Xi'an Jiaotong University, China
Qian He	Guilin University of Electronic Technology, China
Lei Lei	Nanjing University of Aeronautics and Astronautics, China
Junhuai Li	Xi'an University of Technology, China
Zhikun Liu	Xi'an Shiyou University, China
Yan Ma	Beijing University of Posts and Telecommunications, China
Gang Sun	Huawei Technologies Co., Ltd., China
Runyuan Sun	University of Jinan, China
Huobin Tan	Beihang University, China
Shaohua Teng	Guangdong University of Technology, China
Hai Wang	Northwest University, China
Lei Wang	Dalian University of Technology, China

Wendong Wang	Beijing University of Posts and Telecommunications, China
Libing Wu	Wuhan University, China
Xiaoyan Xie	Xi'an University of Posts and Telecommunications, China
Bo Xu	PLA Army Engineering University, China
Ming Xu	National University of Defense Technology, China
Shuangxiu Yi	Northeastern University, China
Haibo Zhang	Higher Education Press, China
Lijun Zhang	Beihang University, China
Xiaoning Zhang	University of Electronic Science and Technology of China, China

Organizing Committee Co-chairs

Baokang Zhao	National University of Defense Technology, China
Hai Wang	Northwest University, China
Huobin Tan	Beihang University, China
Lin Lin	Dalian University of Technology, China
Lei Wang	Dalian University of Technology, China
Cheng Guo	Dalian University of Technology, China
Hong Yu	Dalian University of Technology, China

Organizing Committee Members

Zichuan Xu	Dalian University of Technology, China
Jie Wang	Dalian University of Technology, China
Hao Wang	Dalian University of Technology, China
Jiancheng Chi	Dalian University of Technology, China
Han Liu	Dalian University of Technology, China
Pengfei Wang	Dalian University of Technology, China
Xiaotong Zhang	Dalian University of Technology, China
Xiaowei Zhao	Dalian University of Technology, China
Linlin Tian	Dalian University of Technology, China
Qiufen Xia	Dalian University of Technology, China
Liangtian Wan	Dalian University of Technology, China
Weifeng Sun	Dalian University of Technology, China
Kun Lu	Dalian University of Technology, China

Jiankang Ren	Dalian University of Technology, China
Jing Gao	Dalian University of Technology, China
Liang Zhao	Dalian University of Technology, China
Fangming Zhong	Dalian University of Technology, China
Heng Qi	Dalian University of Technology, China
Lin Yao	Dalian University of Technology, China
Zheng Zhao	Dalian University of Technology, China

Contents

Data Management and Security

Communications and Networking Technologies

Educational Technology and Emerging DomainsTeaching

Teaching Reform and AIGC-empowered Education

The Cultural Confidence Cultivation Plan in the Four New Constructions–A Case Study of the "Computer Networks" Course

Wei Li[1(✉)], Lizhen Cui[1], and Hongji Xu[2]

[1] School of Software, Shandong University, Jinan 250101, Shandong, China
wli1@sdu.edu.cn
[2] School of Information Science and Engineering, Shandong University, Qingdao 266237, Shandong, China

Abstract. Addressing the issue of engineering students do not have enough confidence in traditional Chinese culture, it is proposed to reshape the culture of engineering education, focusing on themes such as national sentiments, cultural literacy, and moral cultivation. By exploring the intrinsic connection between the knowledge system of new engineering courses and traditional Chinese cultural ideas, a systematic plan for cultivating cultural confidence is presented. Taking the "Computer Networks" course as an example, through innovative course content design, teaching methods, and optimization of practical teaching stages, the aim is to help students, while mastering professional knowledge, enhance their identification with and pride in excellent traditional Chinese culture, and cultivate high-quality talents with international vision and cultural confidence.

Keywords: Four New Constructions · Cultural Confidence · Computer Networks · Curriculum Ideological · Political Education

1 Introduction

General Secretary Xi Jinping emphasized during his inspection at Tsinghua University in April 2021 that we should "advance the development of 'Four New Disciplines' – new engineering, new medicine, new agriculture, and new liberal arts". This important statement places the advancement of "Four New Disciplines" in the context of building a first-class university system, making good use of the "catalyst" of interdisciplinary integration, adjusting and upgrading the existing disciplinary and professional system, targeting cutting-edge science and technology and key fields, and accelerating the training of urgently needed talents. It indicates that the development of "Four New Disciplines" is closely linked to the optimization of disciplines and specialties, the improvement of innovation capabilities, the integration of industry, academia, research and application, and the cultivation of new people for the times.

J. Chi et al. (Eds.): CNETCNED 2025, CCIS 2809, pp. 3–10, 2026.
https://doi.org/10.1007/978-981-95-7124-6_1

The development of "Four New Disciplines" is a "Chinese Solution" for talent cultivation in higher education and a strategic layout for the high-quality development of higher education. Further advancing the development of "Four New Disciplines" can promote their interdisciplinary integration and enhance the country's hard power, the health of the whole people, ecological growth capacity, and cultural influence [1].

From the 18th National Congress of the Communist Party of China General Secretary Xi Jinping has mentioned cultural confidence on many occasions, emphasizing the need to "uphold confidence in the path, theory, system, and culture of socialism with Chinese characteristics, adhere unswervingly to the Party's basic line, and continue to advance the great cause of socialism with Chinese characteristics". He pointed out that cultural confidence is the "more fundamental, broader, and deeper" confidence, highlighting the fundamental status of cultural confidence and guiding college students to move from cultural identity to cultural confidence.

From the overall perspective of the Party and the country's cause, the Report to the 19th National Congress of the Communist Party of China put forward the connotation and essence of cultural confidence in the new era: "Without a high degree of cultural confidence and the prosperity and development of culture, there will be no great rejuvenation of the Chinese nation. We must adhere to the path of socialist cultural development with Chinese characteristics, stimulate the vitality of cultural innovation and creation of the whole nation, and build a socialist cultural power." Socialist culture with Chinese characteristics originates from the fine traditional Chinese culture nurtured by the more than 5,000-year-long civilization history of the Chinese nation and is rooted in the great practice of socialism with Chinese characteristics. Contemporary college students are the hope of the country and the future of the nation, so fostering their strong cultural confidence is particularly important, which is the focus of ideological and political education for college students at present.

The Report to the 20th National Congress of the Communist Party of China emphasizes that "we must stay firmly confident in our history and culture" and "continuously enhance China's cultural soft power and the international influence of Chinese culture". Culture is the soul of a country and a nation. Without a high degree of cultural confidence and the prosperity of culture, there will be no great rejuvenation of the Chinese nation. Only when we are confident and self-reliant in culture can we confidently spread our culture to the world.

Contemporary college students are impacted by diverse cultural trends, and some show a tendency of worshipping foreign things while belittling their own. This is manifested in their insufficient understanding of the contemporary value of China's traditional culture, lack of in-depth comprehension of the spiritual connotation of our culture, inadequate overall grasp of China's advanced culture, and a tendency of blind admiration for Western culture. All these are signs of college students' lack of cultural confidence [2]. Due to the characteristics of their majors, most science and engineering students, compared with liberal arts students, are less exposed to and influenced by traditional Chinese culture.

Therefore, it is more necessary to organically integrate the ideas of traditional Chinese culture into the design of professional courses, so as to cultivate professional and technical talents while enhancing students' cultural confidence.

2 The Importance of Cultural Confidence in the Four New Constructions Development

2.1 The Connotation of Cultural Confidence

Cultural confidence refers to a country, a nation, or a political party's full affirmation of the value of its own culture and firm belief in the vitality of its own culture. It is a more fundamental, extensive, and profound confidence, as well as a more basic, deep-rooted, and enduring force. Its connotation is not a one-dimensional cultural identity, but an organic whole composed of historical foundations, value cores, practical orientations, and global perspectives. [3] [4]

2.2 The Significance of Cultural Confidence in the Four New Constructions

The importance of cultural confidence education in cultivating new individuals for the era cannot be overlooked. Through systematic cultural confidence education, students can deeply penetrate the surface of excellent traditional Chinese culture, correctly understand its long-standing developmental context from a historically profound perspective, and deeply comprehend the ideological connotations within, such as the ecological wisdom of "harmony between heaven and man," the philosophy of "unity in diversity," and the national sentiment of "the rise or fall of the world is the responsibility of the individual." From the bottom of their hearts, they develop a strong identification with Chinese civilization, thereby solidifying the spiritual foundation of national pride.

At the same time, in the current era where various cultural trends are interacting, cultural confidence is like a spiritual immune system, significantly enhancing university students' ability to discern and resist Western adverse cultures (such as extreme individualism, materialism, etc.), enabling them to maintain clear cognition in the cultural wave and consciously guard the value baseline of local culture. Especially in the context of globalization, cultural confidence endows contemporary youth with cultural responsibility, assisting them in actively shouldering the era's mission to inherit and innovate advanced socialist culture, leading the direction of cultural development with an open vision and firm beliefs, and becoming a pioneering force with both cultural confidence and a global perspective in the great journey of national rejuvenation.

3 Strategies for Cultivating Cultural Confidence in the "Computer Networking" Course

3.1 Curriculum Content Design

In the teaching of computer network technology, deepening cultural self-confidence education through multi-dimensional teaching strategies can effectively stimulate students' national pride and cultural identity. During teaching, elements of excellent Chinese traditional culture are cleverly integrated into the course content, such as analyzing the essential connection between the design philosophy of network system architecture and the holistic view and systematic thinking in traditional culture, allowing students to deeply understand the intrinsic origin of computer network technology and traditional culture.

At the same time, by combining the outstanding detection capabilities of the "Tianyan" project, the global leading advantages of 5G technology, and the innovative breakthroughs of "Star Flash" technology, major achievements of China in the field of computer networks are explained through vivid cases to showcase the country's technological strength and ignite students' national pride. Furthermore, by systematically comparing the development history of computer network technology between China and foreign countries, students are guided to adopt an international perspective, not only learning from foreign advanced experiences but also strengthening their confidence in indigenous culture, achieving an organic integration of traditional cultural heritage and modern technological development.

3.2 Teaching Method Innovation

Innovative teaching methods are a key path to deepening education in cultural confidence. First, the case teaching method is used to introduce successful experiences of Chinese internet enterprises such as Huawei and Alibaba Cloud, which have broken through international barriers with independent research and development technologies and spread Chinese innovative concepts. This guides students to deeply ponder how cultural confidence can inject spiritual energy into technological development, closely integrating theoretical knowledge with vivid practice. Next, using the group discussion method, topics such as "how cultural confidence can empower innovation in computer network technology" and "insights from traditional cultural thinking on cybersecurity concepts" are discussed, encouraging students to engage in critical thinking and to generate new insights from diverse cultural perspectives through team collaboration.

Furthermore, relying on the project-driven approach, projects with Chinese cultural characteristics like "digital exhibition halls of intangible cultural heritage" and "interactive mini-programs for traditional festivals" are designed and developed. This allows students to transform cultural elements into technological achievements throughout the entire process of requirement analysis, architecture design, and code implementation, thereby significantly enhancing their identification with local culture and their ability to innovate in its application.

3.3 Optimization of Practical Teaching

Constructing a "practice-industry-culture" trinity education model can truly ground the education of cultural confidence. By setting up culture-themed practical projects such as "Network Application Development Based on Traditional Culture", students are guided to integrate cultural elements like the imagery in

The Book of Songs and the Twenty-Four Solar Terms into professional practices such as network interface design and data visualization. In the process of coding and system construction, the in-depth integration of cultural symbols and technical logic is realized, transforming cultural confidence from abstract cognition into tangible innovative achievements. Relying on the school-enterprise cooperation platform, experts from enterprises such as Huawei and Tencent are invited to enter the classroom. Combining practical cases like the "Digital Palace Museum Relics Library" and the "Dunhuang Feitian Virtual Roaming System", they share how to integrate cultural confidence into the technology R&D process and product design concepts. This enables students to understand the internal connection between cultural genes and technological competitiveness from the perspective of the industrial frontline, while improving their practical abilities and cultural awareness.

In addition, organizing cultural exhibition activities such as the "Computer Network Technology and Traditional Chinese Culture" thematic exhibition and the "Digital Cultural Heritage Protection Technology" roadshow, and encouraging students to transform their course project achievements into visual cultural communication carriers—such as cultural relic tracing systems based on blockchain and AR-restored network models of ancient architectures—can deepen their recognition of cultural value through interdisciplinary collaboration and public display, thus forming a closed-loop for cultivating cultural confidence where practice drives innovation, industry enhances cognition, and exhibition strengthens recognition.

4 Case Analysis

This section introduces several cases in which computer network technology is associated with Chinese traditional culture.

4.1 Network Architecture and the Idea of "Unity of Man and Nature"

Network Architecture: Computer networks often adopt a layered architecture, such as the OSI seven-layer model or the TCP/IP four-layer model, where each layer has its specific functions and responsibilities, and they collaborate with each other to achieve data transmission and communication. This layered architecture reflects an orderly and clearly divided system design philosophy.

"The Unity of Heaven and Man" Concept: In Chinese traditional culture, "the unity of heaven and man" emphasizes the harmonious integration between humans and nature, viewing all things in heaven and earth as an interrelated and interdependent whole.

In computer networks, the collaboration between layers is similar to the interdependence of everything in nature, together forming an organic network system to achieve the overall communication function, reflecting a similar holistic and systematic view.

4.2 Data Transmission and the Philosophy of "Harmony in Diversity"

Data Transmission: In computer networks, data is transmitted in various formats and protocols, such as text, images, audio, and video. They are encoded, transmitted, and decoded according to certain rules within the network, eventually being restored to their original form at the receiving end. Different types of data can coexist harmoniously and be accurately transmitted in the network without interfering with each other.

"Harmony in Diversity" Philosophy: Traditional Chinese culture advocates for "harmony in diversity", emphasizing the pursuit of harmony and unity amidst diversity. In data transmission, various types of data are like different individuals or cultural elements in society, each with their unique characteristics and value. Yet, they can cooperate and transmit together in the broader environment of the network, realizing the exchange and sharing of information, embodying the cultural essence of "harmony in diversity".

4.3 Channel Competition Mechanism and the Cultural Landscape of "Modesty and Humility"

Channel Competition Mechanism: Fair Channel Competition Mechanism p-persistent CSMA, where p represents the probability of a station sending data when it detects an idle public channel. The smaller the value of p, the smaller the chance of collision, and the greater the chance of successful transmission for the station. If the value of p is 1, meaning all stations compete for the right to use the channel when they detect it's idle, the likelihood of system conflict increases.

"Humility and Courtesy": Humility and courtesy are the traditional virtues of the Chinese nation and are one of the essences of Chinese culture. In "The Analects·Learning", it is written, "The use of manners is valuable for harmony." This emphasizes that the role of etiquette is to promote harmony, and being courteous is one of the important means to achieve it. In real society, the more one rushes for immediate gain, the more likely it is to backfire, thus guiding students to correctly understand the wisdom of China that spans thousands of years.

4.4 Cybersecurity and the Concept of "Guarding Against Minor Issues Before They Become Major Problems"

Network Security: Computer networks face various security threats such as hacker attacks, virus intrusions, and data leaks. In order to ensure network security, a series of security measures need to be adopted, such as firewalls, encryption technology, and intrusion detection systems. These measures aim to prevent potential security risks and protect the data and resources in the network.

"Preventive Measurement": In traditional Chinese culture, there is a concept of "preventive measurement", emphasizing taking measures to prevent problems when they are still in the budding stage, avoiding their development into serious issues. In the field of network security, deploying various security protection measures in advance is a manifestation of "preventive measurement". By timely identifying and addressing potential security risks, it prevents the occurrence of network security incidents, ensuring the stable operation of the network system.

4.5 Network Communication Protocol and the Norm of "Etiquette"

Network Communication Protocol: Network communication protocols are the rules and standards for data transmission and interaction in computer networks. They specify the format of data, transmission methods, the meaning of signals, etc., ensuring that different devices and systems can communicate accurately and efficiently with each other.

The Norm of "Li"(ritual Propriety): In traditional Chinese culture, "Li" is a behavioral norm and moral standard that constrains people's words and deeds, allowing social interactions to proceed in an orderly manner. Network communication protocols are like the "Li" of the online world, establishing clear behavioral standards for devices and systems in the network. Only by following these standards can network communication proceed smoothly, reflecting a cultural value of order and norm.

4.6 Distributed Systems and the Spirit of "Unity Enables Us to Achieve Long-Term Goals"

Distributed Systems: A distributed system in computer networks consists of multiple nodes distributed across different geographical locations, but interconnected through the network to collaborate and complete tasks together. In a distributed system, each node can share resources and divide the load. Improve the reliability and performance of the system.

"The Spirit of Unity and Progression": In traditional Chinese culture, there are sayings such as "It's hard for one to lift, but easy for many to move forward" and "Many hands make light work", emphasizing the power of teamwork and collective effort. Nodes in a distributed system collaborate like a team, with each node playing its role to achieve the common goal of the system. This embodies the cultural spirit of "unity and progression", where greater achievements can be accomplished through cooperation and collaboration.

5 Conclusions

In the context of the "Four New" construction, integrating cultural self-confidence cultivation into engineering courses such as software engineering is of great significance. "Computer Networks", as a core course in software engineering, has a high degree of practicality and cutting-edge characteristics, serving as an important medium for cultivating students' cultural self-confidence. Through innovative course content design, teaching methods, and optimization of practical teaching segments, students' awareness of cultural self-confidence and professional competence can be effectively enhanced. In addition, several cases linking computer network technology with traditional Chinese culture are also listed. The teaching team should further explore and refine the cultural self-confidence cultivation plan, promote the deep integration of professional courses and cultural self-confidence education, and cultivate more high-quality talents with international vision and cultural self-confidence.

References

1. Stay true to the original aspiration and continue to move forward, Xinhua News Agency series interpretation (2021). http://www.xinhuanet.com/syzt/bwcxjxqj/. Accesssed 10 Mar 2025
2. Pinghua, X.: Party construction work of university foreign language major students from the perspective of cultural confidence. J. Higher Educ. **1**, 183–185 (2018)
3. Chen,. B.: Comprehensively promote the construction of the "Four New" and accelerate the training of outstanding talents for the new era. China's High. Educ. **2020**(1), 4–6
4. Zhang, D.: Leading the high-quality development of higher education with the "Four New" Construction. China's High. Educ. **2020**(2), 12–14

Whole-Process Experimental Assessment Method Based on NFV+SPOC

Bo Xu(✉), Xiulei Wang, Changyou Xing, and Yifan Hu

Command and Control Engineering College, Army Engineering University, Nanjing 210007, China
xubo820@163.com

Abstract. This paper constructs a cyber security experimental platform based on NFV technology. By establishing a virtual network element resource pool and providing functions for automatic deployment of virtual networks and automatic parameter configuration, it helps students quickly set up various experimental environments for cyber security courses. Meanwhile, the experimental platform is integrated with the SPOC teaching system to realize a whole-process experimental assessment for the course. This assessment mechanism can quantitatively evaluate every practical link in the learning process, which not only provides teachers with timely feedback on experimental effects but also helps supervise and stimulate students' learning enthusiasm.

Keywords: NFV · virtual network · cyberspace · SPOC teaching system · whole-process assessment

1 Preface

Cyberspace has gradually developed into the fifth-dimensional strategic space following the seas, land, sky, and air, exerting a crucial impact on national security, economic development, and social stability [1]. Therefore, cultivating application-oriented technical talents in the field of cyberspace security who meet the needs of national security strategies and possess professional skills and innovative awareness is an important responsibility and mission for colleges and universities offering cyberspace security programs [2]. The experiment course plays a vital role in cultivating students' learning, practical, and innovative abilities. However, the experimental teaching courses of the cyberspace security major have high requirements for the experimental environment, which to a certain extent restricts the development of innovative experimental teaching. This is mainly reflected in the following aspects. Firstly, it is impractical to carry out real network attack and defense experiments on the actually operating campus network. The campus network provides communication services for various applications, and any experiment that may cause network instability cannot be conducted in the real network. Secondly, establishing an experimental environment

J. Chi et al. (Eds.): CNETCNED 2025, CCIS 2809, pp. 11–18, 2026.
https://doi.org/10.1007/978-981-95-7124-6_2

that is interconnected with the campus network, can be used for various network attack and defense course experiments, and has the characteristics of a real network is not feasible in terms of time, funds, and management. Thirdly, establishing an experimental environment that is isolated from the campus network, with simple scenarios and small scale, lacks the realism of the network and limits the space and time for students to conduct experimental learning. When students carry out course experiments intensively, the experimental network environment also has shortcomings such as long maintenance cycles, high guarantee costs, and difficulty in summarizing and analyzing experimental results. Therefore, in the face of the problem that a large number of network attack and defense experiments are difficult to carry out effectively, an efficient, economical, and user-friendly innovative technology is needed. It should be able to efficiently and flexibly build various network experimental environments, providing support for experimental teaching environments to cultivate high-level, sophisticated, and cutting-edge professionals in cyberspace security. This paper proposes a method for constructing a virtual experiment platform for cyberspace security based on Network Function Virtualization (NFV) technology [3]. By selecting open-source virtual machine software, it creates virtual routers, switches, and client machines in general-purpose hardware servers to build a virtual network element resource pool. A dynamic scheduling model for virtual resources and a rapid generation method for virtual network experiment environments are designed. According to the XML network environment description files provided by users, the system can quickly generate corresponding experiment environments and complete parameter configuration for each virtual unit [4]. In addition, it integrates with the existing SPOC teaching system through interface calls, facilitating the use of virtual experiment environments for both students and teachers.

2 Experimental Platform Architecture

The design of the system architecture for the virtual experiment platform should adhere to the following basic principles: (1) Implement virtual network experiment environments based on NFV; (2) All types of virtual network devices can interconnect and communicate with each other; (3) The configuration of virtual network experiment environments can be flexibly modified; (4) The functions and performance of virtual networks are consistent with those of real network environments. Based on the above principles, the system architecture of the virtual experiment platform is designed, as shown in Fig. 1. This architecture consists of four layers: the application interface layer, the virtualized network element resource pool, the virtualization software, and the virtualized hardware platform [5]. The virtualized hardware platform refers to physical hardware servers that support the operation of virtualization software. To enable simultaneous experiments across multiple courses and for multiple students, a server cluster is required. The virtualization software mainly includes virtual machines and various virtualization components, such as virtual network components, virtual client components, and virtual security components, which run in virtual machines. The bottom three layers provide basic support for virtualized networks. All virtualization components support the TCP/IP protocol stack and can accommodate experimental environments for various cyberspace security courses. The application interface primarily receives virtual network deployment files sent by users, generates corresponding experiment environments according to the network environment descriptions and parameter configuration information in the files, and displays them to users via web pages.

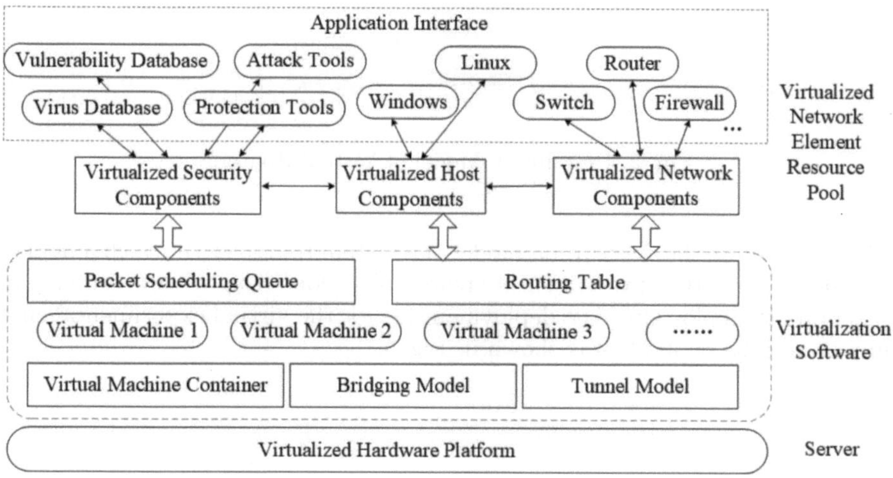

Fig. 1. System Architecture of the Virtual Experiment Platform.

3 Construction of Experimental Environment

In the virtual experiment platform, formal methods are adopted to describe the deployment and control process of the network experimental environment. The application interface receives, interprets and executes the experimental environment description files and control files to complete the deployment and control of the experimental environment, which greatly simplifies the design and use process of various experimental environments.

3.1 Definition and Deployment of Experimental Environment

The interface of the virtual experiment platform provides formal description models for various virtual network elements. Teachers can directly describe the deployment of the experimental environment in XML files according to the definitions of these models, or use the user graphical interface to generate deployment files with software assistance.

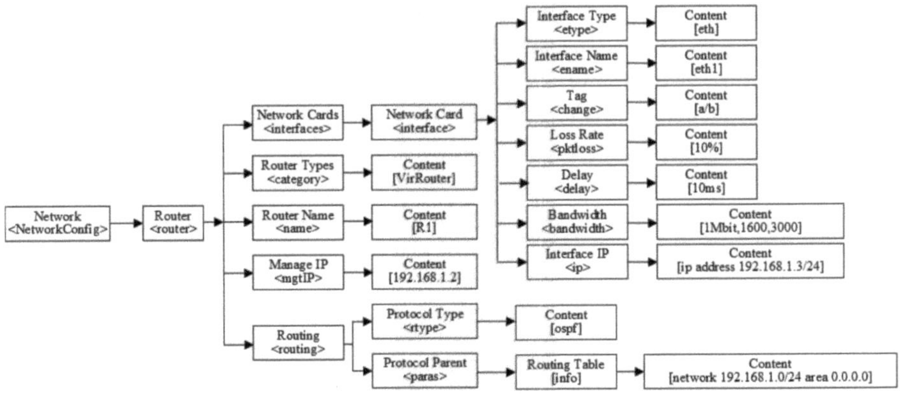

Fig. 2. Description Model of Virtual Router.

Figure 2 shows the description model of a virtual router, with which a deployment file for a virtual experimental environment consisting of two routers can be generated. "deploy.xml" is a deployment file for the virtual experimental environment, and its content is as shown in Fig. 3.

```
<NetworkConfig>
   <router>
      <name>n1</name>
      <Interfaces>
         <interface><ename>eth1</ename>
          <ip>10.0.0.1</ip> </interface>
      </Interfaces>
      <routing><rtype>ospf</rtype></routing>
   </router>
   <router>
      <name>n2</name>
      <Interfaces>
         <interface><ename>eth1</ename>
          <ip>10.0.0.2</ip></interface>
      </Interfaces>
      <routing><rtype>ospf</rtype></routing>
   </router>
</NetworkConfig>
```

Fig. 3. Deployment File Content (deploy.xml).

Submit the virtual experimental environment deployment file "deploy.xml" to the interface of the virtual experiment platform, and the platform will return the virtual experimental environment as shown in Fig. 4.

Fig. 4. Example of Virtual Experimental Environment.

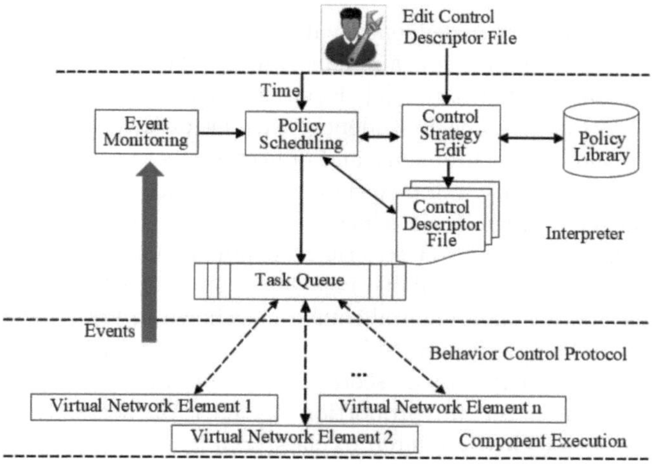

Fig. 5. Behavior Control Architecture of Virtual Network Elements.

3.2 Control of Virtual Network Element Behavior

In some network attack and defense experiments, the defender will take corresponding protective actions based on the attacker's behavior. In this case, teachers need to design the autonomous protection behavior of the experimental environment. The platform provides a method for describing the behavior of virtual network elements based on the XML format. By preparing control description files, the behavior of virtual network elements can be controlled. After receiving the control description file, the platform interface first parses the control file through the behavior control module in the interface, and inserts the parsed control strategies into the task queue. Secondly, when a control strategy is triggered, it communicates with the virtual component through the behavior control protocol to execute the preset behavior actions, thereby realizing autonomous protection. The behavior control architecture of virtual network elements is shown in Fig. 5.

Teachers create control description files using a graphical editing tool. They can either directly create a control description file or copy an existing one, modify it, and form a new file. The created control description file can be submitted to the interpretation and execution program through the user interface for execution at an appropriate time. Driven by events and time, the interpretation and execution program insert control strategies into the task queue in sequence. After the virtual experiment scenario is opened, a unified clock runs to execute control strategies in chronological order. The control platform communicates with virtual components using a behavior control protocol to control their behavioral actions.

4 Whole-Process Course Experiment Assessment

Teaching whole-process management means that teachers pay attention to every link of students' learning process and can evaluate their course grades based on their comprehensive performance [6]. From the start to the end of the course, teachers can keep track of each student's learning quality, progress and effect, timely identify and correct problems, and urge students to complete course learning tasks with high quality. Figure 6 shows the schematic diagram of the whole-process management stage, from which it can be seen that teachers can adopt a variety of different evaluation criteria to conduct quantitative assessment of learning effects. Based on the above idea, we propose a whole-process-oriented assessment method for experimental courses, as shown in Fig. 7. The total score of the experimental course is divided into three categories: extra-curricular experiment scores, in-class experiment scores, and experimental assessment scores, each accounting for a certain proportion of the total score. Extra-curricular experiment scores are closely related to classroom teaching, enabling the assessment of students' experimental abilities in every learning link. In the pre-class preview stage, after students' complete preview experiments, teachers can adjust teaching content based on the results. During in-class experiments, teachers can real-time grasp students' understanding and application of new skills, and assign targeted after-class review experiments. In the after-class review stage, students complete group collaborative experiments to make up for the shortcomings of in-class experiments and ensure the quality of practical teaching. In the experimental process, besides focusing on students' learning effects, attention should also be paid to their emotions, attitudes, and values demonstrated, such as their ability to cooperate with peers, observe and analyze, express themselves, and practice innovation. Therefore, extra-curricular experiments include assessments of experimental contribution and team spirit. Quantitative scoring of each link guides

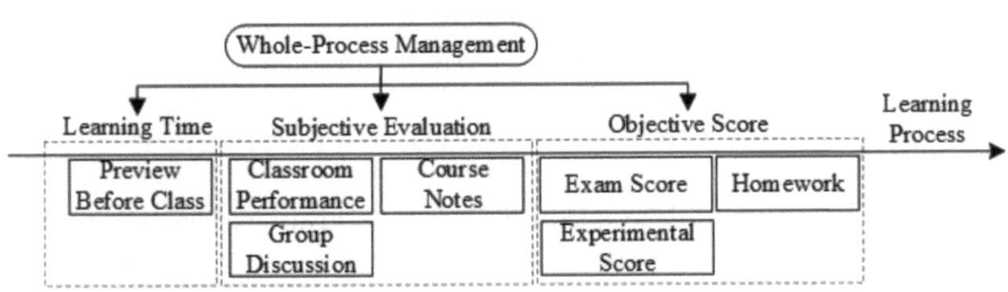

Fig. 6. Schematic Diagram of the Whole-Process Teaching Management Stages.

students to actively complete all experiments and cultivates their comprehensive abilities. The previous final comprehensive experimental assessment score is expanded to mid-term and stage experimental assessments, thereby enhancing students' enthusiasm for completing experiments and the comprehensiveness of experimental assessments.

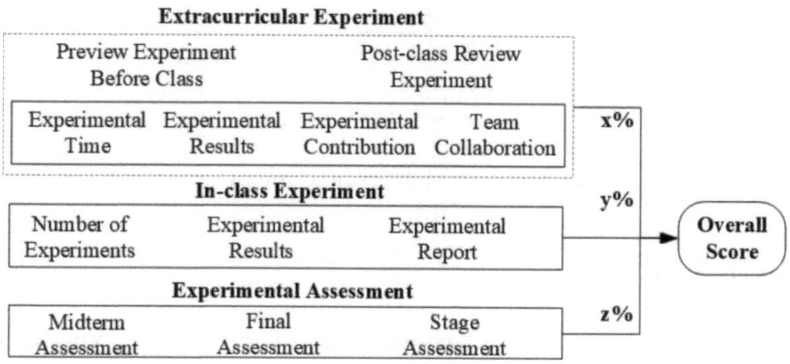

Fig. 7. Schematic Diagram of the Whole-Process Experimental Course Assessment Methods.

5 Coupling with the SPOC Teaching System

The above-mentioned whole-process experiment assessment method places high demands on teachers. To achieve the above assessment goals and reduce teachers' workload, we have designed a user interface in the virtual experiment platform. This interface can conveniently generate experimental environments online based on the experimental environment deployment files provided by students or teachers, and can control the behavior of virtual network elements according to control service files. In addition, we have improved the existing SPOC online teaching system by adding a graphical experimental scenario design function [7], which facilitates teachers in designing experimental scenarios. As long as students and teachers log in to the SPOC teaching system, they can directly open the experimental environment in the virtual experiment platform by clicking on relevant experiment links. In this way, the whole-process assessment of course experiments are realized. The SPOC teaching system provides functions for course experiment management and score analysis, assisting teachers in completing ability tests in each teaching link. Its structural model is shown in Fig. 8.

The improved SPOC teaching system can provide appropriately formatted experimental assessments at each teaching stage, replacing the traditional assessment model of "a single exam determining the final outcome". The assessment results can be directly fed back to teachers, serving as an evaluation of phased teaching effects and providing references for teachers to improve and adjust teaching content.

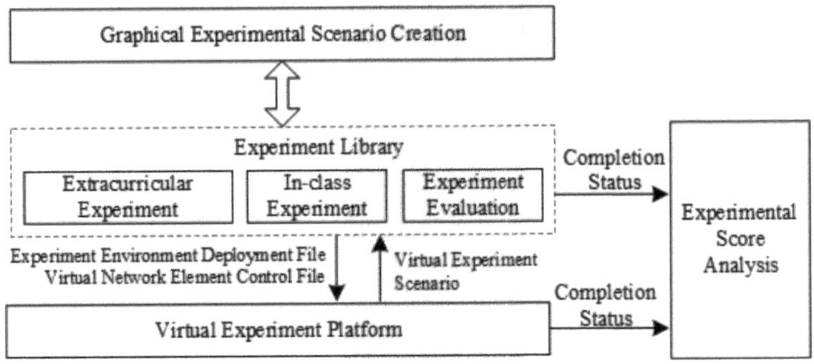

Fig. 8. Experimental Scenario Management and Test Analysis Model.

6 Conclusion

This paper studies the method of constructing a virtualized experiment platform based on the principles of NFV technology, which saves investment in network equipment, reduces the pressure of maintaining experimental environments, and solves the problem of difficulties in carrying out experimental courses for cyberspace security majors. By setting up a coupling interface in the experiment platform and expanding the course experiment management function in the existing SPOC teaching system, it provides teachers and students with powerful virtualized online experiment functions. On this basis, it will further promote the reform of experimental teaching for cyberspace security professional courses.

References

1. People's Daily Online. Xi Jinping's View on Cybersecurity: Without Cybersecurity, There Is No National Security. People's Net-News of the Communist Party of China, 15 Apr 2018. https://news.cri.cn/uc-eco/20220906/d141cfaa-3316-88d3-9159-887ccefaf07a.html
2. Zhang, S., Hui, L.: Research on the training mode of cybersecurity talents for emerging engineering education. Network Secur. Technol. Appl. **9**, 93–94 (2023)
3. Garay, J., Matias, J., Unzilla, J., et al.: Service description in the NFV revolution: trends, challenges and a way forward. IEEE Commun. Mag. **54**(3), 68–74 (2016)
4. Virtual Simulation Experiment Teaching Innovation Alliance. Guidelines for the Construction of Virtual Simulation Experiment Teaching Courses (2020 Edition). Higher Education Press, pp. 134–135 (2020)
5. Zhou, W., Yang, Y., Xu, M.: A survey of network function virtualization technologies. J. Comput. Res. Dev. **55**(4), 675–688 (2018)
6. Liu, P., Chen, W., Li, J., et al.: Reform practice of the whole-process assessment for computer network courses aiming at continuous improvement. Comput. Educ. **353**(05), 154–159 (2024)
7. Huihui, S.: Exploration and practice of a blended teaching model for top-notch innovative mathematics talents based on the SPOC concept. Higher Educ. Explor. **03**, 92–93 (2019)

Teaching Research on Computer Network via SPOC+BOPPPS Model

Bo Xu(✉), Xiulei Wang, Changyou Xing, and Ke Ding

Command and Control Engineering College, Army Engineering University, Nanjing 210007, China
xubo820@163.com

Abstract. This research takes the BOPPPS model as the theoretical core and deeply integrates the SPOC online teaching system to innovatively reconstruct and adaptively expand the traditional teaching model. By leveraging cutting-edge technologies, an intelligent assessment system is established to achieve the intelligent upgrade of pre-instruction testing and in-class evaluation. This significantly reduces the assessment time and remarkably improves the timeliness and accuracy of data feedback. A hierarchical task decomposition strategy is implemented, with tasks designed in layers according to the difficulty of knowledge and students' abilities. Combined with the real-time learning situation feedback mechanism, it stimulates students' enthusiasm for participatory learning. Moreover, a multi-dimensional incentive framework is constructed to boost students' motivation for autonomous learning. Through practical applications, the advantages of this model in enhancing teaching quality have been verified.

Keywords: SPOC Online Teaching System · BOPPPS Model · Whole-process Management · Incentive Mechanism · Teaching Model

1 Overview

The core of teaching activities lies in the two - way dynamic interaction between "teaching" and "learning", and all teaching links are oriented towards achieving the established teaching objectives. In the teaching process, teachers assume multiple roles, including content selection, process planning, classroom implementation, and effectiveness evaluation. On the other hand, students focus on exploring learning paths for deconstructing knowledge systems, grasping key points, and advancing their abilities. The BOPPPS teaching model, originating from North America and widely recognized as a curriculum design paradigm, provides scientific guidance for systematic teaching [1].

To adapt to the trend of digital teaching, our independently developed SPOC online teaching system deeply integrates the concepts of the BOPPPS model, establishing an intelligent education platform that enables collaboration among

J. Chi et al. (Eds.): CNETCNED 2025, CCIS 2809, pp. 19–30, 2026.
https://doi.org/10.1007/978-981-95-7124-6_3

teaching administrators, teachers, and students, thus achieving efficient intercommunication of teaching and management information. Through the meticulous design of three major modules - teaching resource management, curriculum planning, and teaching process control - the system extends the application scenarios of the BOPPPS model to the entire cycle, covering pre - class preparation, in - class interaction, and post - class reinforcement. This innovative architecture not only enhances the quality and efficiency of classroom teaching but also stimulates students' innovative thinking. Meanwhile, the learning evaluation system based on whole - process management allows teachers to precisely control all aspects of teaching, monitor students' learning engagement, participation effectiveness, and academic performance in real - time, and comprehensively assess teaching effectiveness. In addition, the innovative practice platform built by the system provides a showcase for students, ultimately achieving the coordinated improvement of teaching quality, learning effectiveness, and management efficiency.

2 BOPPPS Model

The BOPPPS teaching model is organically composed of six core teaching stages for courses, as shown in Table 1. These stages are interconnected, jointly constructing a complete teaching logical chain. In the Bridge-in (B) stage, it emphasizes naturally introducing the course through means such as creating scenarios and guiding with questions, thus stimulating students' learning interests. The Learning Objective (O) clearly defines the expected knowledge, skills, and literacy goals to be achieved in the course, setting the direction for teaching activities. The Pre-test (P) accurately grasps students' knowledge reserves and cognitive levels through diagnostic tests before class. The Participatory Learning (P) advocates diverse forms such as group collaboration and project - based practices to promote students' in - depth participation in knowledge construction. The Post-assessment (P) dynamically evaluates learning effects during classroom teaching by using means such as immediate quizzes and work presentations. The Summary (S), at the end of the course, systematically sorts out key content to strengthen knowledge internalization and transfer.

Each element not only undertakes unique teaching functions but also has a close mapping relationship with the 5W teaching elements. Why (the significance of learning) runs through the introduction stage, helping students understand the value of learning; Who (the teaching objects) is implicit in the pre-class assessment and participatory learning, assisting teachers in teaching students in accordance with their aptitudes; What (the teaching content) is precisely defined based on learning objectives; How (the teaching methods) is fully reflected in participatory learning; Whether or not (the learning outcomes) is examined through in-class assessment and summary stages. This integration provides a clear framework for teaching implementation.

At the level of teaching practice architecture, the BOPPPS model constructs a closed - loop teaching system. Its operation path starts with the establishment of teaching objectives, which drives the design of teaching strategies and

Table 1. The Meanings of Each Element of the BOPPPS Model.

No.	Name	Main tasks	Elements of curriculum teaching
1	Bridge-in	Introduce the teaching content of this lesson to attract students' attention and stimulate their interest.	Why
2	Learning Objective	Clarify the teaching objectives of this lesson so that students understand what they can do by learning this knowledge.	Who/do Whatunder What/How well
3	Pre-test	Test students to understand their knowledge foundation and lay the groundwork for subsequent teaching.	known What
4	Participatory Learning	The main part of classroom teaching encourages students to participate in classroom activities and learn actively.	Whether or not
5	Post-assessment	Examine whether the teaching objectives of this class have been achieved and what students have learned through various means, and provide feedback on the learning effects.	How well
6	Summary	Course summary: Reflect on what has been learned and introduce the content of the next class.	-

the planning of learning activities. A complete cycle is formed through dynamic evaluation and feedback, enabling teachers to precisely regulate the teaching process and achieve a deep alignment between teaching activities and expected goals. This structured teaching organization model not only ensures the orderly progress of teaching links but also can promptly capture teaching effects through multi - dimensional evaluations, providing data support for continuous optimization of curriculum design [2].

From the perspective of ability cultivation, the BOPPPS model serves as an effective carrier for cultivating computational thinking. This model guides students to systematically master the methodology of problem decomposition and analysis, identification of knowledge difficulties, and reflection on learning misunderstandings during the course of study. Through situational analysis in the introduction stage, collaborative exploration in participatory learning, and self - examination in the evaluation process, students can gradually construct a logical thinking framework in practice and enhance core computational thinking abilities such as abstract modeling and algorithm design, thus achieving a leap from knowledge acquisition to thinking advancement.

3 SPOC Network Teaching System

With the in-depth penetration of Internet technology, the field of education is undergoing an unprecedented digital transformation. The popularization of the Internet has pointed out a networked development path for educational reform. Its openness, distributed architecture, and powerful computing capabilities have broken the temporal and spatial constraints of traditional teaching, endowing the autonomous learning model with new vitality. Against this backdrop, the SPOC teaching system has emerged. With its teaching design that precisely targets knowledge points and personalized autonomous learning support functions, it can not only efficiently integrate teachers' teaching experience but also build a technical bridge for customized teaching activities, becoming a key tool to improve teaching efficiency and cultivate innovative talents.

To further optimize the teaching quality of online courses, we have deeply integrated the SPOC teaching system with the BOPPPS teaching model. Relying on cutting-edge network technologies, the SPOC system extends the six-core links of the BOPPPS model to the stages of pre-class preview and post-class consolidation. By creating diverse interactive scenarios, it fully stimulates students' learning initiative; at the same time, it strengthens teachers' guiding role in the teaching process, builds a management system covering the entire course cycle, realizes the integrated management and control of teaching resources, teaching processes, and learning outcomes, and injects strong impetus into the innovation of teaching models.

3.1 Problem-Driven Extended Classroom

The problem-driven teaching method is rooted in the constructivist learning theory and constructs a problem-oriented teaching paradigm. Adhering to the concept of integrating students' active exploration with teachers' precise guidance, this method stimulates learners' cognitive conflicts and desire for exploration by carefully designing progressive "problem chains" and creating immersive problem scenarios, thereby deeply motivating their enthusiasm for active knowledge acquisition. In teaching practice, teachers play a leading role, using problems as clues to gradually reveal the logic of knowledge generation and application paths, helping students deepen their understanding of knowledge, improve their knowledge system, and accumulate valuable practical experience in the process of solving practical problems [3].

Based on this, we rely on the teaching system to innovate the teaching model, organically integrating the problem-driven teaching method with the BOPPPS model. In the pre-class and post-class sessions, teachers guide students to discuss on the forum platform by issuing inspiring thinking questions. Teachers first conduct in-depth decomposition of the problems to help students grasp the core of the problems; then organize students to carry out diversified exchanges to jointly explore solutions; finally, conduct a comprehensive summary and evaluation of the problems and students' answers. This teaching method not only clearly shows the evolution process of theoretical concepts but also guides students to independently summarize knowledge rules, which greatly stimulates students' enthusiasm for using theoretical knowledge to solve practical problems, effectively enhances their learning self-confidence, and lays a solid foundation for the efficient application of the BOPPPS model in the classroom.

3.2 Process Management and Dynamic Monitoring

The traditional teaching model focuses on the evaluation of students' final grades while neglecting the dynamic monitoring of the learning process. This leads to a lag in teaching evaluation behind the course progress, missing key nodes for optimizing teaching. In contrast, the BOPPPS teaching model achieves real-time diagnosis of teaching effects and problem intervention through pre-class diagnosis, in-class interaction, and immediate assessment. On this basis, leveraging the technical advantages of the SPOC teaching system, the assessment links in the model are extended to the stages of pre-class preview and post-class consolidation, and formative evaluation is integrated with summative evaluation to build a comprehensive teaching evaluation system [4].

Formative evaluation focuses on capturing students' real-time feedback during the teaching process, similar to dynamic records of daily learning performance; summative evaluation, on the other hand, focuses on comprehensive assessment at the end of the course, corresponding to the evaluation of traditional exam results. The SPOC system makes process-oriented evaluation the core of teaching evaluation by accurately recording multi-dimensional data such as students' in-class participation, homework completion quality, autonomous learning trajectories, test results, and experimental operations. This evaluation method can not only timely feedback students' learning progress, assist teachers in judging whether the teaching rhythm is reasonable, but also provide data support for the iterative optimization of teaching methods.

The thus constructed whole-process teaching management mechanism is shown in Fig. 1. Relying on the system's accurate collection and analysis of students' full-cycle learning data, it covers elements such as the frequency of participation in learning activities, investment duration, quality of achievements, and subjective and objective evaluations. Teachers can use this to conduct a three-dimensional assessment of students' learning effects, accurately identify weak links in the teaching process, and then flexibly adjust teaching content and strategies, effectively improving the overall teaching quality, forming a positive cycle of "assessment-feedback- improvement".

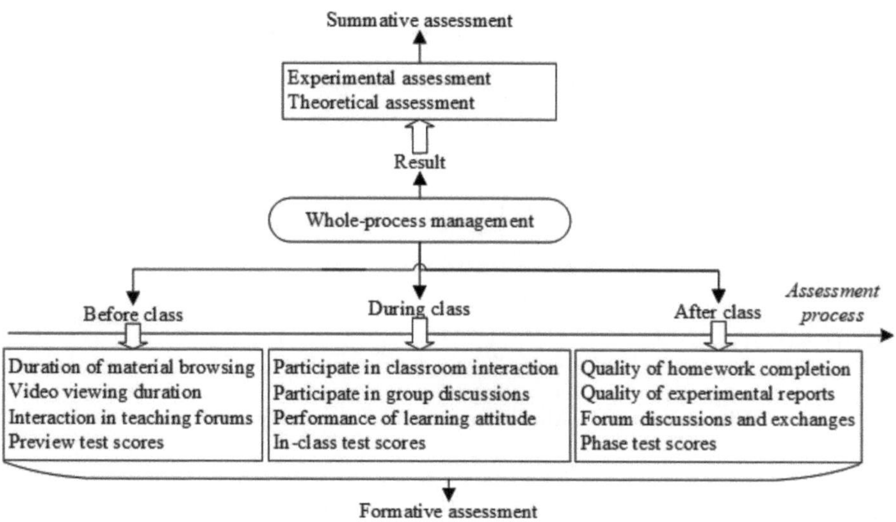

Fig. 1. Schematic Diagram of Stages in the Whole-Process Management Mechanism.

3.3 Online Tests Improve Efficiency

To accurately grasp students' knowledge reserves and teaching effectiveness, the BOPPPS teaching model emphasizes the importance of pre-test and post-test links, among which the quality of classroom teaching is verified by proficiency tests. In response to this demand, the SPOC network teaching system has built a sound question management and online test analysis system, whose systematic structural model is shown in Fig. 2.

In actual teaching scenarios, using the SPOC teaching system to implement the pre-test and post-test tasks of the BOPPPS model can quickly synchronize the evaluation results to teachers, providing an immediate basis for the dynamic adjustment of teaching content and strategies. From the perspective of system function modules, the question management module supports teachers to efficiently input questions, and realizes the phased tracking of learning progress through accurate association with knowledge points or teaching chapters; the test paper composition and testing module covers multiple scenarios such as after-class assignments, chapter assessments, special tests on knowledge points, mid-term and final exams, providing teachers with one-stop services for flexible test paper composition and online testing, which significantly improves the accuracy and intelligence level of testing; the evaluation and analysis module innovatively adopts a combination of automatic scoring and manual review, which can not only complete score processing, but also conduct in-depth analysis of teaching effects and explore potential problems in the teaching process.

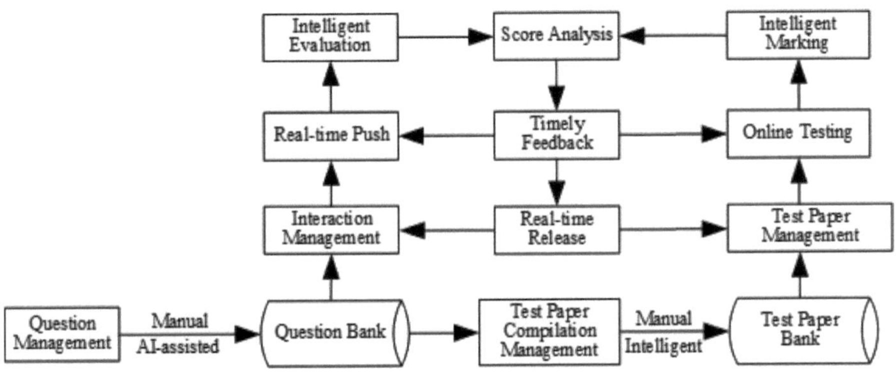

Fig. 2. Question Management and Test Analysis Model.

The collaborative operation of these functions has greatly enhanced the application efficiency of the BOPPPS model, and also created convenient conditions for students' independent learning. By reducing the time, labor and financial input in traditional testing processes, the system ensures that test results are more objective and fairer, effectively promoting the overall improvement of teaching quality.

3.4 Task Decomposition and Real-Time Feedback

To apply the BOPPPS model to practical teaching and achieve a substantial improvement in the quality of practical teaching, we adopt a task subdivision strategy to reshape the teaching process. The content of each practical course is carefully decomposed into a series of independent and operable subtasks. During the experiment, students must strictly follow the curriculum standards, complete each task in sequence, and upload the results to the teaching system in the form of screenshots for retention. This teaching design, which breaks down the whole into parts, effectively reduces the complexity of practical operations, makes learning objectives and progress arrangements clearer and more intuitive, and builds a clear learning path for students [5].

Teachers, relying on the digital management function of the teaching system, can monitor students' task completion in real time. They can not only check the number of completed tasks but also conduct in-depth evaluation of the task quality. For high-quality results, teachers give immediate encouragement through the systems like function, which fully stimulates students' learning enthusiasm and self-efficacy; for tasks with omissions or errors, they timely feedback revision suggestions to guide students to conduct in-depth reflection and optimize their operations. This whole-process dynamic management model has completely reversed the predicament of delayed feedback and lack of guidance in previous practical teaching. With the help of quantitative data and visual presentation, teachers can accurately grasp the teaching rhythm, students' standardization and proficiency in practical operations have been significantly improved, and the teaching efficiency of practical courses has also been enhanced, opening up a new direction for the innovation of practical teaching in the course of "Principles of Computer Networks". The specific task decomposition and real-time feedback teaching model can be seen in Fig. 3.

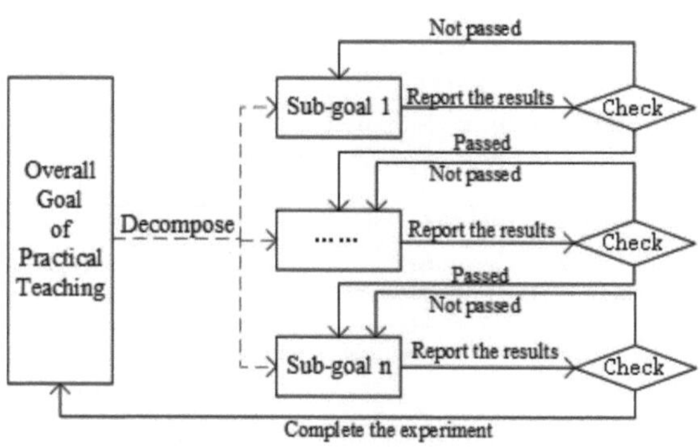

Fig. 3. Schematic Diagram of Task Decomposition and Real-Time Feedback.

3.5 Full-Process Motivation for Active Learning

To activate the endogenous motivation for participatory learning, we have introduced a process-oriented incentive learning model, which deeply embeds teaching evaluation into the entire learning process to arouse students' intrinsic learning drive. Different from the traditional centralized test evaluation, this model, through continuous observation and digital recording, makes evaluation a dynamic engine for promoting learning progress, helping students achieve a positive cycle of autonomous learning and self-optimization [6].

To further strengthen the incentive effect, we have built an all-round and multi-level incentive system. In collaborative learning scenarios, with group discussions as the platform, recording and publicizing discussion videos not only truly restores students' phased learning trajectories but also significantly enhances the enthusiasm of all participants through the demonstration effect of excellent cases; in the result display stage, high-quality after-class assignments and experimental results are regularly publicized, which not only sets a reference learning model for students but also promotes the flow and sharing of knowledge among the group; in the process of classroom interaction, teachers promptly give positive feedback and encouragement, effectively boosting students' learning confidence and enlivening the classroom interaction atmosphere; at the same time, by regularly releasing comprehensive learning rankings, students' sense of competition and enterprising spirit are stimulated. The incentive strategies for each stage are shown in Fig. 4.

Relying on the dynamic data collected by the whole-process teaching management system, these incentive strategies can accurately match students' personalized needs, realizing precise delivery and immediate response of incentives. Practice has proved that this method has significantly improved students' classroom participation and autonomous learning initiative, optimized the teaching interaction ecology, and explored an innovative path for improving the teaching quality of the "Principles of Computer Networks" course.

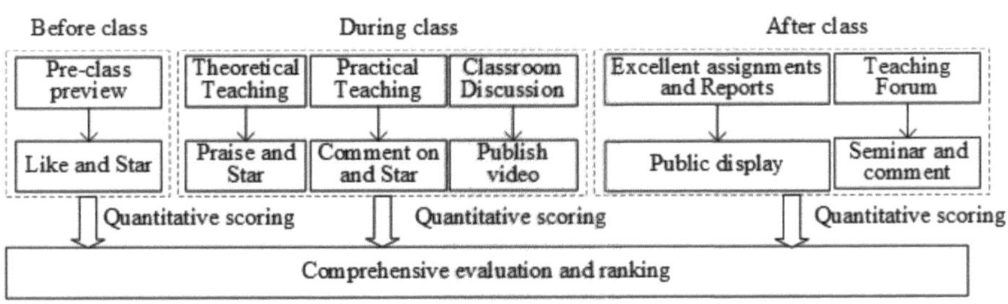

Fig. 4. Incentive Strategies Corresponding to Different Learning Stages.

3.6 Sharing Mechanism Improves Quality

At present, although colleges and universities have established a teaching resource sharing framework and equipped with relevant software systems to support the intercommunication of teaching materials such as lesson plans, courseware, and question banks, this traditional sharing model has obvious shortcomings. Its resource dissemination efficiency is relatively low, making it difficult to meet the needs of the rapid promotion of the BOPPPS teaching model and supporting resources. To break through this predicament, we have constructed a new network teaching resource sharing mechanism in the SPOC teaching system. It adopts a three-stage cyclic interaction model of course resource management, course content management, and teaching implementation process management, promoting the transformation and upgrading from the "course resource library" to the "teaching knowledge base" and accelerating the popularization and application of the BOPPPS teaching model. The resource sharing mechanism is shown in Fig. 5.

Compared with traditional sharing methods, this innovative mechanism gives teachers more initiative. After uploading course resources to the system, teachers can, based on the core concept of the BOPPPS model and combined with their personal teaching experience and course planning, carefully design the implementation plan for each lesson, realizing the deep integration of "teaching" and "learning". For senior teachers, their course implementation plans accumulated over the years are a precious treasure trove of teaching knowledge. Through the online teaching platform, these high-quality resources (including the "teaching knowledge base") can be copied with one click, enabling more teachers to conveniently obtain and learn from them, thereby promoting the improvement of the overall teaching level. This resource sharing mechanism provides an effective path for the rapid spread of teaching methods and resources based on the BOPPPS model among teachers, and has also become an important platform for the promotion of curriculum construction achievements.

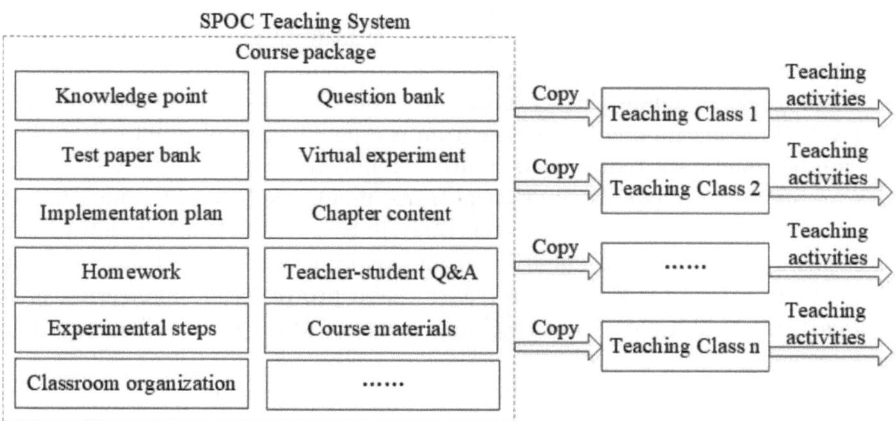

Fig. 5. Resource Sharing Mechanism Based on Network Teaching System.

4 Application Cases

In the teaching practice of the "Principles of Computer Networks" course, we have actively explored innovations in teaching models, deeply integrating the

BOPPPS model with the problem-driven teaching method, and always adhering to the "student-centered" educational philosophy. Relying on the university's SPOC network teaching system, we have broken the time and space limitations of traditional classrooms and built an integrated teaching closed loop covering pre-class, in-class, and post-class stages. This not only creates a convenient online learning space for students but also provides teachers with a full-process teaching management tool.

Taking the teaching design of "Reliable Transmission in the Data Link Layer" as an example, the specific teaching implementation process is shown in detail as follows.

(1) Pre-class autonomous learning to build a foundation: The knowledge points of this course are systematically decomposed into three modules, with 10-minute essential teaching videos recorded for each module. Three checkpoint-style test questions are set for each module, which are pushed to students through the teaching system three days in advance as preview tasks. Students' completion status is automatically included in their usual grades to encourage them to take the initiative in pre-class learning. Teachers can grasp students' self-study progress and effects in real-time through the system, making full preparations for in-class teaching. The high-quality preview session lays a solid foundation for subsequent teaching.
(2) Introduction session to stimulate exploration interest: A life-related thinking question is posted on the SPOC teaching forum to organize students to discuss before class. The easy-to-understand problem scenario arouses students' curiosity. By analyzing the discussion contents and questions raised by students in the forum, teachers can accurately grasp the difficulties in students' learning, making in-class teaching more targeted.
(3) Clear goals to guide the learning direction: Based on students' cognitive level, three learning goals are set from the perspective of practical application: students are required to clearly explain to non-professionals the reasons for the unreliability of physical transmission media and the measures to achieve reliable transmission; accurately judge reliable transmission mechanisms and their effectiveness when analyzing network protocols; and independently design reliable data transmission protocols in engineering practice. This enables students to clarify learning priorities and focus on core knowledge.
(4) Pre-class assessment to accurately grasp students' learning situation: A test paper consisting of 10 multiple-choice questions and 5 judgment questions is carefully compiled, covering important knowledge points of the course, and students are required to complete it within 4 min in class. With the automatic analysis function of the teaching system, teachers can comprehensively understand students' mastery of knowledge points, focus on explaining weak links, and design subsequent teaching content with reference to the test results.
(5) Participatory learning to deepen knowledge understanding: The problem-driven teaching method is used to promote participatory learning, and stu-

dents are guided to participate according to the difficulty level of the problems. Simple questions encourage students to answer directly, while complex questions invite students to explain on stage, with other students raising questions and making supplements. This fully mobilizes students' learning enthusiasm and realizes the transformation from passive acceptance to active exploration.

(6) Diversified assessment to test teaching effectiveness: The learning effect is tested through practical problems. For example, students are required to design a stop-and-wait protocol using reliable transmission mechanisms, and organize classmates to supplement and improve it. At the same time, combined with the key and difficult points of the course and the pre-test results, 4 homework questions are assigned in the SPOC system, and student mutual evaluation activities are carried out to examine students' mastery of knowledge from multiple dimensions.

(7) Summary and extension to promote knowledge internalization: At the end of the class, teachers systematically review the teaching content, refine methods to break through key and difficult points, and guide students to think about the application scenarios of reliable transmission mechanisms. Extended thinking questions are posted on the teaching forum, requiring students to design an efficient data link layer protocol and analyze channel utilization, which not only consolidates the knowledge of the current class but also paves the way for subsequent course learning.

5 Conclusion

Teaching practice data show that the BOPPPS teaching model has demonstrated significant advantages in the field of teaching design. By applying this model, teachers can systematically sort out the knowledge context, accurately identify cognitive difficulties, and then scientifically plan teaching levels and target systems. In the course design process, they can not only clearly establish logical connections between knowledge points but also naturally integrate the core ideas and methodologies of the discipline, effectively improving the efficiency and quality of classroom teaching.

The implementation of the BOPPPS model relying on the SPOC network teaching system platform has further expanded the boundaries of teaching time and space. Teachers can extend teaching links to both pre-class preview and post-class consolidation, realizing refined management of the entire cycle of students' learning. The online testing and intelligent analysis functions equipped in the system have greatly improved the efficiency of evaluation, making teaching feedback timelier and more accurate. By dynamically monitoring the learning process, teachers can adjust teaching strategies in a targeted manner and optimize the learning experience.

This application mode of the BOPPPS model based on the SPOC network teaching system has opened up a new path for the reform of online course teaching. It not only innovates the traditional online teaching paradigm but also provides practical samples and theoretical references for in-depth research on subsequent online teaching methods, which has important demonstration value and guiding significance for promoting the digital transformation of education and improving the quality of online teaching.

References

1. Weiwei, C., Aihua, B., Qing, L., et al.: Teaching Design for Cultivating Computational Thinking Based on BOPPPS Model and Problem-Driven Teaching Method. Industry and Information Technology Education **10**(6), 8–11 (2014)
2. Liu Xingmiao, Liu Chao. Theoretical Basis and Practical Reflection of BOPPPS Teaching Method. Comparative Study of Cultural Innovation, 2020(34): 107-109, 174
3. Popper. Conjectures and Refutations. Translated by Fu Jizhong. Shanghai: Yiwen Press, 1986: 318
4. Li Haidong, Wu Hao. Research on the Whole-Process Blended Teaching Quality Evaluation System: A Case Study of National First-Class Online and Offline Blended Courses. China University Teaching, 2021(5): 65-71.
5. Jingtao, L., Haibin, K., Qixuan, H.: Progressive Project Design of Computer Network Experiments under the Background of New Engineering. Computer Education **5**, 198–201 (2023)
6. Xin, L., Baotian, L., Yuli, X., et al.: Problem-Driven Teaching Reform and Practice Based on OBE Concept: A Case Study of Advanced Data Structure Course. University Education **7**, 114–117 (2022)

Exploration of Reform in Computer Network Experiment Teaching Oriented to Teacher Certification

Zhenxin Hu(✉), Xiaoqing Wang, Yuwen Wan, and Linhui Zhong

School of Artificial Intelligence, Jiangxi Normal University, Nanchang, China
003432@jxnu.edu.cn

Abstract. In response to the problem that traditional computer network experimental teaching is overly focused on protocol analysis experiments, this paper analyzes the common phenomena among graduated students in their work. Combining the three core concepts of teacher education accreditation, it proposes a teaching reform idea of dividing experiments into exploratory experiments, unit experiments, and comprehensive experiments. It also introduces the specific implementation plan of teaching under this reform idea, gradually exploring the talent cultivation model of outstanding teachers, in order to better cultivate information technology education professionals who can meet the needs of basic education and social development.

Keywords: Teacher Education Accreditation · Computer Networking Laboratory · Educational Innovation

1 Introduction

The basis for the certification of teacher education programs lies in the Notice on the Interim Measures for the Certification of Teacher Education Programs in Regular Colleges and Universities issued by the Ministry of Education in 2017. The implementing body is the Higher Education Teaching Assessment Center of the Ministry of Education. The core objective of certification is to ensure that teacher education graduates meet the required standards in knowledge, abilities, and competencies upon graduation. The primary aim is to promote the construction of program substance and focus on the cultivation of teacher education graduates' competencies. The certification is guided by three core principles: student-centeredness, outcome orientation, and continuous improvement, driving sustained enhancement in the quality of teacher education programs. The certification results serve as a reference for policy formulation, resource allocation, funding, employer recruitment, and college admissions. For programs certified at Level 2, graduates may participate in the interview component of the primary and secondary school teacher qualification examinations organized by their respective universities. For programs certified at Level 3, graduates may

J. Chi et al. (Eds.): CNETCNED 2025, CCIS 2809, pp. 31–40, 2026.
https://doi.org/10.1007/978-981-95-7124-6_4

participate in both the written and interview components of the primary and secondary school teacher qualification examinations organized by their universities [1].

Given the significance of the accreditation of teacher education programs, many teacher education institutions in China are actively promoting the accreditation process. The accreditation, with an outcome-oriented approach, requires that graduates achieve certain goals after five years of work in their respective positions. The graduation requirements should be reflected in the course objectives. For students in engineering programs such as computer science and technology for teacher education, the focus should be on the cultivation of practical abilities. Therefore, the traditional teaching and training plans are difficult to meet the requirements of the accreditation for student cultivation. The teaching plans for each course must be reconstructed, which is a problem that all universities promoting the accreditation of teacher education programs must face.

According to the investigation of graduates who have already entered the workforce, it is commonly found that they lack practical abilities and innovative capabilities. This phenomenon reflects the insufficiency of experimental and practical course teaching. Experimental teaching is a key link in connecting theory with practice and enhancing students' comprehensive qualities and innovative abilities. Under the background of teacher education program accreditation, experimental teaching should be strengthened and optimized.

2 Problems Existing in Traditional Experimental Teaching

(1) The experimental methods are monotonous. Traditional computer network experimental teaching is overly focused on protocol analysis experiments. In theoretical classes, the principles of a certain protocol are taught, and during experiments, packet capture software such as Wireshark is used for protocol analysis. Data packets are captured to analyze the data packet format and data flow to verify the correctness and rationality of the protocol principles. This experimental method is a verification experiment, lacking the application of advanced means such as virtualization experiments, which limits the cultivation of students' practical skills and innovative thinking [2].

(2) Lack of hands-on practice. Traditional computer network experimental teaching has relatively few hands-on practice experiments, resulting in insufficient practical skills among students. When facing real problems, they often don't know where to start and lack the ability to apply theoretical knowledge to practical situations [3]. According to a survey of graduates who have already entered the workforce, there is a phenomenon of insufficient practical skills, making it difficult for them to solve practical problems encountered at work well.

(3) Insufficient experimental time. Due to the limitation of class hours, the time allocated for experiments is relatively short, usually two experimental classes per week. Moreover, before students start the experiments, the instructor will

explain the experimental steps and precautions, which further reduces the time available for students to conduct experiments. As a result, it is difficult for students to complete a full experiment within the prescribed class hours, leading to a poor experience and sense of achievement in the experimental classes.

(4) Lack of a unified experimental platform. When using Wireshark for protocol analysis, data packets are randomly captured from the Internet for analysis, making it difficult to obtain clean and tidy data packets that meet the experimental requirements. For example, when analyzing the HTTP protocol, data packets are captured by visiting a webpage on the Internet. However, most websites now use the HTTPS protocol, making it challenging to capture HTTP data packets. Establishing a unified experimental platform to reduce the time spent on setting up the experimental environment is highly necessary.

3 Experimental Teaching Reform Measures

The curriculum design under the OBE philosophy emphasizes output-based standards, aligns with societal needs, and adopts a backward design approach focused on teacher education students' learning outcomes [4]. In the context of teacher certification, the OBE philosophy requires course syllabi to support graduation requirements and implement the cultivation of knowledge, skills, and qualities in teacher candidates [5]. Addressing issues in traditional experimental teaching, it establishes course objectives, correlates these objectives with graduation requirements, restructures experimental teaching content, and adopts innovative instructional methods.

3.1 Course Objectives and Their Relationship to Graduation Requirements

Computer networking is a course that closely integrates theory and practice. In order to improve students' hands-on practical ability and adhere to the output oriented teacher certification concept, computer networking is divided into two courses for teaching: theory and experiment. In the context of teacher education certification, computer network experimental courses place greater emphasis on cultivating students' practical skills, subject literacy, comprehensive education, and communication and cooperation abilities. The following course objectives have been developed for this purpose.

Objective 1: To enable students to use network packet capture tools to verify and analyze computer network protocols and their working principles, and to use network simulation tools to explore the complete process of network communication and the working principles, working characteristics and working processes of various network devices.

Objective 2: Enable students to utilize computer network simulation tools for analyzing, designing, and configuring computer networks; demonstrate proficiency in effectively diagnosing and troubleshooting network issues using theoretical knowledge and relevant tools. Develop the ability to independently research technical documentation to master specific configurations of new computer network hardware and software.

Objective 3: Through the course organization, behavioral etiquette, disciplinary requirements, self-evaluation and peer evaluation, demonstration reports, etc., during computer network experiments, cultivate students in experimental activities, foster good behavioral habits and healthy personalities, and promote the comprehensive development of students.

Objective 4: During hands-on lab sessions, students are encouraged to discuss common challenges within small groups, fostering intellectual exchange rather than plagiarism. Those with stronger academic performance should assist peers facing difficulties, promoting knowledge sharing instead of taking over assignments.

The formulation of course objectives should reflect the indicator requirements for graduation, and Table 1 shows the corresponding relationship between course objectives and graduation requirements.

Table 1. Correspondence between Course Objectives and Graduation Requirements.

Graduation requirements	index point	Support for graduation requirements	Course Objectives
3. disciplinary literacy	3.2 Disciplinary capacity	H	Objective 1
	3.3 Disciplinary applications	H	Objective 2
6. Integrated education	6.2 Educational activities	L	Objective 3
8. Communication and collaboration	8.3 willing to share	L	Objective 4

In Table 1, H and L represent high and low support levels respectively. As shown, Course Objective 1 demonstrates strong support for subject competencies within the graduation requirements framework. To achieve this objective and ensure students meet competency standards, it is imperative to implement corresponding reforms in traditional computer network experimental teaching content and pedagogical approaches.

3.2 Reform of the Experimental Content

Experiments and practical training are essential for developing students' hands-on skills and problem-solving abilities. Emphasizing experimental and practical education helps computer science students enhance their practical competencies and research literacy, enabling them to adapt to professional environments more quickly after graduation. To strengthen hands-on training in experimental teaching, the curriculum is divided into three categories: exploratory experiments, unit experiments, and comprehensive experiments. Exploratory experiments primarily verify computer network protocol principles and investigate network communication processes; unit experiments focus on specific network technology operations and configurations within chapters (e.g., RIP and VLAN configuration); comprehensive experiments involve integrated configurations combining multiple network technologies (e.g., DHCP and VLSM integration). Each category includes multiple experiments, with detailed content shown in Fig. 1.

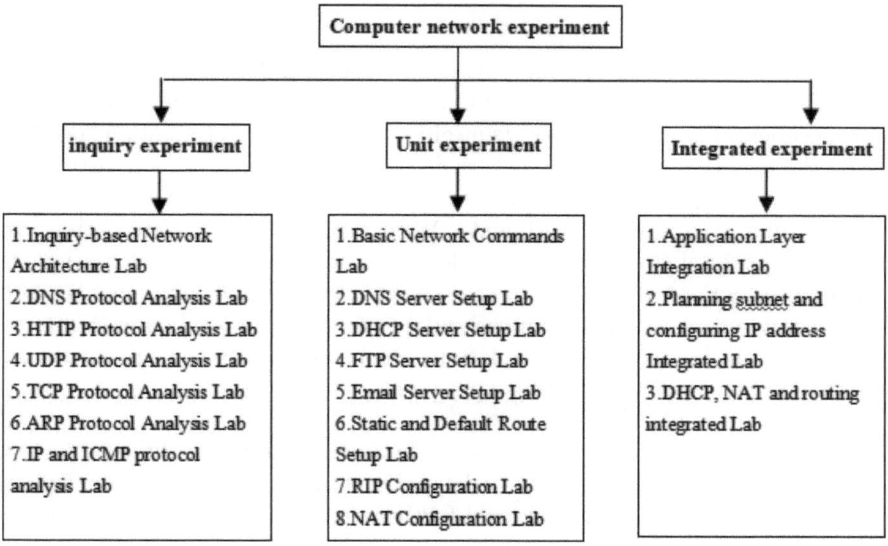

Fig. 1. Computer Network Experiment Content.

Most of the exploration experiments use Wireshark packet capture for protocol analysis, with the aim of achieving course objective 1; Unit experiments can be configured using Packet Tracer or on a virtual experimental platform to achieve course objective 2; The comprehensive experiment requires students to complete independently, with the aim of achieving course objective 3. The comprehensive experiment is mainly conducted in Packet Tracer, as Packet Tracer has a scoring function that can score the experimental results. The score of the comprehensive experiment can be used as the basis for daily scoring. Allow students to communicate and learn from each other during exploratory and unit experiments, with the aim of achieving course objective 4. There are multiple experiments that require students to team up to complete (such as UDP protocol analysis, TCP protocol analysis), with the aim of cultivating students' teamwork spirit.

3.3 Innovation in Teaching Methods

Traditional computer network laboratory instruction primarily involves instructors explaining experimental principles, content, and procedures while demonstrating the process, followed by students replicating the demonstrations. This teaching approach presents several limitations: monotonous methodology, excessive time consumed by teacher-led lectures, and lack of student autonomy and creativity in experimentation. To better achieve course objectives and enhance learning outcomes, the following teaching methods are adopted.

(1) Introducing online teaching
We have created experimental teaching videos and uploaded them to the school's MOOC system. Students are required to watch the corresponding experimental teaching videos themselves before the experimental class. During the experimental class, teachers do not need to teach or demonstrate the experimental process, and students can make full use of the experimental class time to conduct experiments. With sufficient experimental time, the vast majority of students can complete experiments within the experimental class time, which enhances their sense of achievement and confidence in learning. In addition, students can seek advice from teachers when encountering problems during experimental classes, which can quickly solve problems and enhance the experience of the experiment.
(2) Extend experimental time
There are many computer network experiments, and it is difficult to complete all of them within the limited experimental hours. In order for students to master basic network skills and further improve their hands-on practical abilities, some unit experiments can be assigned as homework for students to complete independently outside of class, and the completion of the experiments will be included in their regular grades.
(3) Introduce questions and reflections
Introducing questions in the experimental guidebook for each experiment requires students to complete their answers while conducting the experiment. This approach has two benefits: firstly, it deepens the understanding of computer network theory knowledge; The second is to avoid plagiarism in experimental reports. The experimental guidebook has added thinking questions, requiring students to further study and experiment to answer these questions. This is a deeper learning of theoretical knowledge and a higher level of experimental operation, which can improve students' self-learning and innovation abilities.
(4) Using a demonstration report
During their school years, students majoring in teacher education should practice teaching on the podium and hone their teaching skills. They should have close contact with the podium as soon as possible, in order to cultivate and enhance their comprehensive literacy and professional skills in basic education work [6]. In experimental teaching, selecting students who perform well and have high completion rates to explain their experimental process

and demonstrate their operations on the podium can inspire other students and hone their teaching skills, filling the gap between learning and work.

3.4 Reform of Assessment Methods

Traditional assessment methods in computer network laboratory education remain overly simplistic, primarily relying on final lab exams and daily attendance records for evaluation. This approach tends to overlook the learning process, often resulting in last-minute cramming sessions to pass exams, which is a one-sided approach. Furthermore, using identical questions for final lab exams increases the risk of plagiarism. To address these issues, the following assessment measures will be implemented.

(1) Adopt process assessment
Teacher education program accreditation places greater emphasis on sustained learning, and the implementation of process-based assessment effectively motivates students to maintain continuous academic engagement. This evaluation system incorporates daily attendance, classroom participation, regular assignments, lab reports, and comprehensive lab scores into the overall grade, significantly increasing the weight of regular performance. Under this framework, regular grades and final computer-based exam scores each account for 50%, with daily attendance and classroom participation making up 10%, regular assignments and lab reports contributing 10%, and comprehensive lab work representing 30%. Given the substantial weight of regular grades, students now prioritize consistent learning, completing all assigned tasks including homework and lab reports with greater urgency than before.

(2) Use a different set of final exam questions
In order to prevent students from copying each other, different final exam questions are used. The questions are randomly generated in Packet Tracer, which can play a role in preventing students from copying during the exam.

(3) Calculation of test score discount
To encourage students to master network technology proficiently, the exam scoring system is designed as follows: Top 30% of students who submit exam materials receive full marks (100%), the next 30% to 60% receive 98%, and the remaining students receive 96%. To maximize their scores, students diligently practice network operations before the exam. This assessment mechanism effectively enhances students' practical skills through hands-on experience.

4 The Effectiveness of Experimental Teaching Reform

In the context of teacher education certification, the teaching syllabus has been revised, a virtual simulation teaching platform has been designed, and experimental teaching videos have been produced, resulting in improved learning outcomes for students compared to traditional teaching methods.

4.1 Revised Course Outline

The certification of teacher education majors requires course objectives to support graduation requirements, emphasizing output orientation and valuing the cultivation of students' practical abilities. In the newly revised curriculum outline, course objectives should be set according to graduation requirements, and the achievement of course objectives should be reflected in specific teaching content. Therefore, it is necessary to revise the curriculum teaching outline again.

The newly revised curriculum outline includes basic course information, course introduction, course objectives, correspondence between course objectives and graduation requirements, correspondence between teaching content and course objectives, course teaching methods, course assessment and evaluation, and other related content.

4.2 A Virtual Simulation Teaching Platform Is Designed

A unified virtual simulation platform for computer network experiments has been developed based on PNETLab, as shown in Fig. 2. This platform supports three types of experiments: exploratory experiments, unit experiments, and comprehensive experiments. During exploratory experiments, students can access clean network data packets free from external interference, which facilitates protocol analysis and reduces time spent setting up experimental environments. The network configuration under this platform closely mimics real-world network environments, effectively enhancing students' mastery of network device operations.

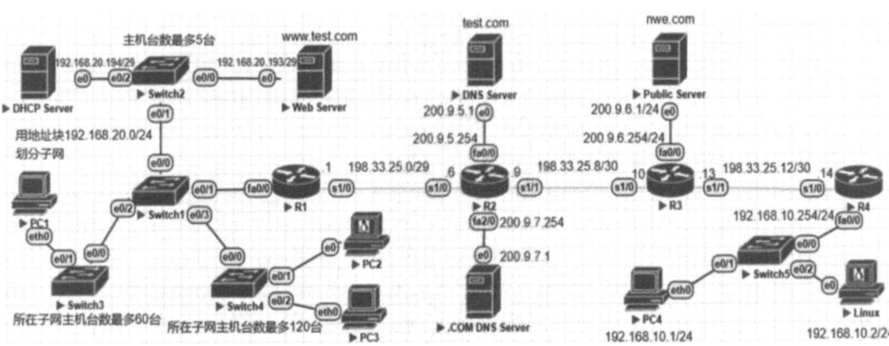

Fig. 2. Computer network virtual simulation experiment teaching platform.

4.3 Produced Experimental Teaching Videos

To implement blended online-offline teaching and expand learning resources for self-directed study, we developed 20 experimental instructional videos. These include 7 inquiry-based experiments, 10 unit experiments, and 3 comprehensive experiments, each demonstrating core principles, objectives, and step-by-step procedures. All videos are uploaded to the university's MOOC platform. Before lab sessions, students can access these materials for previewing, which significantly enhances both the efficiency of completing experiments and the overall learning experience, making the process more engaging and rewarding.

4.4 The Course Objectives Were Well Achieved

The degree of achievement in curriculum objectives reflects both teaching quality and the fulfillment of graduation requirements. Table 2 presents the achievement status of curriculum objectives in teacher education programs over the past two years, demonstrating that overall objective attainment remains satisfactory. This indicates that experimental teaching reforms under teacher certification have achieved some success. However, ongoing research is needed to further explore how teacher education accreditation impacts practical teaching reforms [7,8].

Table 2. Course Objective Attainment Status.

Class	number of students	Objective 1	Objective 2	Objective 3	Objective 4	Overall objective
2022 Computer Science and Technology (Normal) Class	41	0.8826	0.8618	0.8741	0.94	0.87
2023 Computer Science and Technology (Normal) Class	35	0.9424	0.9232	0.9347	1	0.93

Course objective evaluation serves as the foundation for graduation requirement assessment, where its reliability and achievement directly determine the authenticity of evaluations and actual attainment [9]. The rationality and comprehensiveness of course objective evaluation still require long-term practical validation, while further research is needed regarding the assessment of objective achievement [10–12].

5 Conclusion

Traditional computer network experimental teaching has been overly focused on protocol analysis experiments, neglecting the cultivation of students' practical skills. This results in graduates lacking scientific literacy for problem analysis and resolution when entering the workforce. Under the accreditation framework for teacher education programs, reforms in computer network experimental teaching have adopted student-centered approaches, outcome-oriented strategies, and continuous improvement principles, emphasizing hands-on network practice and pedagogical competencies. While these innovations have shown some success compared to conventional teaching models, evaluation systems for meeting graduation requirements require further refinement. Teaching content and methodologies should also be continuously improved based on graduate feedback and survey data.

Acknowledgements. This study was funded by Teaching reform research project of Jiangxi Normal University (JXSDJG2301, JXSDJG2501) and Provincial-level Teaching Reform Research Project for Higher Education Institutions in Jiangxi Province (JXJG-22-2-24).

References

1. Ministry of Education, PRC: Implementation measures for the accreditation of teacher education programs in regular higher education institutions (interim) (2017), http://www.moe.gov.cn/srcsite/A10/s7011/201711/t20171106_318535.html, jiao Shi No.13
2. Chen, K., et al.: The mechanism, scenarios, challenges and countermeasure of conversational artificial general intelligence in education. J. Distance Educ. **41**(3), 21–41 (2023). https://doi.org/10.15881/j.cnki.cn33-1304/g4.2023.03.003
3. Ling, J., Zhang, L., Chen, H., Jin, B., Lin, M.: Application of generative artificial intelligence in computer experiment teaching. Comput. Educ. (5), 28–32 (2025). https://doi.org/10.3969/j.issn.1672-5913.2025.05.007
4. Tian, T., Liu, R.: The construction of teacher education curriculums in the perspective of obe accreditation. J. South China Normal Univ. (Social Science Edition) (1), 41–52,205 (2022)
5. Guan, K., He, L., Zhao, Y., Zhao, S., Tan, S.: Curriculum outline reconstruction under the background of teacher education certification——taking the course of "theoretical mechanics" as an example. Phys. Bull. (1), 11–15 (2024). https://doi.org/10.3969/j.issn.0509-4038.2024.01.003
6. Zheng, C.: Application research on teaching mode of "learning by competition, training by competition and teaching by competition". Read Write Periodical **12**(10), 252 (2015). https://doi.org/10.16071/j.cnki.cn51-1650/g4.2015.10.237
7. Fang, Y.: Research on the curriculum reform of teacher education in normal colleges based on the accreditation of teachers' major. Theor. Pract. Educ. **40**(27), 41–43 (2020)
8. Wang, F.: An analysis of the teaching model reform of the teacher education theory courses. Modern Educ. Manage. (4), 92–98 (2021). https://doi.org/10.16697/j.1674-5485.2021.04.012
9. Zhang, A.: Evaluation of the degree of achievement of curriculum objectives, graduation requirements and training objectives based on obe concept. Higher Educ. Dev. Eval. **40**(6), 1–11 (2024). https://doi.org/10.3963/j.issn.1672-8742.2024.06.002
10. Xiang, F., Wang, F., Xiang, J.: Evaluation of curriculum goal achievement and continuous improvement strategy under the background of teacher education major certification. China Univ. Teach. (7), 74–79 (2021). https://doi.org/10.3969/j.issn.1005-0450.2021.07.014
11. Liu, H., Yang, S., Shi, X.: Research on teaching evaluation system of computer science and technology under teacher education in obe concept. Comput. Educ. (4), 235–239, 246 (2025). https://doi.org/10.3969/j.issn.1672-5913.2025.04.047
12. Liu, X., Li, B., Tang, Y., Xue, Y.: Assessment and achievement evaluation of algorithm introduction course based on obe. Comput. Educ. (1), 163–167 (2021). https://doi.org/10.3969/j.issn.1672-5913.2021.01.040

A Preliminary Exploration of Network Engineering Curriculum Content Organization and Teaching Method Optimization in the Era of Intelligence

Sun Weifeng[1(✉)], Gao Jie[1], Gao Zunjing[1], Xu Zichuan[1], and Lu Bingxian[2]

[1] Dalian University of Technology, Dalian 116620, China
wfsun@dlut.edu.cn

[2] Northeastern University, Shenyang 110000, China

Abstract. In the era of ubiquitous and embodied intelligence, areas such as intelligent algorithms, the Python programming language, and data processing are gaining increasing popularity. Consequently, adjustments are needed in the training system of the Network Engineering curriculum, and the content of core professional courses also needs to be updated. This paper explores the optimization of the Network Engineering curriculum system, taking three professional courses—Computer Networks, Cloud Computing, and Network Attack Defense and Practice—as examples. It provides targeted strategies for course content selection, teaching methods, and assessment schemes in the intelligent era. It also discusses the practical application of knowledge graph technology in the Computer Networks course.

Keywords: Ubiquitous Intelligence · Target Assessment · Practice Support

1 Introduction

Network Engineering is one of the specialized directions in the field of Information Science. It officially appeared in the 2012 list of undergraduate majors in general universities, aiming to train students to systematically master the basic theories and engineering principles and methods of computers, communications, and networks. Amid the wave of artificial intelligence, internet companies and traditional IT firms have also undergone transformations, with many venturing into the field of AI. There is a close connection between AI and computer network technology, and they complement each other. Meanwhile, as algorithms, AI requires support from large-scale data in the field of data science and from computing power and networks (primarily cloud computing) to be effective. The three areas mutually promote each other, providing greater overall value. To adapt to the changes in technology and skill requirements in the AI era, adjustments are needed in the curriculum setup and course content of the Network

J. Chi et al. (Eds.): CNETCNED 2025, CCIS 2809, pp. 41–53, 2026.
https://doi.org/10.1007/978-981-95-7124-6_5

Engineering major. These adjustments are intended to meet the needs of an innovative nation by cultivating innovative, interdisciplinary, and application-oriented talents in network systems engineering and management.

In 2024, the Central Committee of the Communist Party of China and the State Council issued the Outline of the Plan for Building a Strong Educational Nation (2024–2035) [1], which explicitly identifies artificial intelligence as the core driving force of education reform. The plan calls for building the "Four Horizontals and Five Verticals" national smart education platform system as proposed at the 2024 World Digital Education Conference. For higher education (both undergraduate and graduate), it requires comprehensive development of students in moral, intellectual, physical, aesthetic, and labor education. It also stipulates further deepening of undergraduate education and teaching reform, comprehensive improvement of course quality, actively developing "Internet+ Education" and "AI+ Education", exploring new forms of intelligent education, and promoting a revolution in classroom teaching.

Meanwhile, AI technology is booming, and generative AI (AIGC) tools are emerging in endless streams, including large language models such as OpenAI's GPT-3 and GPT-4, Baidu's Wenxin Yiyan, ByteDance's Douban, Youdao Writing Assistant, Kimi, etc. Notably, this year the open-source lightweight large language model DeepSeek has become globally popular; it can perform semantic analysis, computational reasoning, code generation, and more. Due to its open-source nature, many cloud platforms (such as Baidu AI Cloud, Huawei Cloud, Alibaba Cloud, Tencent Cloud, Volcano Engine, 360 Cloud, etc.) have already launched the DeepSeek large model, and numerous mobile apps have appeared. For college students, the channels to obtain information have increased greatly; for instance, the problems or exercises in a course can be obtained easily. However, AIGC-generated texts are generally content-rich but lack emphasis on key points, making it increasingly difficult for students to find the specific knowledge they need from a vast amount of data.

Facing this transformation, the Network Engineering major has been impacted significantly in the AI era. According to data from Soft Science, around 300 universities nationwide offered the Network Engineering major in 2012, but by 2025 only about 180 remain— a decrease of over 40%. Some universities, such as Hunan University and Xidian University, have already transformed this major into specializations like "Internet of Things Engineering" or "Cyberspace Security". For the development of first-class universities and their majors and curriculum settings, determining how to better adapt to the needs of the era has become a crucial problem [4].

Some core courses of the Network Engineering major will continue to be offered in related programs, such as Computer Networks, Cloud Computing, and Network Attack Defense and Practice. Among these, some are fundamental required courses and others are advanced electives. All three courses will be integrated with AI, incorporating AI technologies in teaching methods. AI is a double-edged sword for course learning: while it allows students to conveniently obtain answers, it deprives them of the training involved in collecting and organizing information and engaging in reflective thinking. For both teachers and students, knowledge graphs serve as useful tools to organize knowledge points and clarify their interrelationships. This paper also explores the application of knowledge graph techniques in courses like Computer Networks.

2 Major Features and Curriculum System Improvements

2.1 Measures of a First-Class Network Engineering Program

Dalian University of Technology School of Software launched the Network Engineering major in 2004. In 2018, this major passed the first batch of China's engineering education accreditation and was recognized as a national first-class undergraduate demonstration major. The program offers two specialty tracks: network security and Internet of Things technology. It integrates elite education with engineering education to build a diversified and innovative training system for network engineering technical talents. The program's characteristic features include alignment with long-term national school–enterprise cooperative education, systematic monitoring and tracking of teaching quality, innovative practical training driven by technology competitions and research, enhanced foreign language proficiency and international exchange, and continuous improvement through both in-school and off-campus cycles. The training objectives of the Network Engineering major require students to master theoretical knowledge with an emphasis on practice, achieving an integration of theory and application. To meet these objectives, most specialized courses are accompanied by corresponding computer lab and experiment courses, continuously deepening the integration of industry and education. (Specific courses are not enumerated here.) In addition to the fundamental Computer Networks course, AI-related courses include Artificial Intelligence, Internet of Things Technology, and Cloud Computing; there are also hands-on courses such as Python and Data Analysis and a Comprehensive Network Laboratory. The major's distinct characteristics enable it to systematically cultivate the abilities and qualities of undergraduate students in network engineering, enhance their professional competitiveness, and prepare students with strong practical competence and social adaptability.

2.2 Curriculum System Optimization

To embrace the AI boom, the Network Engineering curriculum has been correspondingly optimized [5]. For example, Beijing Jiaotong University offers courses such as Artificial Intelligence Security, AI + Network Offense and Defense, and Deep Learning and Big Data; Guangzhou University offers AI Principles, Machine Learning, and Deep Learning; and Fuzhou University offers Introduction to AI and Data Mining, among others. Our department has also introduced courses like Python Programming and Cloud Computing, integrating AI-related content. Additionally, students can select electives from the Software Engineering program, such as Fundamentals of AI and Machine Learning and Deep Learning.

Specifically, the Software Engineering college's electives "Fundamentals of Artificial Intelligence" and "Machine Learning and Deep Learning" include network-oriented modules (such as network traffic analysis, fault prediction, intelligent routing, and traffic engineering) to help Network Engineering students master core methods of using AI to optimize network performance. Given the relatively lower caliber of incoming Network Engineering students, the curriculum implementation should place greater emphasis on skill development and task-based learning. For example, we take the required course "Computer Networks" and the elective "Cloud Computing" to illustrate changes in course content, instructional methods, and assessment.

3 Application of Knowledge Graph in Curriculum Content Optimization

3.1 Application of Knowledge Graph in Teaching

Knowledge graphs address the issues of fragmented knowledge and unclear associations in teaching, which make it difficult for students to form a structured cognitive framework. A knowledge graph is a graphical structure for representing knowledge, which includes descriptions of entities, relationships, and attributes, and the connections between them. It uses information visualization techniques to vividly display the overall knowledge architecture of a discipline. A knowledge graph can thus structure course knowledge and provide more effective guidance and support. Furthermore, students themselves can analyze their own learning history and, based on differences in memory and interests, choose appropriate levels of the knowledge graph, thereby customizing their learning plans and review content [6]. This paper proposes and designs a customized hierarchical knowledge graph scheme. Taking the Computer Networks course as an example, we construct a multi-layer knowledge graph for computer networks. Depending on different learning goals and coverage of knowledge points, the scheme displays either the core knowledge graph or more detailed ones, helping students purposefully select the knowledge points to strengthen during self-study.

To reflect the relationships between entities, mind maps and knowledge graphs are two commonly used tools. Although their overall purposes are similar, they differ in how knowledge is organized and expressed, each carrying unique functions and values. A knowledge graph is a highly structured method of knowledge representation: it displays entities, concepts, and their interrelations in graphical form. Built on a semantic network, a knowledge graph uses nodes to represent entities or concepts and edges to depict their connections. Knowledge graphs are not only suitable for storing and retrieving large-scale knowledge, but also play an important role in understanding and reasoning about complex relationships among knowledge. A mind map, on the other hand, is a nonlinear, tree-structured diagrammatic tool. It uses a central theme as the core and radiating branches to expand related concepts and ideas. Each branch represents a concept or idea closely connected to the central theme. The advantage of a mind map is that it promotes divergent thinking and associative thinking, helping users organize their thoughts, deepen memory, and clearly display the thinking process. Figure 1 shows an example mind map for the network layer of a computer network.

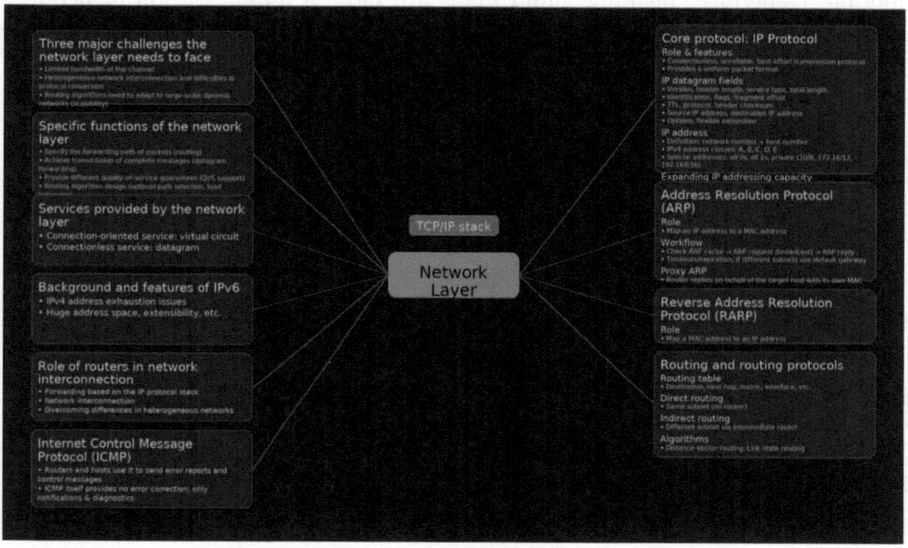

Fig. 1. A mind map of the network layer knowledge points in a computer network.

However, different tools have different understandings of knowledge graphs. As shown in Fig. 2, it is the knowledge graph presentation of the Chaoxing platform, which is more inclined to represent the word frequency cloud graph. There are four ways: graph, ring graph, tree graph, and map. The importance of keywords can be seen in all of them, but the path and logical relationship are not reflected. That is to say, the existing knowledge graph tools still have some deficiencies and cannot be flexibly used.

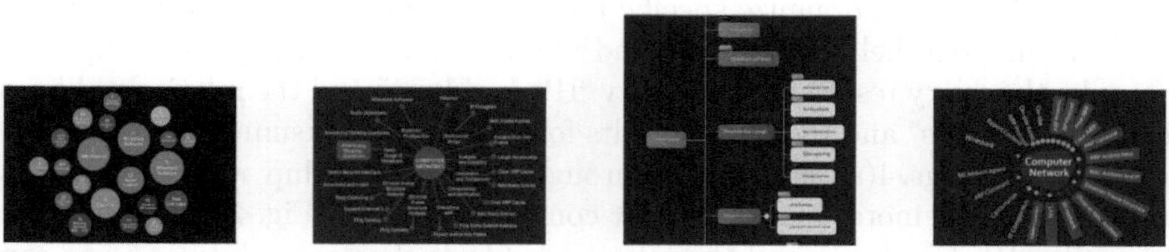

(a) Network Graph (b) Ring Graph (c) Tree Graph (d) Geographical Graph

Fig. 2. The knowledge graph representation of network layer experiments on the Chaoxing platform

In summary, knowledge graphs focus on the systematic organization, storage and retrieval of knowledge, emphasizing the clarity and logic of the relationships between entities. Mind maps, on the other hand, focus on the visual display of an individual's thinking, emphasizing the creativity and associative nature of thinking. Generally speaking, mind maps are more a manifestation of people's subjective logical relationships, and there are corresponding mapping assistance tools. Knowledge graphs can be automatically generated using tools and adjusted as needed based on self-generated and scalable triples. Therefore, this paper uses knowledge graphs as a tool to conduct research on the mining and application of knowledge point relationships in computer-related courses.

3.2 Exploration of the Application of Knowledge Graph in the Computer Networks Course

For example, in Professor Xie Xiren's Computer Networks textbook, we organized the knowledge points and designed triples to construct a multi-layer knowledge graph. The complete graph is shown in Fig. 3, which illustrates the relationships among various knowledge points arranged in progressive hierarchy. The Chinese knowledge points generated for Chinese textbooks follow the same principle if they are applied to English.

Relationship Mining and Role of Computer Network Knowledge Graph. (1) Basic knowledge point organization. In practice, the teaching team and students use the knowledge graph for summarization or self-testing, which clarifies the relationships among the various knowledge points. Table 1 lists two categories of knowledge point indexing indicators summarized by teachers and students. (Other specific knowledge points at each network layer—such as representative protocols and characteristics of each application layer; transport layer protocols like TCP, UDP, SCTP, QUIC, MP-TCP, MP-QUIC; network layer technologies like SDN, OSPF, BGP, RIP; data link layer technologies like CSMA and ALOHA; and ideological and political education content at each layer—are not fully enumerated here.)

(2) Deeper mining. Through reflective analysis during implementation, the knowledge graph can organize specific technologies for a given knowledge point and learning goal, helping teachers and students fill in missing knowledge. For example, the query results for the entity "IPv4 address" and the relation "address shortage solutions" and the query results for "Internet checksum related entities" are shown in Figs. 4(a) and 4(b). Through this relationship mining, teachers and students can more clearly sort out connections. From Fig. 4(a), focusing on the entity "IPv4 address" and the relation "address shortage solutions," one can deduce that from a time-development and technological perspective: DHCP can dynamically allocate IP addresses to reduce waste of fixed IP resources; CIDR breaks the limitations of IP address classes by allowing variable-length subnet masks; NAT uses multiple private IPs mapped to a single public IP, enabling hundreds or thousands of devices to share one IP address to connect to the Internet;

Fig. 3. Complete knowledge graph of computer networks.

Table 1. Index Indicators in Computer Networks.

Index Category Name	Expected Outcome	Purpose	Depth
Network Classification	1. Classification by transmission range (e.g., LAN, WAN, MAN) 2. Classification by transmission medium (e.g., wireless, DSL wired, HFC wired) 3. Classification by network bandwidth (e.g., 10 Mbps, 100 Mbps) 4. Classification by network protocol (e.g., ATM, Ethernet, IPv4 network, IPv6 network)	Understand various methods of network classification.	Medium
Network Layers	5-layer reference model, OSI 7-layer reference model, TCP/IP 4-layer model, etc.	Understand network layering and functions.	Medium

and IPv6, the next-generation IP protocol, uses a 128-bit address space to solve the IPv4 address exhaustion problem. Among these four technologies, NAT and DHCP are often used simultaneously, which is the main reason why new users with IPv4 addresses can still connect to the Internet today. This kind of relationship mining helps learners organize the connections among these solutions. Furthermore, following the indications of the knowledge graph relationships, one might also identify related technologies such as VLSM, tunnels/dual-stack transition, SRv6, SDN, etc., which is helpful for supplementing course content and guiding self-study.

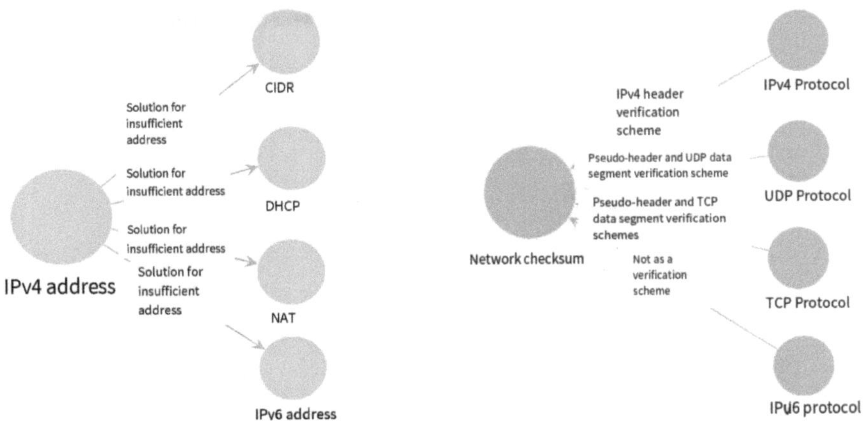

(a) Results for querying the entity "IPv4 address" and the relation "Solution for insufficient address"

(b) Results for querying "network checksum related entities."

Fig. 4. Results of Cypher queries on the Neo4j database

For the query results in Fig. 4(b) on Internet checksums, we can observe different usage methods of the same underlying technologies. For example, IPv4's checksum is calculated over the IPv4 header (20–60 bytes); UDP and TCP include the entire data segment plus the pseudo-header in their checksum; and IPv6 headers have no checksum field. From these differences in how similar technologies are used, one can analyze that TCP and UDP inherently break layer isolation by using the network layer's IP address in their checksums. IPv6, as the successor to IPv4, actually removed the checksum field. Instructors can guide students to analyze why this "simplification" was made, encouraging them to discuss and conclude that more error-checking is not always better. This introduces the issue of "redundant" checks in the protocol stack: besides the application layer, the transport, network, and data link layers all perform checks, and this repetition consumes system resources. In terms of transmission results, it is like inspecting a delivered package: the end-user ultimately checks the actual received item (verifying the correctness of the delivered message); in the transmission process itself, the data frame already contains all upper-layer information, and the

CRC check can detect almost all errors. Since the IP header, TCP header, and payload are already verified by CRC, redoing the error-check (in IPv4) becomes unnecessary—this is the main reason the IPv6 header omitted the checksum field.

There are many similar relationship mining cases, and students provided feedback such as: both TCP and IP have header length fields, whereas UDP and IPv6 do not; IP and UDP have a total length field while TCP does not (IPv6 uses payload length instead); OSPF, RIP, and BGP all require the transmission of routing-related information, but they respectively use IP, UDP, and TCP as their carriers; HTTP, DNS, instant messaging, and file transfer protocols (FTP, TFTP) all have versions or use cases that run over UDP and TCP, etc. Due to space constraints, we do not show all these knowledge graphs here. By mining common content with knowledge graphs and learning through analogy and comparison, learners can better understand certain technologies and design principles in computer networks.

4 Application of Artificial Intelligence in Course Teaching

4.1 Summary and Investigation of AIGC Tools and Their Applications

As a course assignment, students are required to research and summarize mainstream AIGC tools and their applications in a given scenario. Students conduct actual investigations and present the results in class; teams of students review AI tools and their characteristics together. The students' summaries include:

Mainstream AIGC tools such as ChatGPT, DeepSeek, Tongyi Qianwen, iFlytek Essay Correction, Zhiyuan Qingyan, Wenxin Yiyan, Kimi, and Doubao exhibit unique strengths in different scenarios. In data analysis, ChatGPT and DeepSeek are a key comparison: ChatGPT performs more stably and accurately when processing large amounts of data and can efficiently summarize analysis results, whereas DeepSeek, though occasionally misunderstanding, can produce satisfactory results after correction; both involve technologies like natural language processing and data parsing. In education contexts, AI-based essay correction tools like iFlytek Essay Correction and Wenxin Yiyan rely on BERT models, syntactic tree analysis, and other techniques. Each has different emphases in grammar correction and content evaluation: iFlytek aligns more with exam standards, while Wenxin Yiyan adapts to multiple language styles. In mathematics assistance, Zhiyuan Qingyan excels at handling trivial and difficult math problems, while Tongyi Qianwen has an advantage in dynamically updating knowledge. Both support the design of intelligent learning assistants. In the legal field, DeepSeek and Doubao are used for contract review and legal text retrieval: DeepSeek has fast search speed, and Doubao can identify risk points in contracts, but the completeness of details still requires reference to professional databases. In research, Kimi and ChatGPT assist with literature analysis and experimental design: Kimi can extract methodologies from academic papers, ChatGPT can generate controlled experimental plans, though ethical review must be considered. In creative design, Doubao and ChatGPT generate advertising slogans and product scenario descriptions, combining user preference analysis to optimize marketing strategies. In healthcare, Quark Health Assistant and Alipay AI Health Butler interpret routine blood test reports: Quark focuses on medical professionalism, whereas Alipay is more oriented toward everyday health management. In programming, ChatGPT and DeepSeek each excel in code generation and review: ChatGPT is suitable for rapid prototyping, while DeepSeek is adept at reasoning through complex logic. Additionally, there are AI systems for sign language translation that break communication barriers through motion capture and NLP, and OpenCV-based applications for image recognition in research and medicine. Through hands-on testing and comparative analysis, students not only summarized each tool's strengths (such as efficiency improvements and precision) but also identified limitations (such as lack of creativity and limited capability for handling complex problems), providing valuable guidance for tool selection and future optimization.

4.2 Examples of Countermeasures Against AIGC Dependence

For example, in the Computer Networks laboratory, students are required to complete a basic experiment, an advanced experiment, and a challenge experiment [2]. In the basic experiment, students are asked to configure a web server on the lab machine and create a personal webpage. During inspections, we found that some students' generated webpages included techniques that the students themselves did not actually understand or master; some students did not even include their own names on their webpages. When checking the correctness of the IIS configuration, students were instructed to browse to the homepage at 127.0.0.1 and to the homepage at the machine's local IP address to verify that the server was configured correctly. For students who had errors, when questioned, they said they had simply followed a tutorial provided by DeepSeek, which did not meet the actual requirements. In the cloud computing course, students were instructed to use AIGC tools to look up key cloud computing technologies and to list several keywords each. In practice, because AIGC tools provided many answers, extracting keywords from large passages of text proved to be a significant effort. Students used word clouds or sampling methods to select keywords for analysis, prompting critical thinking. Students also reported that sometimes using AIGC tools does not solve even moderately challenging problems.

4.3 Other Measures

To highlight the characteristics of the Network Engineering major, students are encouraged to actively participate in programs and competitions such as the College Student Innovation and Entrepreneurship Program, "Internet+" competitions, the National College Student Information Security Competition, the

Huawei Network Technology Competition, the Liaoning Cybersecurity Penetration Testing Competition, etc., thereby training through competition to solidify their foundation. In addition, after completing theoretical classes in the spring semester, Network Engineering students take a "Network Comprehensive Laboratory" course in the following summer. In theoretical teaching, we also emphasize in advance the main content they will face in the lab, such as specific network protocols, routing algorithms, and switch configurations. Practical application of theory includes cabling, packet capturing, router/switch login and configuration, and experiments involving DNS, link aggregation, RIP/OSPF, firewalls, and ACLs. During the pandemic, our lab system was also deployed "on the cloud," allowing remote access and operation [3]. The assessment for the Network Comprehensive Laboratory course is an exam, in which students must build and configure a comprehensive network scenario and then draw questions to answer three theoretical problems in computer networks.

5 Implementation Effects

According to the grade data of relevant classes in the Computer Networks course at Dalian University of Technology (Table 2), after implementation of the curriculum reforms, the class average scores, proportion of high scores, and pass rates have all shown significant improvement. For example, in the class that adopted the "knowledge graph–assisted knowledge point organization plus staged lab assessment" approach, the average score increased by about 6–8 points compared to classes without the reform, the proportion of high scores (≥90) rose to 25%–30%, and the pass rate stabilized above 90%, significantly higher than in classes without systematic reform measures.

Table 2. Comparison of class performance before and after improvements in the "Computer Networks" course.

Metric	Class with Improvement Measures (e.g., Class 2411)	Class without Improvement Measures (e.g., Class 2403)
Average Score	79.02	71.52
High Score Rate (≥90)	34%	18%
Pass Rate	96.03%	86.59%
Complex Protocol (e.g., TCP/IP, ARP) Understanding Score Rate	82%	63%
Practical Operations Question Score Rate	85%	52%
Retake Students Average Score	63.5	51.7

Classes that used customized knowledge graphs (e.g., hierarchical knowledge point graphs for computer networks) showed improved student understanding of complex protocols (such as TCP/IP and ARP): the score rates on related knowledge points were 15%–20% higher than in traditional teaching classes. The knowledge graph had a significant organizing effect on strongly related knowledge points such as "IPv4 address shortage solutions" and "network checksum mechanism," helping students establish a systematic knowledge framework and reducing rote memorization; scores on subjective questions improved markedly. Through the layered design of "basic experiment (server configuration) + advanced experiment (routing protocol configuration) + challenge experiment (firewall and ACL configuration)", students' scores on practical operation questions exceeded 80%, which was 30% higher than in the class that relied solely on AIGC-generated theoretical answers. Especially for practical tasks like Wireshark packet capture analysis and Ethernet frame structure interpretation, students with strong hands-on skills showed significant advantages, confirming the conclusion that "practical operations cannot be replaced by AIGC." Students who overly relied on AIGC to complete assignments (for example, directly using DeepSeek to generate lab reports without modification) scored only 50%–60% on questions requiring logical deduction and detailed operations (such as IP datagram fragmentation calculations or analysis of the TCP three-way handshake), and their performance became polarized: some students scored low because they blindly copied AIGC content (which contained redundancies or errors), while those who reasonably used AIGC to assist in organizing their thoughts performed better.

In this analysis, we found that retaking students still had unsatisfactory scores. Investigation revealed that their dependency on AIGC was over 70%, and their scores on questions involving protocol principles and comprehensive lab design were only 40%–50%, lowering the class average by about 3–5 points. Additionally, although some students could use the knowledge graph to master the associations among knowledge points, they still lacked flexible application abilities in practical problem-solving (such as complex network troubleshooting), reflecting that the conversion of "theory to practice" needs further strengthening.

It is worth noting that computer networks are the foundation for cloud computing, and cloud computing is the platform for AI computation; these technologies are tightly linked at the application level and are driven by networks. After the curriculum reform, Network Engineering students showed increased willingness to participate in AI competitions based on their Computer Networks foundation; for example, a team led by student Sun participated in the Artificial Intelligence Global Open Competition. This is due to our introduction of AI-related technologies and concepts in the network courses, allowing students early exposure so that they can prepare in advance for relevant competitions.

6 Conclusion

This paper explores the adaptive adjustments of the Network Engineering curriculum system in the era of intelligence, systematically explaining specific paths for course content optimization, teaching method innovation, and assessment mechanism improvement. At the curriculum system level, by integrating AI fundamentals, machine learning, and deep learning content, the convergence of network engineering and intelligent technology is strengthened. This preserves the professional foundation of core courses such as Computer Networks, Cloud Computing, and Network Attack Defense and Practice, while aligning traditional knowledge with the demands of the intelligent era. In teaching practice, the focus is on exploring the application value of knowledge graphs in the Computer Networks course: by constructing a hierarchical knowledge point graph, students are helped to organize the associative logic of complex protocols, improving the efficiency of systematic knowledge mastery. In response to the learning challenges posed by AIGC tools, a layered assessment model of "basic experiment + advanced experiment + challenge experiment" is adopted, combined with measures such as "training through competitions" and deploying the network lab on the cloud. These measures strengthen the cultivation of practical operation ability and effectively prevent the thinking inertia caused by over-reliance on tools. Finally, by evaluating the implementation effects, we can see that these improvements have led to enhancements in students' learning performance and practical abilities in the Network Engineering major. These improvement measures can also be applied to other similar courses, and our approach has been implemented at the College of Information, Liaoning University as well. However, some students still exhibit significant issues in learning attitude and academic performance, and how to improve the learning motivation of retaking students remains a future research direction [1].

References

1. Committee, C.C., Council, S.: Outline of the plan for building China into an educational strong nation (2024–2035). Policy document (2024)
2. Li, G., Guo, H., Li, X.: Optimization design and practice of the experimental teaching system of a first-class course in computer networks. Exp. Sci. Technol. **22**(04), 90–95, 119 (2024)
3. Sun, W., Zhang, L., Yao, L.: Exploration and implementation of the "three new" in the computer networks course in the new era. Softw. Guide **21**(7), 27–32 (2022)
4. Yang, C., Li, X.: Exploration and practice of blended teaching reform of computer networks under the background of engineering education accreditation. J. Jilin Eng. Technol. Normal College **39**(05), 84–86 (2023)
5. Zhang, S., Han, Q., Sun, S.: Exploration of the practical teaching system for the network engineering major in the context of new engineering. J. Zhoukou Normal Univ. **40**(5), 122–125 (2023)
6. Zhao, Y., Zhang, L., Yan, S., et al.: A survey of disciplinary knowledge graph construction and application in personalized learning. Comput. Eng. Appl. **59**(10) (2023)

Project-Driven Enhancement of Innovation Capacity: Teaching Reform Practice of Generative AI Courses

Jiao Tian[1(✉)], Wei Xia[1,2], Shuxian Liu[1], and Haoxiang Huang[1]

[1] School of Computer Science and Technology, Xinjiang University, Urumqi 830017, China
{jiaotian,liushuxian,hhx_cs}@xju.edu.cn, wx@uestc.edu.cn

[2] School of Information and Communication Engineering, University of Electronic Science and Technology of China, Chengdu 611731, China

Abstract. To deepen the construction of new engineering disciplines in the intelligent era and explore the discovery and cultivation mechanism of national top-notch innovative talents, universities are required to focus on the strategic needs of the country and emerging fields, continuously optimize the curriculum, and strive to enhance the practical and innovative abilities of reserve talents. This study proposes a project-driven general elective course named Basic AIGC. This course aims to continuously stimulate students' internal driven holistic and critical innovative with project practice. Through the reform of the project-led curriculum system and teaching content, it ensures that students can keenly perceive and engage in this technological revolution, and enhance their core competitiveness literaly.

Keywords: Project-Driven · Practical Innovation Ability · Generative AI Course · Teaching Curriculum Reform

1 Introduction

Since the release of ChatGPT, generative artificial intelligence (Artificial Intelligence Generated Content, AIGC) has received high attention from governments, universities, research institutions and enterprises around the world. The emergence of DeepSeek is a sign of the intensification of the competition between China and the United States. As the main battlefield for cultivating top-notch innovative scientific research talents, the main force of basic research and the source of major scientific and technological breakthroughs, Chinese universities should seize the opportunity and comprehensively enhance social productivity, promote the construction of a strong country and realize the great rejuvenation of the nation through teaching reform, talent cultivation and scientific and technological innovation [3]. The report of the 20th National Congress of the Communist Party of China pointed out that according to the new trends in scientific and

Supported by School of Computer Science and Technology, Xinjiang University.

J. Chi et al. (Eds.): CNETCNED 2025, CCIS 2809, pp. 54–66, 2026.
https://doi.org/10.1007/978-981-95-7124-6_6

technological development, the discipline settings and talent cultivation models of higher education should be optimized to cultivate urgently needed talents for developing new productive forces and promoting high-quality development [6]. As the first year of AIGC, 2023, its ability to create new content and integrate existing knowledge to solve new problems not only provides unprecedented assistance for the innovation of college students in the new era, but also puts forward more comprehensive and critical ability requirements. Offering a general elective course "Introduction to Generative Artificial Intelligence (AIGC)" to all majors in the university and focusing on cultivating students' macro-innovation ability in the teaching process is the only way to accurately grasp the priority development of education, promote independent and strong science and technology, and achieve talent-driven development.

The General Course on "Fundamentals of Generative AI (AIGC)" is a comprehensive course designed to systematically introduce the basic theories, practical methods, cross-disciplinary applications, and professional applications of AIGC. Through detailed concept explanations, algorithm evolutions, and case analyses, it helps students understand its development history and the latest research and application trends. The course aims to cultivate students' theoretical foundation and practical application abilities in the field of AIGC, and enhance their cross-disciplinary critical thinking and innovation capabilities. Against the backdrop of rapid technological iterations and deep industry transformations in AIGC, traditional simple knowledge search and integrative innovation have gradually been replaced by large models [5]. Students urgently need to possess the abilities of project-level task decomposition, macro-control, and efficient combination [4]. Moreover, the potential falsity and bias in the content generated by big data pose higher requirements for users' judgment and integration capabilities [2]. In the early stage of AIGC course offerings, no preferential improvements have been made in the curriculum system and teaching methods. This study takes this as an entry point and proposes suggestions and opinions for deepening project-driven course teaching reform to cultivate students' macro-innovation capabilities needed for future career development.

2 Thoughts on the Construction of Project-Driven Generative Artificial Intelligence Curriculum System

Offering AIGC courses to students of all majors can maximize the popularization of cutting-edge technologies and encourage them to actively explore and apply new knowledge. However, given the nature of general elective courses and the relatively weak background in artificial intelligence of the students, AIGC focuses on understanding macroscopic knowledge, broadening professional horizons, and enhancing practical innovation capabilities. The course is organized in a sequence from simple to complex content, from basic to comprehensive functions, and from life-related project practices to professional fields. The first and second chapters provide the background of this technology; the third chapter covers the key to human-machine co-intelligence technology [4]- the carrier of AI thinking transformation; the fourth to eighth chapters are, in turn, the basic office skills, basic research skills, and cutting-edge professional skills needed for students to complete their studies efficiently and with high quality; the ninth chapter is the comprehensive application and fine-tuning of all basic skills, further deepening the knowledge learned; the last chapter summarizes and looks forward to the research field of AIGC. The depth and difficulty of the content in subsequent chapters can be adjusted according to the students' cognitive levels and learning progress to meet the needs of students at different levels [1]. The teaching chapter settings are shown in Table 1.

Table 1. Curriculum Design for Generative Artificial Intelligence Courses.

Chapter/Section	Main Teaching Contents
One	An Overview of Generative Artificial Intelligence and Large Language Models
Two	Laws, regulations and technical usage norms related to generative artificial intelligence
There	Prompt engineering and structured prompt words
Four	Generative artificial intelligence empowers smart office
Five	AI-driven program design assistance
Six	The Basics of Image Generation AI Technology
Seven	The Basics of Video Generation AI Technology
Eight	The Basics of Audio Generation AI Technology
Nine	AI multimodal hybrid creation
Ten	Foreseeing the Future: The Beginning of New Explorations

3 Curriculum Design for Generative Artificial Intelligence

The course is designed with four major projects: professional science popularization, Little Red Book bloggers, employee salary reports, and game character creation. The main task of the professional science popularization project is to select popularization topics, create understandable popularization content in various forms, and combine less commonly encountered knowledge in natural science and art design in daily life. The content will be evaluated based on accuracy, ease of understanding, and dissemination effect. The Little Red Book blogger project requires students to clarify the blogger's positioning and theme based on survey statistics, formulate a content creation plan, and regularly release high-quality text, images, and videos to achieve fan growth, interaction, and brand cooperation. Students majoring in marketing, psychology, and statistics can better apply their knowledge. The main task of the employee salary report project is to collect and organize employee salary data, conduct in-depth analysis, and write detailed reports. The main evaluation criteria for this project are data accuracy, logic, analysis depth, and report quality. This project is suitable for students majoring in economics and management as well as mathematics. The game character creation project assesses the setting of character attributes, skills, logical integration, and display effects based on creativity, model quality, animation effects, and special effects performance. This project combines techniques from fields such as art design, computer graphics, and literary creation. Different sub-projects at various stages are divided as shown in Fig. 1 (the same project is marked with the same color). Basic functions are completed in the third to eighth chapters along with course practice, while innovative effect exploration is done in after-class practice. Comprehensive applications are completed in the ninth chapter and the final major assignment.

Fig. 1. Schematic Diagram of Project-Driven Curriculum Structure.

3.1 An Overview of Generative Artificial Intelligence and Large Language Models

Chapter One introduces the background and technical schools of thought of the birth of large language models through the popularity of DeepSeek, presents the basic concepts of AIGC and the development framework of the content industry, and encourages students to envision the potential of AIGC in the future and its impact on various industries and future job requirements based on the current development status of their own majors. It then dialectically summarizes the short-term unemployment wave brought about by technological revolutions and possible countermeasures. The chapter also provides an overview of the course and the four projects that run throughout, guiding students to put themselves in the shoes of the users to complete the demand analysis and make corresponding project plans in line with the course progress. Through this interaction and the active guidance of the teacher, students are cultivated with a broad vision of new technologies and the ability to lead projects comprehensively.

3.2 Laws, Regulations and Technical Usage Norms Related to Generative Artificial Intelligence

Since the advent of AIGC, there have been no shortage of disputes over digital ethics and intellectual property rights. This chapter focuses on learning the relevant laws and regulations, namely the "Interim Measures for the Administration of Generative Artificial Intelligence Services" and the "Measures for the Identification of Content Generated and Synthesized by Artificial Intelligence". The students who have chosen this course are all potential tech talents and will inevitably use AIGC in their future careers. The ethical standards mixed in are expounded from a macro perspective of national security, cyber security, and privacy protection to illustrate the importance and necessity of regulating AIGC [7]. It guides students from external discipline to self-discipline and helps them establish correct values and a sense of social responsibility through ethical and moral cases. Through case analysis teaching methods involving interaction with AI, it alerts students to the issues of AI reshaping human perception and social judgment and amplifying inherent biases, and cultivates their critical thinking in the problem-solving process.

3.3 Prompt Engineering and Structured Prompt Words

The foundation of human-machine co-intelligence lies in humans' ability to effectively convey their needs to machines, endowing them with a certain degree of creativity while setting clear boundaries for their outputs. This innovative concept differs from the simple command control in traditional machine learning and transcends the scope of cybernetics and information theory. It is the core technology of this course [9]. In the third chapter, by drawing an analogy to a patient seeking medical advice at a hospital, the four key elements of prompt words, as well as the prompt strategies for single-word and multi-round questions, are introduced. In the popular science project, the text description practice of a history teacher explaining the causes and impacts of World War II to children is dissected, leading to the introduction of the classic CRISPE framework and the application and effects of the thought chain in large language models. This helps students master the design principles and steps of structured prompt words. In the operation of students seeking help from large language models when encountering problems in simulated after-class assignments, they are first required to provide results based on independent thinking prompts; then, the teacher provides framework prompts based on course guidance, compares the results to draw conclusions, and leaves time for students to freely explore after identifying areas for improvement. Students then discuss and evaluate each other's achievements, fostering their ability to identify problems, make improvements, and engage in further critical innovation.

3.4 Generative Artificial Intelligence Empowers Smart Office

Chapter Four mainly elaborates on the application of AIGC in daily office work, including text generation, table processing, presentation, and the usage steps and techniques of tools such as mind mapping and data excerpting for students. It analyzes the key links and prompt engineering techniques of high-traffic text generation through trendy self-media creative writing (increasing followers through travel sharing on Xiaohongshu) and game character strategy generation (introduction of skills for characters in San Guo Sha), and provides detailed steps and code generation modifications for AIGC assistance in Microsoft Office and WPS Office, such as table construction, data filling, formula application, macro commands, data output format conversion, chart generation, and recommendations. It connects with the teacher's lesson preparation project in the previous chapter to automatically generate PowerPoints using structured text and VBA code, and uses third-party AI tools for polishing. It introduces and compares different PowerPoint presentation effects through plugins, add-ins, iterative use of multiple AI tools, and the one-stop AI assistant Sider, and raises questions to explore the differences in effect, potential hidden information misguidance, and even false information caused by different integration methods of the same resources. It combines the majors of the students who have selected the course to provide comprehensive projects, such as the renovation and sustainable development of old communities, and organizes students from different majors to try innovations and showcase their achievements, with case comparisons and analyses among groups. This interactive learning method not only enhances students' exploration interest but also promotes their in-depth understanding and critical application ability of related technologies.

3.5 AI-Driven Program Design Assistance

In Chapter Five, the basic information, development history, and advantages and disadvantages of the main programming tools are mainly introduced using Python as the programming language. Through the elaboration of the four major advantages of programming with large language models, namely natural language understanding, automatic code generation, detection and correction, and cross-platform application of multiple programming languages, the necessity, advantages, and application scenarios of programming are explained. The practical section introduces the configuration, usage steps, and completion of representative practical tasks such as sorting algorithms, annuity calculation, and web front-end design using plugins like GitHub Copilot, Codeium, and Wenxin Kuaima based on VS Code. Teachers guide students to conduct multi-result comparison and reflection, engage in classroom Q&A interactions, and assign cases related to data analysis in their major to enable students to fully master the techniques of automatic code generation and correction. Additionally, the occurrence of erroneous code during the process illustrates the phenomenon where some AIs ignore the interpreter environment and provide seemingly error-free code and possible dead loops in human-machine interaction feedback in complex programming, fostering students' ability to solve problems independently and stimulating their critical and innovative thinking in integrating their professional knowledge with programming techniques.

3.6 The Basics of Image Generation AI Technology

Chapter Six showcases AI images of different styles to enable students to initially understand the basic principles of AIGC in multimedia generation. It introduces the concept of latent variables in potential diffusion models and their application in image generation, as well as the text-to-image working mechanism and application methods of the CLIP model. In practical operations, teachers first introduce the characteristics and operation interface usage processes of different AI drawing tools (such as Midjourney, Stable Diffusion, LoRa), loading modules, parameter adjustments, and result previews. In demonstrations such as PowerPoint illustration design, video cover design, poster design, and game IP design, attempts are made to generate consistent and diverse content. Based on the generation results, effective prompt word optimizations for images are provided, guiding students to summarize the characteristics of better-performing prompt words. Through theoretical learning and practical operations, students can critically select appropriate auxiliary tools for future scenarios and efficiently and accurately guide AI to complete tasks, laying a solid foundation for more complex content integration.

3.7 The Basics of Video Generation AI Technology

Starting from the core principles of AI video generation, through the practical achievements in Chap. 6, students will understand how smooth and coherent videos are generated from images through precise prompt words, diffusion models, and parameter adjustments. They will also learn about the roles of basic video terms such as resolution, frame rate, and generation duration, as well as techniques like keyframe redrawing and AI frame interpolation. In the practical stage, three types of tools are introduced in order of increasing difficulty: beginner-friendly ones like Synthesia and D-ID for quickly generating virtual person explanation videos; creative advanced ones like Runway and Pictory for creating cinematic vlogs to further operate on sharing travel experiences on Xiaohongshu; and technical geek ones like Stable Video Diffusion and its plugins Deforum and AnimateDiff for demonstrating basic skills of game characters with high consistency and smoothness in the visuals. In the prompt word optimization section, the effects of ordinary and advanced prompt words are compared to guide students to derive the "subject + scene + detail + style + parameter" magic formula, enhancing their ability to write prompt words. By completing the improved Xiaohongshu travel project in practice, students can consolidate what they have learned, achieve the leap from theory to practice, and quickly master AI video generation technology while trying out new features of the tools.

3.8 The Basics of Audio Generation AI Technology

This chapter delves into the core principles of audio generation, the two major directions of AI in audio generation: Text-to-Speech (TTS) and Voice Conversion (VC), and various technical routes and advancements in AI-generated audio. By using the analogy of a band performance, students are guided to understand the collaborative roles of prompts (sheet music), AI models (musicians), and parameters (rhythm and tempo). Subsequently, audio generation is categorized into three types based on function: voice synthesis, demonstrated with the open-source SVC software for customizing personalized voice cloning; music composition, illustrated with SUNO creating background music for the game IP in Chap. 6; and sound effect generation, exemplified by Boomy and Noise.app for producing natural environmental sounds. Through comparing prompts in music composition tools, students learn to select musical styles, input melody directions to generate music, and are introduced to the precise adjustment of the "content + style + detail + parameter" formula. Practical projects are set up, including voice announcements and creating background music for short videos based on the previous chapter, allowing students to consolidate their knowledge and quickly master AI-assisted audio generation techniques through practice.

3.9 AI Multimodal Hybrid Creation

Based on the learning from the first eight chapters, students are required to comprehensively apply the knowledge they have acquired by using the analogy of "stage play arrangement" for multimodal creation: text is the script, images are the set design, audio is the background music, video is the performance of the actors, and the AI model is the director who coordinates everything. This helps students understand the collaborative logic of each element. A demonstration is provided to show the basic operations of an interactive science popularization short film that can achieve image style-driven audio melody and text emotion-controlled video tone. The prompt word design stage focuses on showing the effect comparison between cross-modal association instructions and general instructions, and the teacher and students interact to summarize the key points. In the classroom practice, the content creation of science popularization short films related to the major is improved, enabling students not only to master the entire process of multimodal creation proficiently in practice but also to have a comprehensive understanding of the position and importance of each part of this course in the overall framework.

3.10 Foreseeing the Future: The Beginning of New Explorations

Chapter Ten introduces some new explorations in the current AIGC industry and the possibilities of future technological development. Based on the professional backgrounds of the students enrolled in the course, it combines text, images, and videos to introduce the applications of AIGC in various fields. For example, for students majoring in cyber security, it showcases the current development status of AI simulating real network attack scenarios, real-time threat detection, and automated response [8]. It stimulates students to think about the innovative technologies that can be initially accomplished by integrating the technologies learned in this course with their respective majors. It encourages students to further engage with cutting-edge technologies and develop the habit of regularly following current events, self-study, and lifelong learning.

4 Project-Based Practices for Stimulating Intrinsic Motivation for Innovation

4.1 Exhibition of Selected Accomplishments from Student Projects

The project-driven student work showcases of AIGC include the automatic generation of summary texts from literature, text-to-outline generation, outline-to-PowerPoint conversion, and PowerPoint polishing techniques in the professional science popularization project as shown in Fig. 2; background style transformation technology in the game character creation and Little Red Book blogger project, which lays a solid foundation for image-to-video generation and video style unification prompt engineering as depicted in Fig. 3; and screenshots of the popular tourist attractions introduction video in the Little Red Book blogger project, including digital human narration and subtitle generation technologies as illustrated in Fig. 4.

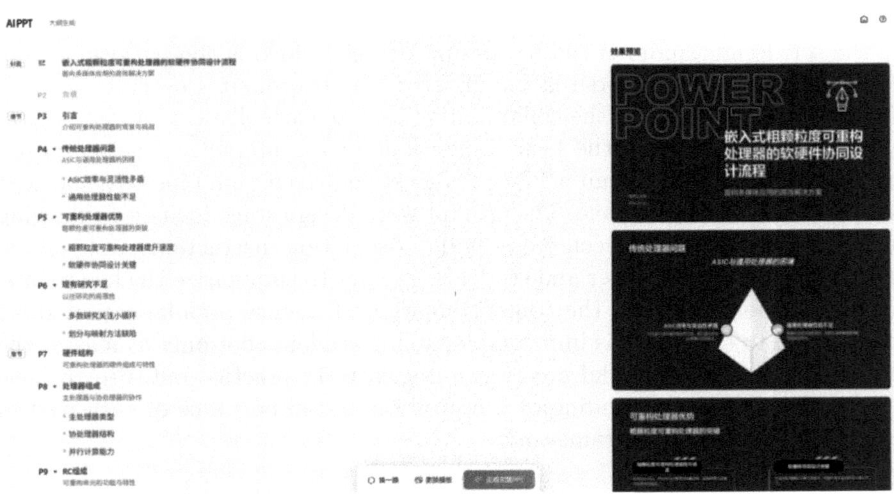

Fig. 2. Student Practice: Automated Generation of PowerPoint Presentations from Academic Literature Reviews.

Fig. 3. Student Practice: Implementing Painting Style Transfer Using LoRA.

4.2 Comparative Analysis of Academic Transcripts and Academic Performance

The AIGC teaching reform set up an experimental class driven by projects and a control class taught by traditional methods. Both classes had 100 students. Figure 5 shows the statistics of the students' majors in the two classes. Students from Network Space Security and Information Security were the majority, accounting for 48% and 54% respectively. To test whether there was a significant difference in the distribution of students' majors, a chi-square test was conducted. The probability value was obtained as $p=0.110>>0.05=\alpha$, and the null hypothesis could not be rejected: there was no significant difference in the distribution of majors between the two classes.

The learning evaluation results and analysis are shown in Table 2. The average score of the experimental class is 78.4, which is 6.8 points higher than that of the control class. Meanwhile, the standard deviation of the experimental class is smaller, and the distribution ratio of the scores in the 0–60, 60–79, and 80–100 score ranges is more concentrated in the 80–100 score range, indicating that the students' scores are more concentrated in the high-score range. A T-test was conducted on the average score, with a Satterthwaite degree of freedom of 163. When the significance level $\alpha=0.05$ is taken, $t=2.071>1.654=$tcritical value, the null hypothesis is rejected, indicating that there is a significant difference in the average scores of the two groups of students. Combined with the detection that there is no significant difference in the professional distribution of students in the experimental class and the control class, it can be concluded that the experimental class as a whole shows better teaching effects.

Fig. 4. Student Practice: Tourist Video with Digital Human Narration.

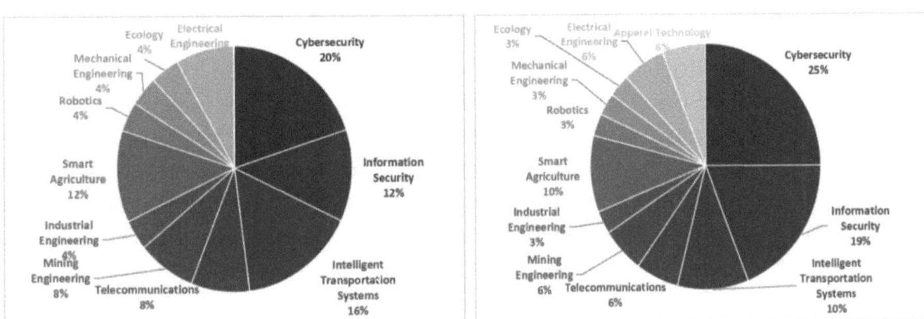

(a) Experimental Group (b) Control Group

Fig. 5. Statistics of students' majors in the class.

Table 2. Comparative Analysis of Academic Performance Evaluations between the Experimental Group and the Control Group

Class	Grade distribution				
	Mean Score	Standard Deviation	0–59 Points	60–79 Points	80–100 Points
Experimental Group	78.4	17.0	7%	21%	72%
Control Group	71.6	28.1	14%	28%	58%

4.3 Evaluations of Project-Based Instruction by Students and Faculty

Some students reported during their classroom presentation of practical achievements that "I was just thinking of creating a Little Red Book account, but I didn't know what to share. Using AI to generate multiple results gave me different inspiration for choices, and the generated content came with popular tags and emojis, saving me a lot of time." Another student said, "The assistance in office work and programming is very helpful for the entry-level autonomous driving in the intelligent transportation major. The introductory course on artificial intelligence offered by our college is too brief. Even if I understand it, I still don't know how to apply it. However, the project-driven approach taught me how to break down difficult tasks, which is very helpful for self-study and hands-on practice."

From the feedback of teachers, it is observed that the students in the project-driven teaching class have shown a significant improvement in their class participation compared to those in the traditional teaching class. The interlinked practical activities not only allow for multiple reviews of the previous learning content but also encourage students to actively participate in identifying problems and expressing their viewpoints. The innovation in students' homework has also been significantly enhanced.

The student evaluation of teaching on the teaching quality management platform shows that the experimental class gave the course a score of 93.25, while the control class scored 81.76. All in all, it indicates that students highly recognize the project-driven teaching method that enhances their innovation ability, and it has achieved good results when applied to the AIGC course.

5 Conclusion

Project-based innovation ability is the key for students to embark on a sustainable career path in the future. Through this teaching reform practice, we have not only witnessed a significant improvement in students' technological innovation and application capabilities, but also been delighted to see the critical thinking and interdisciplinary knowledge integration abilities they demonstrated when facing problems. These abilities are precisely the core requirements of society for professionals in all fields in the context of AI. Looking back on the entire teaching process, we have deeply realized that project-driven teaching can not only effectively stimulate students' interest in learning and intrinsic motivation, but also guide them to closely combine theoretical knowledge with practical operations, thereby continuously transferring and innovating in the process of solving practical problems. At the same time, AIGC, this cutting-edge technology, has opened a door to the future technological world for students, giving them the opportunity to personally experience and participate in this technological revolution.

Looking forward, we will continue to deepen teaching reform, constantly explore more efficient and practical teaching methods and means, in order to achieve more significant results in cultivating students' innovation ability and comprehensive quality.

Acknowledgements. This paper was supported by the Autonomous Region Graduate Education and Teaching Reform Project (Grant No. XJ2023GY12), the Ministry of Education Industry-Academia Cooperative Education Program (Grant No. 231007559194459), and the 2025 Xinjiang University Undergraduate Education and Teaching Research and Reform Project (Grant No. XJU-2025JG68).

References

1. Ding, G., Wang, S., Ma, S., Zhang, J.: Exploration on construction mode of industry-education integration curriculum system based on knowledge graph. Res. High. Edu. Eng. (02), 79–83+90 (2024)
2. Liu, Y., et al.: Exploration and practice of ideological and political teaching in computer network experiment course. Comput. Edu. (05), 44–48+54 (2025). https://doi.org/10.16512/j.cnki.jsjjy.2025.05.008
3. Ministry of Education of the People's Republic of China: [china youth daily] statistics on ten years of education: Universities have become the main force of basic research and the source of major scientific and technological breakthroughs (2022), http://www.moe.gov.cn/fbh/live/2022/54875/mtbd/202209/t20220927_665358.html, Accessed on 02 Jul 2025)
4. Tu, T., Zhang, Y.: Teachers' teaching wisdom driven by human-machine co-intelligence: Value implication, action mechanism and generation path. Journal of Southwest University (Social Sciences Edition) **50**(05), 204–212 (2024). https://doi.org/10.13718/j.cnki.xdsk.2024.05.017
5. Wu, H., Zhou, H., Li, G.: Research on the application of generative ai in the teaching of "introduction to artificial intelligence" course. Comput. Knowl. Techn. **20**(31), 158–160 (2024). https://doi.org/10.14004/j.cnki.ckt.2024.1605
6. Xinhua News Agency: Xi jinping: Hold high the great banner of socialism with chinese characteristics and strive in unity to build a modern socialist country in all respects–report to the 20th national congress of the communist party of china (2022), https://www.gov.cn/xinwen/2022-10/25/content_5721685.htm, Accessed on 02 Jul 2025
7. Xu, Y., Ren, Y., Qiu, J., Qiu, H.: Endogenous construction of ideological and political education in all courses for cyberspace security majors. Netw. Sec. Technol. & Appl. **05**, 90–94 (2025)
8. Xu, Y., Liu, X., Wang, W.: Cybersecurity risks and countermeasures of generative artificial intelligence. China Information Security **03**, 22–24 (2025)
9. Zhang, Y., Wang, Y., Zhang, H., Zhang, C.: Design of curriculum content system driven by multi-party needs in the era of generative ai: A case study of "information analysis" course. Libr. Tribune **45**(11), 83–94 (2025)

Adaptive Reform for Computer Network Experimental Teaching in the Era of LLMs

Haipeng Dai[1], Jiaqi Zheng[1(✉)], Jia Liu[1], Yuben Qu[2], Meng Li[1], Ying Jin[1], Shizhe Liu[1], Si Shen[1], and Guihai Chen[1(✉)]

[1] State Key Laboratory for Novel Software Technology, Nanjing University, Nanjing, China
{haipengdai,jzheng,jialiu,meng,jinying,gchen}@nju.edu.cn,
{shizheliu,sishen}@smail.nju.edu.cn

[2] College of Electronic and Information Engineering, Nanjing University of Aeronautics and Astronautics, Nanjing, China
quyuben@nuaa.edu.cn

Abstract. Large language models (LLMs) pose unprecedented challenges to courses centered on experimental teaching in areas such as computer networks. Students may use LLMs to complete coding tasks and technical reports, which not only diminishes the effectiveness of experimental training but also impacts the fairness of assessments. To address this challenge, this paper proposes a "Three-Dimensional Competency Development" framework tailored for computer network experimental teaching. The framework reconstructs computer network experiments from three dimensions: consolidating foundational skills, enhancing analytical abilities, and elevating innovative capacities, through a progressive design. Implementing this experimental framework in specific teaching practices shows that over 70% of students can effectively grasp the underlying principles and knowledge of computer networks.

Keywords: Computer Network · Experimental Teaching · Large Language Models · Adaptive Reform

1 Introduction

The rapid development of large language models (LLMs) such as ChatGPT [1] and DeepSeek [2] is transforming experimental teaching in computer science majors. Leveraging the powerful code generation, debugging, and explanation capabilities of LLMs, students can easily obtain experimental solutions through multiple rounds of interaction with LLMs. However, if students submit these answers without critical thinking, it deviates from the original intent of experimental teaching. Especially in computer network practical courses, relying on LLMs' outputs can hinder students' understanding of network protocols, preventing true development of their programming and systemic thinking skills.

J. Chi et al. (Eds.): CNETCNED 2025, CCIS 2809, pp. 67–76, 2026.
https://doi.org/10.1007/978-981-95-7124-6_7

During the experimental teaching process, we observed that misuse or reliance on LLMs for students can lead to the following three issues:

(1) **Superficial code understanding.** Although students can quickly obtain experimental code from LLMs, they lack in-depth understanding of network protocols (*e.g.*, TCP congestion control and BGP routing), making them prone to the dilemma of "knowing what it is without understanding why."
(2) **Hollowed practical skills training.** Key practical skills such as algorithm design, debugging, troubleshooting, and performance optimization are delegated to LLMs, resulting in the erosion of students' ability to solve problems independently. As a result, practical skills training becomes hollowed out.
(3) **Learning assessment distortion.** Traditional evaluation systems based on the results of submitted code are hardly able to identify content generated by LLMs, leading to our struggling to recognize students' true abilities. As a result, the current experimental feedback mechanism becomes ineffective.

However, the reasonable use of LLMs also presents new teaching opportunities, reshaping learning methods and promoting the upgrade of teaching modes [3]. For example, multimodal experimental report auto-correction systems driven by LLMs [4] can transcend time and space limitations; intelligent Q&A systems [5] can provide personalized learning support; and adaptive programming teaching platforms [6,7] have the potential to realize tailored instruction.

Thus, we face a key issue that urgently needs to be solved: *how to embrace the technological revolution brought by LLMs while maintaining the core goal of education, ensuring students solidly grasp the basic concepts and principles of computer network?* This paper aims to explore adaptive reform pathways for computer network experimental teaching in the era of LLMs, creating a new teaching model that leverages the advantages of intelligent tools while safeguarding the cultivation of students' core abilities.

2 Reform Motivation

2.1 Reform Urgency of Experimental Teaching

LLMs pose unprecedented opportunities and challenges to the traditional experimental teaching [8]. Nowadays, many experimental tasks can be solved with relatively accurate answers generated by LLMs. Notably, simply prohibiting students from using LLMs is neither practical nor consistent with the educational purpose of enabling students to recognize and embrace cutting-edge technologies. Remarkably, we believe that if LLMs are reasonably used as intelligent auxiliary tools, their powerful generative capabilities can significantly improve teaching effectiveness. Thus, we need to reconstruct the current teaching model with a more open mindset.

To achieve the organic integration of LLMs and experimental teaching, it is necessary to address two fundamental contradictions: on the one hand, fully leveraging the empowering role of LLMs, and on the other hand, preventing students from forming excessive technological dependence. The key lies in promoting the transformation of LLMs from a potential "shortcut tool" into a "cognitive enhancer." For the field of computer network experimental teaching, reform needs to focus on three aspects: enhancing students' understanding of network protocols and underlying implementations, improving their ability to locate and solve problems, and cultivating innovative and critical thinking.

In addition, LLMs also pose severe challenges to the evaluation system of experimental teaching, which can be reflected in two significant aspects.

(1) **Compromised fairness in grading.** Traditional evaluation methods based on the final code results (for example, pass rates of test cases in online judging systems) or the completeness of experimental reports have become inadequate in the face of the strong generative capabilities of LLMs. During the teaching process, it was observed that students who seriously and independently completed experiments might score lower than those who excessively relied on LLMs. This severely undermines grading fairness. Moreover, current AI code detection techniques remain imperfect. Students can bypass detection through multiple rounds of interaction or by modifying code fragments, making the evaluation system overly dependent on academic integrity.

(2) **Ineffective competency development measurement.** The core value of experimental education lies in enhancing students' problem-solving thinking and hands-on skills. However, when students use LLMs to obtain answers, they skip critical steps such as reasoning, trial-and-error, and iteration (*e.g.*, understanding protocol details, designing data structures, and debugging boundary conditions). As a result, the final submitted code and reports cannot accurately reflect students' true abilities in code comprehension, problem analysis, and debugging. This severely hinders the development of students' skills, preventing instructors from grasping teaching priorities based on their submissions and from identifying deficiencies in current instructional methods.

Therefore, reforming the experimental teaching evaluation system to effectively assess students' real learning processes and mastery of core abilities in the context of LLMs has become an urgent priority.

2.2 Requirements for Computer Network Experimental Design

To effectively respond to the challenges and impacts brought by LLMs, and to maximize their potential as auxiliary tools (*e.g.*, rapid knowledge acquisition and automatic generation of basic code frameworks), the core goal of experimental course design has shifted from simple knowledge verification and skill imitation to the construction of authentic problem scenarios that foster deep understanding, critical practice, and innovative capacity. This shift places three new requirements R1-R3 on experimental course design, as illustrated in Fig. 1.

R1: Mining blind spots of LLMs. It is necessary to design experimental tasks with defensive capabilities against LLMs by deliberately creating gaps

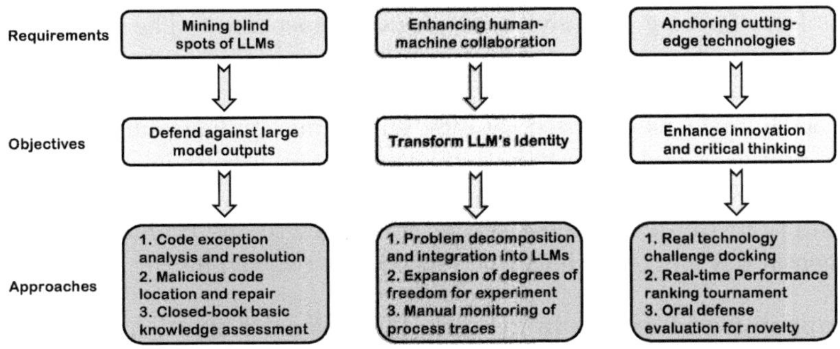

Fig. 1. Requirements, objectives, and approaches for computer network experimental design in the era of LLMs.

between course knowledge and model outputs. Specific methods include: providing code that cannot fully pass test cases and requiring students to analyze and solve the problems; offering code with artificially introduced errors for students to locate and repair; and conducting closed-book assessments on fundamental knowledge and key experimental details.

R2: Enhancing humanmachine collaboration. The focus should be shifted toward problem-driven learning and complex problem analysis, transforming the role of LLMs from solution providers into assistants for task completion. Specific methods include: decomposing complex problems into multiple sub-problems, with some sub-problems integrated into LLMs to solve; expanding the flexibility of experimental topics by allowing students to select key indicators and establish evaluation methods; and strengthening manual monitoring of learning traces to ensure fairness and rationality in grading.

R3: Anchoring cutting-edge technologies. The emphasis should be on selecting valuable cutting-edge topics for practice in order to improve students' innovative and critical thinking abilities. Specific methods include: integrating real-world challenges into experimental topics (*e.g.*, routing table lookups with tens of millions of IP addresses); encouraging students to pursue performance optimization from multiple evaluation perspectives and organizing leaderboard competitions; and conducting oral defenses to evaluate students' efforts and learning outcomes.

Note that the three requirements are interrelated and progressive. Designing computer network experiments that meet these requirements can transform experimental teaching into a capability forge in the era of LLMs, thereby cultivating computing talents capable of mastering and harnessing LLMs technologies.

3 Restructuring Experimental Teaching

3.1 Teaching System

Figure 2 illustrates the teaching system for computer network experiments in the era of LLMs. This system constructs a "Three-Dimensional Competency Devel-

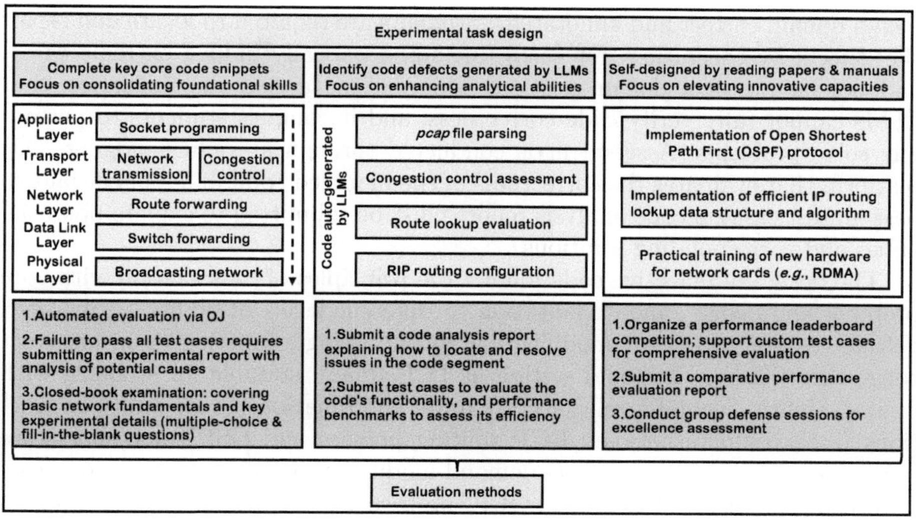

Fig. 2. Teaching system for computer network experiments in the era of LLMs.

opment" framework. Through a hierarchical design that consolidates fundamental abilities, enhances analytical abilities, and advances innovative abilities, it is supported by a multidimensional evaluation mechanism that emphasizes process, validation, and innovation. The specific implementation pathways of this system are as follows.

Consolidating Fundamental Skills. In this dimension, experimental teaching adopts a top-down layered design approach, following the principles of "progressing from shallow to deep" and "advancing step by step." Core experimental modules from different protocol layers are carefully selected. Each experiment provides detailed descriptions, test cases, state transition diagrams, and flowcharts, while requiring students to complete key code segments. Such a design aims to help students master basic knowledge of computer networks.

To prevent students from obtaining answers directly through LLMs, the assessment criteria introduce a closed-book computer-based test focusing on fundamental knowledge and key experimental details. To reduce students' preparation burden, the computer-based test is limited to multiple-choice and fill-in-the-blank questions. For students who achieve high experimental scores but low closed-book test scores, face-to-face assessments are conducted, and their experimental scores are adjusted accordingly.

Enhancing Analytical Abilities. In this dimension, experimental teaching aims to cultivate students' debugging, troubleshooting, and fault localization skills. Experiments deliberately employ defective code generated by LLMs, with modifications applied to critical function bodies (while non-essential code segments remain correct and annotated). Students are required to locate and repair the defects by consulting test cases (including partially hidden extreme cases) and official protocol documentation. This design targets the limitation that LLMs cannot fully verify code correctness, and it compels students to personally solve problems. Assessment is conducted through an online judging (OJ) platform that evaluates the correctness of the modified code. If a student fails to pass all test cases, a code analysis report must be submitted to explain potential issues and corresponding solutions.

The design of defective code follows the principles of "association with core protocol knowledge" and "adaptation to different levels of ability." First-level defects require parameter modification within a single function (*e.g.*, incorrect congestion window threshold setting in TCP Reno), suitable for students with weaker ability. Second-level defects require coordination across multiple functions (*e.g.*, conflicts between BGP routing policies and OSPF neighbor state interactions). Third-level defects demand module-level architectural reconstruction (*e.g.*, coupling faults between QUIC protocol flow control and retransmission logic), suitable for students with strong innovative abilities.

Elevating Innovative Capacities. In this dimension, experiments are designed to expose students to cutting-edge networking technologies, improve their ability to read English papers and technical documentation, and fully develop creative and critical thinking skills. We provide students with the latest top-conference papers on efficient IP routing lookup, newly released design documents on Open Shortest Path First (OSPF), and product manuals of new network interface cards (*i.e.*, RDMA, SmartNIC, and BlueField). Based on these materials, students are required to independently design and implement specific functional programs.

Due to the limitations of LLMs in knowledge timeliness, they cannot provide high-quality output for the implementation of the latest algorithms or for practical cases involving new hardware. This compels students to invest time and effort to explore and solve the implementation challenges of related functional modules. To enhance openness and inclusiveness, assessments are conducted in the form of performance leaderboard competitions, where students can also submit custom test cases, thereby fostering positive competition. In addition, students are required to submit technical reports elaborating on design concepts and performance evaluation. Finally, the course organizes oral defenses to identify outstanding work.

3.2 Experimental Environment

The experimental environment is built on the Linux operating system and the Mininet network emulation platform [9], with C language as the primary programming language. The rationale behind this choice lies in the fact that Linux provides abundant network programming interfaces and toolchains, Mininet can efficiently simulate complex network topologies, and the C language enables

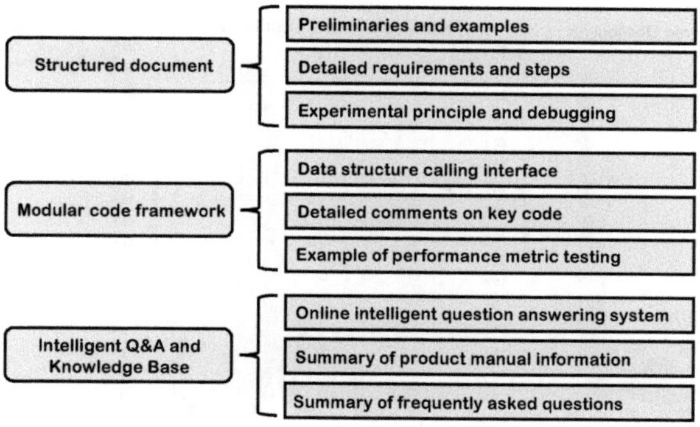

Fig. 3. Design of teaching support for computer network experiments.

direct manipulation of system-level resources, making it suitable for protocol stack implementation. The environment is uniformly configured through a virtual machine image, ensuring that students perform experiments under consistent development conditions and avoiding issues caused by heterogeneous environments.

3.3 Design of Teaching Support

The course provides structured documentation, modularized code frameworks, and intelligent Q&A with knowledge bases to help students quickly start experimental tasks. As shown in Fig. 3, structured documentation includes prerequisite knowledge, detailed requirements and steps, experimental principles, and debugging strategies (*e.g.*, using tcpdump and Wireshark for protocol flow analysis to validate model outputs). The modular code framework provides interfaces for core data structures, detailed annotations of critical code, and examples for testing performance metrics. The intelligent Q&A and knowledge base include an online Q&A system (an AI agent built on open-source LLMs to answer computer network questions), summarized key information from hardware product manuals, and frequently asked questions. Through this comprehensive support system, students' efficiency in completing experiments is improved, and their understanding of fundamental knowledge and underlying protocols is enhanced.

3.4 Presentation of Teaching Outcomes

Figure 4 shows the score distribution of students after incorporating the proposed reform scheme into the course. In the distribution of experimental course scores, 4.62% of students scored below 60, 19.23% scored between 60 and 80, 33.08% scored between 80 and 95, and 43.08% scored above 95. This distribution indicates that the majority of students successfully mastered the fundamental concepts, principles, and technologies of computer networks under the current teaching practice. Moreover, students with higher experimental course

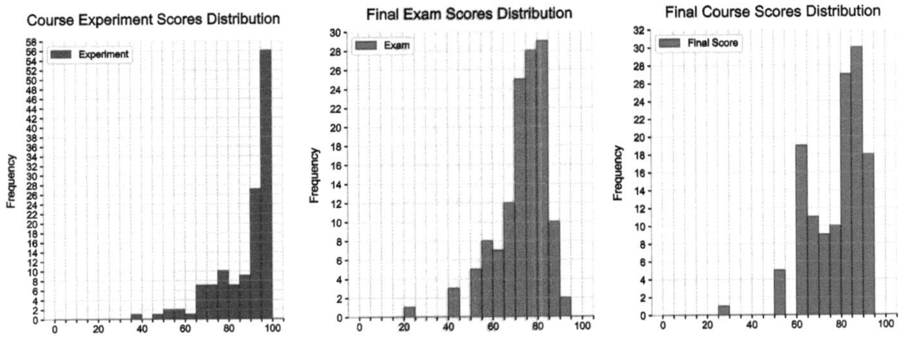

(a) Experimental scores (b) Final exam scores (c) Overall course scores

Fig. 4. Score distribution of students in the computer network course.

scores also achieved relatively higher final exam scores (note that the final exam primarily focuses on fundamental knowledge and open-ended problem-solving ability), suggesting that the current experimental teaching promotes students' understanding of course knowledge.

The score distribution provides direct evidence that the current teaching system has achieved remarkable results in ensuring solid mastery of core competencies. Interviews with students further revealed that many explicitly stated "they gained a deeper understanding of the TCP state machine during the process of debugging defective code." In addition, in the technical reports submitted during the innovative experiments, students presented proposals for improving network protocol methods. These qualitative results substantiate the effectiveness of the competence cultivation framework.

4 Implementation Challenges and Feasible Solutions

We actively and meaningfully explore the design of computer network experiments under the influence of LLMs. A "Three-Dimensional Capability Development" framework has been constructed and multidimensional evaluation reforms have been implemented. However, during the deep advancement of teaching reform, several serious challenges still remain. Facing these challenges and seeking feasible solutions is the key to achieving sustainable experimental teaching. Specifically, the challenges can be summarized as follows.

4.1 Defending Against Outputs Generated by LLMs

The foremost challenge lies in defending against the answers generated by LLMs. Currently, the evolution cycle of LLMs is extremely short, while the update cycle of experiments often lags behind the iteration speed of LLM technologies. This discrepancy leads to the diminishing effectiveness of carefully designed experiments—such as debugging defective code generated by LLMs, integrating with cutting-edge research papers, and interfacing with hardware—in resisting LLM outputs over time.

To address this, it is necessary to establish a "model capability monitoring and teaching response" mechanism. This includes forming interdisciplinary teams to continuously track the progress of mainstream LLMs in areas such as protocol implementation, debugging, and optimization; periodically evaluating the "vulnerability" of existing experiments and iterating new experimental modules quickly; strengthening the "integration degree of frontier technologies"; and closely aligning with the latest industrial and open-source community technologies (e.g., DPU programming, QUIC protocol details, AI-driven network configuration). Leveraging the natural temporal gap and information asymmetry of these technologies as the cornerstone of experimental design can compel students to engage in active exploration during experiments.

4.2 Rationality and Convenience of Process-Based Evaluation

The second challenge is ensuring both the rationality and convenience of process-based evaluation. Although this course emphasizes process-oriented assessment (e.g., debugging reports, design documents, and oral defenses), distinguishing students' attitudes toward completing experiments and evaluating their independent thinking and creativity requires substantial effort. In large-class teaching with more than 100 students, achieving refined evaluation is nearly impossible. Future efforts should focus on developing AI-enabled intelligent evaluation tools that can automatically analyze students' process data (e.g., version control histories of code, keyword patterns in debugging logs, and logical structures of design documents) to assist grading. Other strategies include exploring small-class refined teaching, formulating more detailed process evaluation standards, and designing peer review mechanisms to establish a multi-level evaluation system that ensures both rationality and convenience.

4.3 Fairness of Resource Allocation

The third challenge concerns fairness in resource allocation. Experimental environments rely on high-performance hardware as well as stable cloud computing resources (e.g., for online evaluation and LLM interactions). The high costs of these resources make it difficult to provide full-time allocation for every student, leading to uneven distribution of experimental resources and further affecting students' motivation for hands-on learning. To address this, instructors can apply for on-campus high-performance computing resource pools and high-speed campus network access, make use of open educational resource-sharing networks and CloudLab platforms [10], and seek industrial support for additional resources.

5 Conclusion

This paper proposes a "Three-Dimensional Capability Development" framework tailored for computer network experimental teaching in the era of LLMs.

This framework adopts a progressive design that solidifies foundational skills, enhances analytical abilities, and elevates innovative capacities. Besides, coupled with a multi-dimensional assessment mechanism that emphasizes process, verification, and innovation, we carefully crafted experiments to defend against LLMs' outputs. This new teaching shifts the focus from simple knowledge verification and skill acquisition to cultivating students' abilities in critical thinking, debugging, validation, and creative exploration. Implementing this experimental framework in specific teaching practices shows that over 70% of students can effectively grasp the underlying principles and knowledge of computer networks.

Acknowledgements. This work was supported in part by the National Key R&D Program of China under Grant No. 2023YFB4502400, and in part by the National Natural Science Foundation of China under Grant 62272223.

References

1. ChatGPT. https://chatgpt.com/. Accessed 12 Sept 2025
2. DeepSeek. https://www.deepseek.com/en. Accessed 12 Sept 2025
3. Liu, M., Wu, Z., Liao, J., Ren, Y., Su, Y.: Educational applications of large language models: principles, status and challenges - from light-weighted BERT to conversational ChatGPT. Mod. Educ. Technol. **33**(8), 19–28 (2023)
4. Xu, J., Huang, N., Song, H.: Automatic correction of multimodal experimental reports driven by LLM. Mod. Inf. Technol. **9**(12), 79–84 (2025)
5. Zhang, L., et al.: Design and implementation of large language model retrieval-augmented generation-based computer network experiment course QA system. Exp. Technol. Manage. **41**(12), 186–192 (2024)
6. Zhang, H., Zhou, X., Xu, Y., Yang, Q.: Generative artificial intelligence empowers teaching innovation in computer programming courses. Comput. Educ. **7**, 44–48 (2024)
7. Zhao, Y., Ling, X., Zhu, H., Zhou, F., Deng, Z.: Exploration of computer programming teaching reform based on large language models. In: 11th International Conference on Computing and Artificial Intelligence, pp. 359–363. IEEE, Kyoto, Japan (2025)
8. Zhang, J., Gong, X., Gao, X., Duan, F., Xiong, H.: Innovative experimental design of computer systems based on general large language models. Exp. Technol. Manage. **41**(10), 1–9 (2024)
9. Mininet. https://mininet.org. Accessed 12 Sept 2025
10. CloudLab. https://www.cloudlab.us. Accessed 12 Sept 2025

Generative AI in Undergraduate Finance Education: Curriculum and Teaching Reform

Xianru Ma[1(✉)], Yan Cheng[2], and Jiancheng Chi[3]

[1] School of Law, Dongbei University of Finance and Economics, Dalian, China
maxianru@dufe.edu.cn

[2] School of Education, Tianjin University, Tianjin, China
yan.cheng@tju.edu.cn

[3] School of Software, Dalian University of Technology, Dalian, China
chijiancheng@dlut.edu.cn

Abstract. With the rapid advancement of generative artificial intelligence (AI), particularly large language models (LLMs) such as ChatGPT and ERNIE Bot, higher education is undergoing a paradigm shift from knowledge transmission to competence formation. Finance education, characterized by its semantic density, rule-based logic, and decision-driven scenarios, is especially well-aligned with the cognitive capacities of LLMs. However, current undergraduate curricula remain fragmented, with insufficient integration of AI technologies, outdated pedagogical models, and a misalignment between technical skills and domain-specific applications. This paper proposes a three-tier integrated curriculum framework—comprising foundational theory, practical application, and frontier exploration—tailored for AI-empowered finance education. It introduces a generative pedagogical loop based on a human–task–model triadic interaction system, reshaping learning from passive reception to active cognitive construction. Furthermore, the study emphasizes the importance of platform infrastructure, interdisciplinary collaboration, and institutional coordination to support sustainable curriculum innovation. By addressing key challenges in curriculum coherence, pedagogical adaptation, and ethical governance, the proposed framework offers a systematic pathway for transitioning finance education toward an AI-augmented, capability-driven ecosystem.

Keywords: Generative Artificial Intelligence · Finance Education Reform · Curriculum Integration Framework · Human–AI Collaborative Pedagogy

1 Introduction

In recent years, artificial intelligence (AI) has undergone a transformative leap from perceptual intelligence to cognitive intelligence. Among the most disruptive innovations are large language models (LLMs), such as ChatGPT, Claude, and

J. Chi et al. (Eds.): CNETCNED 2025, CCIS 2809, pp. 77–89, 2026.
https://doi.org/10.1007/978-981-95-7124-6_8

ERNIE Bot, whose rapid evolution is deeply permeating every aspect of modern society. With capabilities spanning language generation, semantic understanding, multimodal interaction, and human–machine collaborative decision-making, LLMs exhibit highly generalized, cross-domain cognitive capacities. This technological revolution not only reconfigures industrial structures [2,3] and social collaboration mechanisms but also profoundly reshapes the foundational organization and epistemological frameworks of education. In the context of higher education, LLMs are no longer confined to marginal, assistive functions; instead, they are emerging as central engines of pedagogical transformation, driving systemic changes in curriculum design, instructional paradigms, learning strategies, and even the underlying philosophy of education [19].

Among various academic disciplines, finance and economics (hereafter collectively referred to as "finance education") are among the most profoundly affected by generative AI. The semantic density and rule-based structure of core financial domains—such as capital markets, accounting and auditing, and tax regulation—closely match the capabilities of LLMs, enabling these models to participate effectively in tasks like policy interpretation, financial analysis, and decision support [4]. At the same time, finance education increasingly demands a hybrid competency structure that includes critical thinking, institutional understanding, technological fluency, and ethical reasoning—capabilities that traditional curricula often fail to cultivate in an integrated manner. These tensions are driving finance education to evolve beyond linear, textbook-centered models, which are becoming increasingly inadequate in rapidly changing environments shaped by digital economies, platform regulation, and intelligent governance. Problems such as outdated course content, inflexible pedagogy, and insufficient integration of emerging technologies continue to hinder both instructional quality and disciplinary competitiveness. In this context, AI-enhanced educational systems are shifting toward open, adaptive, and co-creative learning environments, which restructure the roles of teachers and students alike by fostering prompt-driven dialogue, semantic-level engagement, and reflective learning practices [17].

Despite the transformative potential of generative AI, its application in undergraduate finance education remains constrained by several limitations. First, on the level of curriculum architecture, many universities have yet to establish a coherent and staged AI course system. AI-related courses often exist in isolation, commonly embedded as general education modules or coding workshops, without meaningful integration with core finance subjects. Second, traditional teaching methods—dominated by one-way lectures and closed-form assessments—continue to prevail, lacking the interactivity, task-driven structure, and reflective mechanisms required for generative AI–enabled learning. Third, a misalignment persists in curriculum content, with a tendency to overemphasize programming while underemphasizing modeling, or to focus on generic technical skills while neglecting contextualized applications in finance. This weakens students' ability to form cognitively integrated, domain-aware AI literacy. Additionally, outdated faculty training, insufficient interdisciplinary collaboration, and fragmented teaching resources exacerbate the disconnect between finance AI education and real-world demands [18].

Against this backdrop, there is an urgent need to construct a finance-oriented AI curriculum cluster that is structurally coherent, competency-driven, and iteratively sustainable. Such a system must embed AI technologies across the full spectrum of educational processes, addressing multiple objectives in both vertical and horizontal dimensions. Vertically, it should establish a three-tier progression of competencies: foundational theory, practical application, and frontier exploration. Horizontally, it must integrate financial knowledge structures, AI technological frameworks, and ethical governance principles to build an educational ecosystem driven by tasks, supported by transfer learning, and anchored in system-level evaluation. This curriculum cluster should not only encompass fundamental AI topics such as algorithmic principles, data processing, and model training, but also design generative learning tasks around professional finance scenarios, including financial statement analysis, auditing oversight, financial modeling, and tax planning. By aligning semantic structures and logical reasoning between financial knowledge and intelligent systems, such a design fosters the synergistic development of AI literacy, disciplinary competence, and generalist thinking.

Beyond serving as a content-generation tool, generative AI is increasingly evolving into an engine of cognitive construction and logical reasoning in the classroom. This paradigm shift requires finance education to transcend surface-level technology adoption and instead embed AI within the epistemological fabric of teaching and learning. Under the affordances of LLMs, the instructor's role transitions from unilateral knowledge transmission to that of task architect, prompt engineer, and cognitive coach [5]. Simultaneously, students evolve from passive recipients to active problem framers, process debuggers, and critical evaluators of model outputs. This instructional dynamic—anchored in a learning loop of "prompting, interaction, generation, and reflection"—not only enhances the depth of financial understanding and precision of expression but also cultivates students' capacity for systematic problem formulation and ethical reasoning in technology-rich contexts.

2 Literature Review

The field of AI itself, originating from the 1956 Dartmouth Conference [11, 15], has developed through multiple stages—from the artificial neuron model to machine learning and deep generative models [20]. Key technologies such as neural networks [10], deep learning [1], and GANs [9] have laid the groundwork for the emergence of Generative AI (GAI) as a transformative tool in education [16].

The integration of AI into higher education began in the early 1990s. Entering the 21st century, this field has witnessed significant evolution alongside breakthroughs in deep learning and natural language processing. Since 2018, the emergence of pre-trained language models such as BERT, GPT, and T5 has continued to push the boundaries of natural language understanding and generation, demonstrating strong capabilities in language interaction and content customization within educational environments. Peláez Sánchez et al. [14] point out that in order to adapt to this transformation, curriculum systems must adopt a three-tiered progression: from foundational AI literacy, to technical practice, and then to professional application. This structure forms a closed loop covering topics from "AI ethics and data literacy" to "prompt engineering and natural language processing" and finally to "financial statement analysis and intelligent auditing". Li et al. [21] further emphasize that such a system promotes the integration of interdisciplinary knowledge graphs and AI capabilities in finance students.

In terms of pedagogical paradigms, many researchers have proposed that LLMs should be viewed as "cognitive collaborators" rather than static support tools. They advocate a closed-loop instructional model composed of task formulation, prompt interaction, content generation, teacher feedback, and student reflection. Miranda et al. [12], drawing on the Education 4.0 framework, found that such a loop can significantly enhance students' metacognitive skills and collaborative competencies. In the finance domain, related studies have shown that multi-round prompt interaction in tasks such as financial summarization, investment logic construction, and risk assessment can significantly improve students' analytical and expressive abilities.

Regarding governance mechanisms and ethical standards, existing research has consistently emphasized the risks associated with LLMs in educational settings, including hallucinated outputs, information bias, and academic integrity concerns. Jiao et al. [7], through an analysis of policies from 80 universities, stress that establishing clear accountability for generated content and implementing robust error correction processes are essential to maintaining educational quality. At the same time, Mzwri et al. [13] argues that in order to ensure fairness and privacy, finance-related generative tasks should incorporate algorithmic transparency and data protection standards. Krause D. [8] highlights the need for a well-rounded grasp of AI and data analytics, while also emphasizing the value of ethical awareness, regulatory insight, effective collaboration with AI tools, technological proficiency, and the cultivation of a lifelong learning mindset.

In terms of platform development and collaborative mechanisms, research suggests that educational platforms should be equipped with interfaces for data integration, prompt template libraries, generation tracking, and learning behavior analysis functions. A review published by Springer underscores that multifunctional teaching platforms are essential for achieving instructional closure and resource sharing. Additionally, reports indicate that several universities have deployed AI teaching assistants to manage thousands of student queries, significantly improving responsiveness and educational equity. In recent years, there has also been a surge of interest in prompt engineering strategies. Gozzi and Di Maio [6] found that multitask prompt strategies are more efficient than single-task designs in financial analytics.

Overall, research on the integration of AI in finance education has yielded preliminary achievements, but several gaps remain. First, there is a lack of studies on the systematic design of curriculum clusters, with most initiatives still focused on individual course-level reforms. Second, the pace of pedagogical innovation lags behind technological advances, as traditional lecture-based instruction and case analysis dominate classrooms, lacking adaptation to the characteristics of LLMs. Third, evaluation systems and platform support remain underdeveloped, with limited integrated practical environments and data-driven learning tracking tools. Building on existing research, this study proposes a well-structured, fully functional, and operational curriculum cluster framework tailored for AI-enhanced finance education, aiming to provide a theoretical model and practical roadmap for embedding generative AI in the training of future-ready finance professionals.

3 Constructing a Three-Tier Integrated Model for AI-Enabled Undergraduate Finance Curriculum Clusters

Amid the rapid evolution of generative AI, finance and economics education is undergoing a fundamental shift from knowledge-oriented instruction to a competence-oriented paradigm. To effectively integrate AI technologies into undergraduate finance curricula, it is essential to restructure both the curriculum architecture and the instructional mechanisms. This requires the systematic development of AI-embedded course clusters that incorporate tiered progression, capability alignment, and normative guidance. Drawing on curricular practices from leading institutions such as the Central University of Finance and Economics, Nankai University, and Shanghai University of Finance and Economics in China, and in light of current AI-driven educational trends, the curriculum can be structured into three progressive tiers: foundational theory, practical application, and frontier exploration. These tiers collectively form a logically coherent, capability-driven, and spiral progression model for talent development.

3.1 Construction of a Three-Tier Curriculum Cluster

At the foundational level, the curriculum targets lower-year undergraduates and emphasizes conceptual initiation and technical understanding. Courses such as Introduction to AI, Python and Financial Big Data Analysis, Foundations of Statistical Learning, and Information Literacy and Data Ethics are designed to equip students with a basic understanding of AI principles, cultivate data awareness, modeling logic, and ethical sensitivity. These courses extend beyond technical theory, focusing on the logical interface between AI methodologies and the financial context, thereby laying a multidisciplinary groundwork for future specialization.

As students progress to the application tier, the focus shifts to the deployment of AI tools in concrete financial tasks. Upper-year students are expected to master the use of LLMs and related technologies in domains such as financial report analysis, tax interpretation, market forecasting, and financial writing.

Core offerings include Applications of LLMs in Financial Statement Analysis, Intelligent Auditing and Tax Decision Support, Algorithmic Strategies in Financial Markets, ChatGPT and Practical Financial Writing, and Designing Intelligent Financial Q&A Systems. These courses incorporate real-world enterprise data, regulatory texts, and platform governance rules, implementing task-based and project-oriented pedagogies to foster students' practical problem-solving and system-level reasoning skills.

At the frontier exploration level, course content addresses emerging issues at the intersection of AI and finance, emphasizing systemic thinking and interdisciplinary integration. Courses such as AIGC and Financial Communication, AI in Financial Regulation, Platform Economics, and Digital Economy Law encourage students to engage with topics including AI governance, algorithmic ethics, and regulatory frameworks. Through policy analysis, case-based evaluation, and simulated inquiry, students are guided to critically assess the implications of AI within institutional environments, thereby enhancing their strategic thinking, normative reasoning, and sense of social responsibility (Fig. 1).

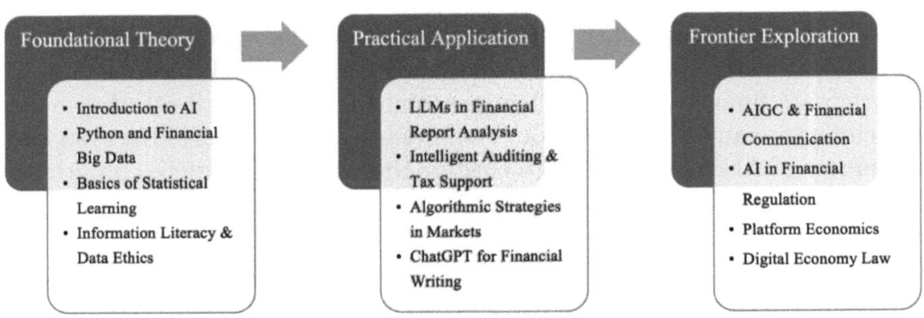

Fig. 1. The Three-Tier Synergistic Model of New Finance-AI Curriculum Clusters.

3.2 Formulation of Guidelines for the Development of Undergraduate AI Curriculum in Finance

To ensure the effective implementation of this curriculum framework, it is critical to develop standardized course development and execution guidelines that align course objectives, instructional resources, and technical workflows. Following a "backward design" principle, course objectives should be clearly articulated along three dimensions: knowledge, skills, and dispositions. Knowledge goals encompass AI fundamentals (e.g., machine learning, NLP), core finance knowledge (e.g., financial statement analysis, risk management, regulatory policy), and integrated domains such as algorithmic finance and intelligent auditing. Skill development includes data analysis, model invocation, prompt engineering, and financial problem modeling. Dispositional objectives address ethics awareness, systems thinking, interdisciplinary collaboration, and digital security literacy. Based on these dimensions, a curriculum-capability mapping should be constructed to ensure that every course contributes to the broader professional training goals and builds incrementally along the student learning trajectory.

During implementation, a tripartite assessment framework integrating knowledge, skills, and dispositions should be established to ensure closed-loop quality management and adaptive improvement. Knowledge mastery may be evaluated through quizzes, conceptual mapping, and stage assessments. Skill formation should rely on task-based assessments, such as financial case modeling, policy writing, and AI tool execution. Dispositional growth can be tracked through peer reviews, reflective journals, and participation metrics. To enhance precision, a data-driven learning analytics system should be employed to synthesize digital interaction logs—including time-on-task, query frequency, and model invocation records—providing individualized feedback and cognitive pathway analysis.

The technical implementation of these courses also requires standardized instructional procedures and teaching strategies, especially as LLMs become increasingly integrated into educational practice. Clear protocols must be established for invoking LLMs (e.g., ChatGPT, Wenxin Yiyan), including interface selection, task matching, and usage boundaries. Instructional content should explicitly teach the principles of prompt construction—clarity, task alignment, and controllability—as well as common formats such as contextual scaffolding, directive cues, and role assignment. Additionally, output validation standards should be developed for the finance domain, encompassing linguistic appropriateness, financial logic consistency, policy reference accuracy, and information security thresholds. Ethical norms must also be established to govern AI use, with clear boundaries to prevent content misuse, excessive model reliance, and data breaches.

Building on these foundations, it is recommended that an Instructional Manual for AI-Enhanced Finance Courses and a Handbook for AI Teaching Tools be developed. These resources should provide end-to-end guidance for instructors and curriculum developers, covering content design, technical integration, classroom interaction, and assessment procedures. Modularized teaching components and script libraries can further support scalability and ease of adoption across institutions, enhancing the adaptability and transferability of AI-powered finance curricula.

4 Pedagogical Reconstruction and Methodological Innovation in AI-Enabled Finance Education

4.1 Redefining Knowledge Construction: From Content Transmission to Generative Processes

The emergence of generative AI has brought about a paradigm shift in how knowledge is conceptualized, constructed, and communicated in finance education. Traditionally, learning in finance has followed a linear model of "transmission–reception–reproduction," where instructors serve as knowledge transmitters and students as passive recipients. With the integration of LLMs, however, knowledge is increasingly perceived as a "structured generative outcome." Through prompt engineering, AI interaction, and human revision, students actively participate in generating, refining, and validating content. This shift necessitates reconfiguring curricula around generative tasks rather than static content modules. In this new paradigm, the core educational objective transitions from content coverage to process controllability and output quality, emphasizing students' ability to engage in dynamic cognitive processes rather than rote memorization.

4.2 Designing the Generative Pedagogical Loop: A Competence-Centered Learning Framework

To cultivate AI-era competencies, finance education must adopt a new pedagogical model—referred to here as the Generative Pedagogical Loop. This loop comprises four interconnected stages: (1) task identification and problem formulation, (2) prompt design and model interaction, (3) output deconstruction and logical revision, and (4) result transformation and applied migration. Each cycle of this loop fosters not only domain-specific understanding but also transferable skills in logical expression, model debugging, and scenario adaptation. Rooted in social constructivism and tool-mediated learning, this model positions knowledge construction as a collaborative process between the student, the AI system, and the task context. For example, in a course like Intelligent Auditing and Financial Statement Analysis, students might be tasked with generating a financial fraud warning report using an LLM. The process includes constructing prompts from real data, interpreting model output, identifying reasoning errors, and aligning insights with real-world auditing procedures—thus combining cognitive, technical, and applied learning outcomes.

4.3 Restructuring Instruction and Assessment: From Teacher Facilitation to Generative Evaluation

The successful implementation of generative pedagogy in AI-enabled finance education requires a fundamental redefinition of both instructional roles and evaluation systems. In this paradigm, instructors move beyond the traditional role of content deliverers to become designers of prompt-based tasks, facilitators of cognitive processes, and supervisors of ethical AI usage. This pedagogical shift demands two core competencies: first, generative instructional design, which involves translating complex financial problems into AI-compatible task structures with prompt templates that align with students' cognitive development; and second, generative content supervision, which focuses on identifying logical inconsistencies, factual inaccuracies, and ethical risks in model outputs while providing real-time feedback and guidance. In parallel, traditional product-based assessments are no longer adequate to capture the multidimensional nature of learning that unfolds through interaction with language models. Instead, a process-oriented and multimodal assessment framework must be established to evaluate students' generative competence. This framework consists of three key categories of indicators: structural indicators, including prompt clarity, task definition accuracy, and the rationality of parameter configuration; behavioral indicators, such as the frequency of model interaction, iteration depth, and revision cycle patterns; and output indicators, including financial logic coherence, factual correctness, and structural integrity of the generated content. These evaluations are supported by the analysis of generation logs, interactive behavior data, and student reflection narratives, which together enable the construction of comprehensive learner profiles and the provision of personalized, data-informed feedback for continuous improvement (Fig. 2).

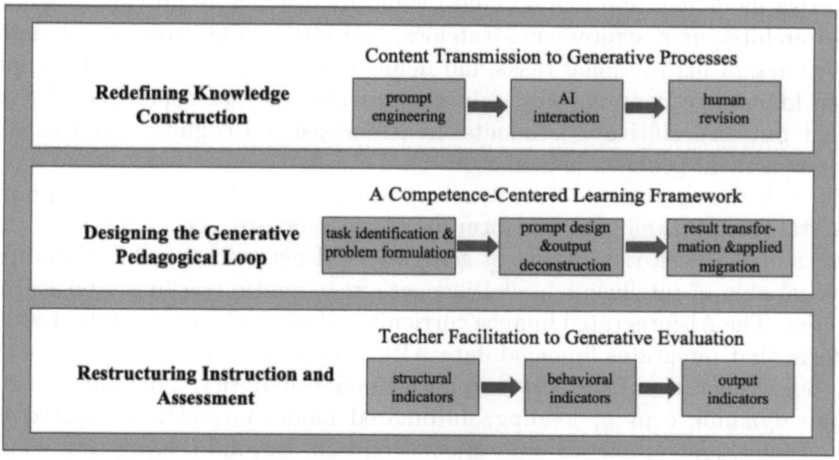

Fig. 2. LLM-Driven Teaching Innovation Framework for AI-Finance Education.

5 Collaborative Mechanisms and Platform Infrastructure for AI-Enabled Finance Curricula

Curricular reform in higher education is not merely a matter of reorganizing teaching activities, but a systemic reconstruction that demands multi-actor, multi-level, and multi-resource collaboration. The finance-oriented AI curriculum cluster—an emerging pedagogical architecture integrating generative AI with disciplinary finance education—requires robust interdisciplinary, interorganizational, and inter-platform coordination to ensure its sustainable operation. In the era of LLMs–dominated human-machine collaboration, educational activities are transitioning from isolated "curricular units" to integrated "interactional systems." Thus, course development must go beyond pedagogical design to encompass institutional arrangements, platform functionalities, and cognitive governance strategies. The effective implementation of such curricula depends on the construction of embedded coordination mechanisms to support adaptive evolution, broad applicability, and deep curricular integration.

First, the collaborative foundation of AI-enabled finance curricula lies in their capacity to integrate interdisciplinary knowledge systems. The adoption of LLMs in finance education is not a superficial technological enhancement but a structural transformation that dissolves disciplinary boundaries and promotes a problem-centered, technically integrated, and ethically oriented educational paradigm. Successful course execution necessitates deep collaboration between finance and AI disciplines—not through equal partitioning of content, but through a "problem–task–competence" mapping model that guides curriculum logic. For example, in a course like Constructing Intelligent Investment Strategies, finance instructors contribute domain knowledge such as product logic, risk modeling, and market rules, while AI instructors provide insights on model architectures, expression strategies, and interaction protocols. Together, they co-design instructional tasks and define evaluation standards. This multi-source knowledge coupling not only ensures the internal coherence of course content but also cultivates students' multidimensional cognition and capacity for cross-domain problem articulation.

Second, the operational infrastructure of the curriculum must be supported by a stable and intelligent platform-based architecture. The interactive, non-linear, and feedback-rich nature of generative AI necessitates educational platforms capable of intelligent model invocation, semantic tracking, and learning analytics. The AI-integrated finance curriculum should adopt a modular teaching platform that integrates financial data APIs, model services, prompt orchestration tools, generation logs, and learning behavior analytics. This infrastructure enables dynamic content loading, automated model interactions, nested task management, and visualized assessment feedback. Beyond serving as a conduit for content delivery and model execution, the platform becomes a central system for faculty collaboration, personalized learning, behavioral data collection, and responsive scheduling. Its embedded structure facilitates portability and adaptability, paving the way for cross-institutional and cross-disciplinary diffusion of AI-enabled finance education.

Third, the curriculum's sustainable development hinges on robust institutional governance mechanisms. Traditional course administration follows a linear, department-based model for faculty assignment and resource allocation. In contrast, AI courses function as inherently cross-boundary initiatives requiring coordinated responsibility, joint governance, and integrative incentive systems. In terms of course ownership, dual-institutional structures (e.g., co-construction and joint-supervision schemes) should be established to recognize AI courses as both technical and disciplinary assets. For faculty development, cross-training and interdepartmental teaching exchanges can enhance instructors' dual literacy in finance contexts and AI methods. Regarding resource distribution, mechanisms for shared funding, joint task allocation, and performance-based compensation are essential to ensure high-quality and continuous course delivery. Ultimately, these institutional designs shift responsibility from individual instructors to organizational systems, catalyzing a transition from localized reform to structural transformation.

The coordination mechanism must also address differentiated learner trajectories. In generative learning environments, students exhibit highly individualized patterns in starting points, learning paths, and cognitive outcomes. To accommodate this variability, curricula must incorporate personalized learning management modules that analyze student behaviors during prompt construction, model interaction, content generation, and reflection. These analytics inform dynamic content adjustments, resource recommendations, and task escalation, thereby forming a semantic behavior–based adaptive feedback system. This mechanism underpins the shift from uniform progress to stratified advancement and introduces a novel pathway for educational equity—optimizing individual cognition while maintaining resource equality.

Furthermore, the coordination mechanism should extend to industry–academia collaborative ecosystems. Since AI applications in finance are highly context-sensitive, course content, case resources, and assessment criteria must be grounded in real-world scenarios. A practice community involving universities, tech firms, and financial institutions should be formed to convert real-world business practices into educational resources. Use cases such as automated annual report generation, intelligent tax interpretation, or regulatory text analysis can be transformed into generative tasks within the curriculum. Students thereby engage in a full-cycle training process: industry-driven problem definition – academic modeling and analysis – AI-enabled expressive generation. This model not only enriches curricular realism and complexity but also enhances the translational efficiency of academic resources and fosters deep mutual embedding between educational and industrial systems.

6 Conclusion

AI—particularly LLMs—is fundamentally reshaping the knowledge frameworks, pedagogical paradigms, and competency orientations of undergraduate finance education. Driven by technological advancement and disciplinary convergence, finance education is undergoing a profound transformation: from knowledge transmission to capability generation, from discipline-centered instruction to problem-oriented learning, and from teacher-led teaching to human–AI collaborative cognition. The construction of AI-integrated curriculum clusters has become a key pathway for institutional reform in finance education, with their core architecture grounded in vertical progressive competence structures (i.e., foundational–applied–exploratory) and horizontal cross-domain integration (i.e., technology–finance–ethics). This forms a task-driven, feedback-responsive, and intelligent instructional ecosystem.

Such transformation not only redefines the structure and logic of curriculum design but also positions finance education as a dynamic cognitive system. However, critical challenges remain—chiefly, ensuring the accuracy of generated content, the internal consistency of financial logic, and adherence to ethical norms. Future research must deepen theoretical development across prompt design, assessment mechanisms, and cognitive modeling to achieve effective alignment between AI capabilities and human educational objectives. Ultimately, this will facilitate the transition of finance education from a craft-based paradigm to an intelligence-driven system, capable of thriving in the era of generative AI.

Acknowledgements. This paper was supported by the Basic Scientific Research Project of Colleges and Universities of the Education Department of Liaoning Province (Grant No. LJ112410173046) and the Liaoning Provincial Economic and Social Development Research Project (Grant No. 2025lslqnkt-006).

References

1. Bengio, Y., Lecun, Y., Hinton, G.: Deep learning for AI. Commun. ACM **64**(7), 58–65 (2021)
2. Chi, J., Qiu, T., Xiao, F., Zhou, X.: Atom: adaptive task offloading with two-stage hybrid matching in MEC-enabled industrial IoT. IEEE Trans. Mob. Comput. 1–17 (2023)
3. Chi, J., Zhou, X., Xiao, F., Lim, Y., Qiu, T.: Task offloading via prioritized experience-based double dueling DQN in edge-assisted IIoT. IEEE Trans. Mob. Comput. **23**(12), 14575–14591 (2024)
4. Da Xu, L., Lu, Y., Li, L.: Embedding blockchain technology into IoT for security: a survey. IEEE Internet Things J. **8**(13), 10452–10473 (2021)
5. Druga, S., Otero, N., Ko, A.J.: The landscape of teaching resources for AI education. In: Proceedings of the 27th ACM Conference on on Innovation and Technology in Computer Science Education, vol. 1. pp. 96–102 (2022)
6. Gozzi, M., Di Maio, F.: Comparative analysis of prompt strategies for large language models: Single-task vs. multitask prompts. Electronics **13**(23), 4712 (2024)
7. Jiao, J., Afroogh, S., Chen, K., Atkinson, D., Dhurandhar, A.: The global landscape of academic guidelines for generative AI and large language models. arXiv preprint arXiv:2406.18842 (2024)
8. Krause, D.: Adapting the finance curriculum for an AI-driven future (2023). SSRN 4448143
9. Liu, M.Y., Huang, X., Yu, J., Wang, T.C., Mallya, A.: Generative adversarial networks for image and video synthesis: algorithms and applications. Proc. IEEE **109**(5), 839–862 (2021)
10. Majewski, M., Kacalak, W.: Intelligent system for natural language processing. In: Huang, D.-S., Li, K., Irwin, G.W. (eds.) ICIC 2006. LNCS (LNAI), vol. 4114, pp. 742–747. Springer, Heidelberg (2006). https://doi.org/10.1007/978-3-540-37275-2_93
11. McCarthy, J., Minsky, M.L., Rochester, N., Shannon, C.E.: A proposal for the Dartmouth summer research project on artificial intelligence, August 31, 1955. AI Mag. **27**(4), 12–12 (2006)
12. Miranda, J., et al.: The core components of education 4.0 in higher education: three case studies in engineering education. Comput. Electr. Eng. **93**, 107278 (2021)
13. Mzwri, K., Turcsányi-Szabo, M.: Bridging LMS and generative AI: dynamic course content integration (dcci) for connecting LLMS to course content-the ask me assistant. arXiv preprint arXiv:2504.03966 (2025)

14. Peláez-Sánchez, I.C., Velarde-Camaqui, D., Glasserman-Morales, L.D.: The impact of large language models on higher education: exploring the connection between AI and education 4.0. In: Frontiers in Education, vol. 9, p. 1392091. Frontiers Media SA (2024)
15. Sanabria-Navarro, J.R., Silveira-Pérez, Y., Pérez-Bravo, D.D., de Jesús-Cortina-Núñez, M.: Incidences of artificial intelligence in contemporary education. Comunicar: Media Educ. Res. J. **31**(77), 93–103 (2023)
16. Shah, C.: Generative AI and the future of information access. In: Proceedings of the 32nd ACM International Conference on Information and Knowledge Management, pp. 3–3 (2023)
17. Tomczak, J.M.: Why deep generative modeling? In: Deep generative modeling, pp. 1–13. Springer, Cham (2024). https://doi.org/10.1007/978-3-030-93158-2_1
18. Zakaria, S., Manaf, S.M.A., Amron, M.T., Suffian, M.T.M.: Has the world of finance changed? A review of the influence of artificial intelligence on financial management studies. Inf. Manag. Bus. Rev. **15**(4), 420–432 (2023)
19. Zhai, X., et al.: A review of artificial intelligence (AI) in education from 2010 to 2020. Complexity **2021**(1), 8812542 (2021)
20. Zhang, C., Chen, Y.: A review of research relevant to the emerging industry trends: Industry 4.0, IoT, blockchain, and business analytics. J. Industr. Integr. Manag. **5**(01), 165–180 (2020)
21. Ziemba, E.W., Maruszewska, E.W., Grabara, D., Renik, K.: Acceptance and use of chatgpt among accounting and finance higher education students. In: Hernes, M., Wątróbski, J. (eds.) ECAI 2023. LNNS, vol. 1079, pp. 185–202. Springer, Cham (2023). https://doi.org/10.1007/978-3-031-66761-9_16

Innovation and Practice of AIGC-Empowered Teaching Mode for Comprehensive Course Design of Network Software

Xiaofang Wang(✉), Kun Liu, Shan Jing, and Yan Zhao

School of Information Science and Engineering, University of Jinan, Jinan 250022, Shandong, China
ise_wangxf@ujn.edu.cn

Abstract. Addressing issues in current software development courses such as outdated teaching content, difficulty in meeting students' personalized needs, and insufficiently scientific evaluation methods, this paper proposes an innovative teaching mode for the comprehensive course design of network software based on Artificial Intelligence Generated Content (AIGC) technology. By reconstructing teaching objectives, content, and the evaluation system, a "dual-line integration, three-stage progression" teaching framework was constructed. Integrating intelligent tools like GitHub Copilot and SonarQube, AI empowerment throughout the entire software development lifecycle was achieved. Empirical research shows that this model significantly enhances students' system development efficiency, code quality, engineering practice ability, and innovation capability. The study provides a referential teaching solution for cultivating software development talent in the intelligent era.

Keywords: AIGC · Software Development · Teaching Mode Reform · Intelligent Programming · Practical Ability Cultivation

1 Introduction

With the rapid development of artificial intelligence technology, AIGC is profoundly changing the methods and processes of software development [1,2]. In the

Supported by the Shandong Undergraduate Teaching Reform Project (Grant Nos. Z2022322, Z2023094), the Shandong Graduate Education High-Quality Teaching Resource Project (Grant No. SDJKC2023016), Shandong Province Graduate Education and Teaching Reform Research Funding Project (SDYJSJGBZ2024004, SDYJSJGC2024097), the Ministry of Education Industry-University Cooperation Collaborative Education Program (Grant Nos. 220606008212310, 220305332225056, 220906272130231, 22067099231405, 231102802275445), and the Second Batch of Artificial Intelligence Interdisciplinary Undergraduate Course Establishment Project of University of Jinan (Jinan University Academic Affairs Office [2024] No. 20 (General No. 71)).

J. Chi et al. (Eds.): CNETCNED 2025, CCIS 2809, pp. 90–101, 2026.
https://doi.org/10.1007/978-981-95-7124-6_9

field of higher education, traditional practical teaching of software development faces prominent problems such as lagging updates in teaching content, single teaching methods, and insufficiently scientific evaluation methods. Especially in highly practical courses like the comprehensive course design of network software, how to effectively integrate emerging technologies to cultivate students' innovation ability and engineering literacy has become an important topic in current teaching reform [3,4].

The traditional teaching mode for the comprehensive course design of network software is teacher-led, primarily focusing on the impartation of basic theory and training of conventional software development skills. Students complete software projects assigned by the teacher according to unified requirements. This approach suffers from outdated teaching content, difficulty in matching students' personalized learning needs, and constraints on cultivating students' independent inquiry and creative thinking [5–7]. Against the backdrop of new technologies like AIGC, the traditional teaching mode can no longer meet the current software industry's demand for software development talent. Therefore, there is an urgent need to explore a new teaching mode for the comprehensive course design of network software empowered by AIGC technology.

2 Construction of an AIGC-Empowered Course Teaching Mode

AIGC uses generative AI technology to automatically create multimodal content. Based on pre-trained large language models, it can demonstrate excellent language understanding and context awareness capabilities, efficiently and conveniently generating required content through natural language interaction [8]. The current software development process is undergoing a paradigm shift centered on AIGC. From requirements analysis, design, coding, testing, to deployment and maintenance, AI programming tools can automatically generate documentation, code, and test cases, greatly improving software development efficiency [9]. The core functions and applicable scenarios of current mainstream AI programming tools are shown in Table 1 below.

The Comprehensive course design of network software is a intensive practical course offered for the Network Engineering major. It has 32 teaching hours and is scheduled in the 6th semester. The course is demand-oriented, led by industry applications, and adopts a school-enterprise cooperation collaborative education model. Based on enterprise cases from the QST U+ New Engineering Smart Cloud Platform, it introduces AI tools to assist the entire software development process, carries out project-driven teaching, and cultivates students' independent learning ability and innovative practical ability.

The course utilizes AIGC technology to empower teaching reform, reconstructs course teaching objectives, updates teaching content, reforms the teaching mode, and innovates the evaluation system. Teaching is conducted around eight aspects: intelligent requirements acquisition and analysis, intelligent software design, automated code generation, intelligent code recommendation, software defect prediction and automatic repair, automated code testing, automated

Table 1. Mainstream AI Programming Tools

AI Programming Tool	Core Function	Applicable Scenario	Language Support
ChatGPT	Natural language code generation, requirements analysis, document generation	Requirements analysis/Prototype design/Code explanation	Python, Java, JS and other mainstream languages
GitHub Copilot	Code auto-completion, function generation, unit test generation	Daily coding/Rapid prototyping	Python, JS, Go and 50+ languages
Tongyi Lingma (Aliyun)	Code generation, explanation, commenting, optimization, documentation	Rapid prototyping, enterprise system development, code maintenance & optimization, education/beginners	Python, Java, JS/TS and other mainstream languages
Amazon CodeWhisperer	Code suggestions, security vulnerability detection, API integration	Full-stack development/Cloud service integration	Java, Python, JS, C# and 15 languages
Tabnine	Localized code completion, team knowledge base learning	Enterprise development/Private code repository maintenance	All mainstream languages, emphasis on Python/Java/C++
SonarQube	Static code analysis, vulnerability detection, code smell identification	Code review/Quality assurance	Supports 27 languages, including Java, C#, Python, JS
Visual Studio IntelliCode	Context-aware code recommendations, AI-assisted refactoring	IDE integrated development/Architecture design	With a focus on mainstream enterprise development languages (C#, Java, JS/TS, Python, C++)
Testim.io	Self-healing test script generation, intelligent test case maintenance	Web/Mobile automated testing	JS/TS
Swagger AI	API document auto-generation, interface test case generation	RESTful API development & documentation	All languages supporting OpenAPI specification
Jira AI	Task auto-classification, progress prediction, risk warning	Agile project management	Language independent

document generation, and intelligent assisted decision-making. AI tools are used to assist in generating Q&A teaching resources, customizing personalized learning plans, and through data analysis of student learning behaviors and effects, providing personalized evaluation of students. The course reform plan is shown in Fig. 1.

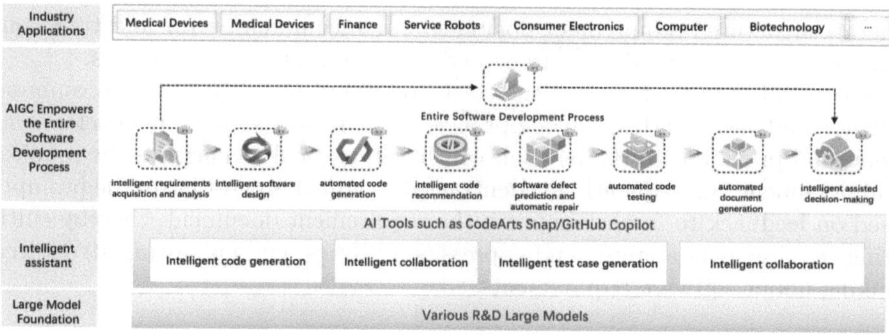

Fig. 1. Course Reform Design Diagram.

2.1 Reconstruction of Teaching Objectives

Based on the OBE (Outcome-Based Education) concept, the course incorporates the application ability of AIGC tools into the teaching objective system. It enables students to master the core functions and usage methods of mainstream AIGC tools, learn the application of various typical AIGC tools throughout the software development lifecycle, and cultivate abilities such as decomposing, abstracting, and describing problems, proficiently expressing software development intent, understanding the results generated by AI tools, discriminating and judging the generated results, and adjusting prompts based on the feedback from AI tools. This thereby enhances students' self-learning ability, innovation ability, and ability to solve complex engineering problems.

2.2 Update of Teaching Content

Centering on the entire software development lifecycle, the course designs 8 key AIGC-empowered teaching segments: intelligent requirements acquisition and analysis, intelligent software design, automated code generation, intelligent code recommendation, software defect prediction and automatic repair, automated code testing, automated document generation, and intelligent assisted decision-making. AIGC empowerment throughout the software development process can significantly improve development efficiency while providing students with rich learning opportunities. Through the rational use of AI tools, students can not only master traditional software development skills but also cultivate comprehensive abilities such as problem analysis, optimization decision-making, and teamwork, laying a solid foundation for future career development.

Intelligent Requirements Acquisition and Analysis. Intelligent requirements acquisition and analysis mainly includes automated requirements collection, understanding, and validation. AIGC tools can help developers better understand user needs based on natural language descriptions, automatically generate structured requirement documents, reduce human error and time consumption, and improve the accuracy and completeness of requirements.

After fully understanding the task requirements, students decompose, abstract, and describe the problem, proficiently express the software development intent, and provide it to the AI tool, which automatically generates the requirement document. Subsequently, students need to adjust and optimize the prompts based on feedback to further improve the requirement document, thereby cultivating requirements analysis and expression abilities, and enhancing structured thinking about software requirements.

Intelligent Software Design. Intelligent software design mainly includes software architecture generation and recommendation, design evaluation, and optimization. Based on the results of requirements analysis, it automatically generates software architecture and design documents. AIGC tools can generate system architecture diagrams, module divisions, and interface designs based on requirements, and provide optimization suggestions based on historical data and best practices, accelerating the design process and improving system scalability and security.

After the AI tool provides suggestions for design patterns and architectural styles that meet the requirements, students need to evaluate and optimize the results, analyze the cost, performance, and maintainability of different design solutions, and ensure the design meets the requirement specifications. This process cultivates students' software architecture design ability and trade-off decision-making ability, enabling them to master how to choose the optimal design solution under different constraints.

Automated Code Generation. AI programming tools use AI models and natural language processing technology to automatically generate software code based on natural language descriptions or other specifications. This covers code generation at different granularities and stages, from system architecture to code snippets, from business logic to test verification.

Students need to analyze the correctness of the generated code and evaluate its readability, performance, and security, making optimizations and adjustments if necessary. This process enhances students' code review ability and awareness of programming standards, enabling them to maintain strict control over code quality even with AI assistance.

Intelligent Code Recommendation. By learning from students' programming habits and the current context, AI can recommend required code snippets or templates from existing codebases, supporting efficient reuse of high-quality existing code and assisting the software development process.

Students need the ability to understand and evaluate code, judge the applicability, efficiency, and security of the recommended code, and master code reuse and integration techniques to avoid redundancy or conflicts. By comparing AI-recommended code with manually written code, students can cultivate an optimization awareness and gradually improve their ability to independently write high-quality code.

Software Defect Prediction and Automatic Repair. AIGC tools use machine learning algorithms to analyze historical defect data, predict potential defect locations and types in software, and provide repair patches through search methods or generative models, reducing the overhead of manual review and repair.

Students need to master code debugging and logical analysis skills, understand the defects predicted by AI, and verify the correctness of repair patches. By analyzing AI's repair solutions, students can learn common defect patterns and repair strategies, accumulating experience to prevent similar problems. At the same time, critical thinking needs to be cultivated to avoid over-reliance on automated tools and ensure the rationality of repair solutions.

Automated Code Testing. Automated code testing includes automatic test case generation, test execution, and result analysis, covering unit testing, integration testing, and system testing levels. AIGC tools can generate test cases based on functional requirements, cover more scenarios, and quickly generate analysis reports, helping developers discover and fix problems promptly.

Through the test cases generated by AI, students learn test case design principles (such as boundary value analysis, equivalence partitioning) and master test coverage analysis methods to ensure key logic is fully verified. At the same time, it cultivates students' problem localization ability, quickly identifying the root cause of defects based on test results, and optimizing test code to make it more aligned with actual requirements.

Automated Document Generation. AIGC tools, based on learning from large-scale code and natural language text, can automatically generate and maintain requirement documents, design documents, API documents, etc., based on source code or other software artifacts, reducing the effort developers spend on document maintenance.

Students need the ability to review and refine documents, judge the accuracy and completeness of AI-generated documents, and manually supplement key details. By comparing the consistency between requirements, code, and documents, students' systematic thinking is strengthened, understanding the relationship between documentation and software development. Furthermore, students learn standardized document expression and optimize the structure of AI-generated documents to comply with technical standards.

Intelligent Assisted Decision-Making. Based on software development data, AIGC tools can support project managers in making more reasonable decisions in areas such as development timeline planning, resource allocation, and risk assessment.

Students need to learn resource planning and risk assessment capabilities through suggestions provided by AI, such as how to balance development cycles with quality requirements. At the same time, they should develop data-driven decision-making awareness, adjust project plans based on AI analysis results, and exercise teamwork and communication skills to translate AI's decision support into executable team tasks.

2.3 Teaching Mode Innovation

This study constructs a "dual-line integration, three-stage progression" AI-empowered teaching mode, as shown in Fig. 2. Through the integration and organic coordination of online (Qingsoft U+ platform) and offline (software lab) dual lines, it achieves an intelligent reconstruction of the entire software development process through three progressive stages: pre-class, in-class, and post-class. In the pre-class stage, teachers use AIGC technology to generate dynamic learning cases and record instructional videos; students watch the videos and complete independent knowledge construction through an intelligent Q&A system. The in-class stage adopts the 8 key segments described in Sect. 1.2, relying on AI tools to achieve human-machine collaborative programming, and deepens knowledge internalization through group discussions and code reviews. Post-class, based on intelligent detection tools like SonarQube, layered expansion tasks are assigned, constructing a diversified intelligent evaluation system covering the entire process. This mode enhances students' engineering practice ability and forms a student ability cultivation path of "AI tool application - problem solving - innovation ability".

3 Teaching Implementation and Evaluation

3.1 Teaching Implementation

The development of an "Online Examination System" project is used as an example to illustrate how the course uses AI to empower the entire software development process. As shown in Table 2, for the 8 stages of software development, the AI tools used, specific AI-assisted operations, students' main tasks, and the abilities cultivated are introduced respectively. Through course teaching, the teacher's role is transformed from a knowledge imparter to a learning guide, and students change from passive learning to autonomous inquiry learning through AI tools. Through the experience of the entire software development process, students' engineering practice ability is strengthened, and their ability to independently analyze and solve problems is cultivated.

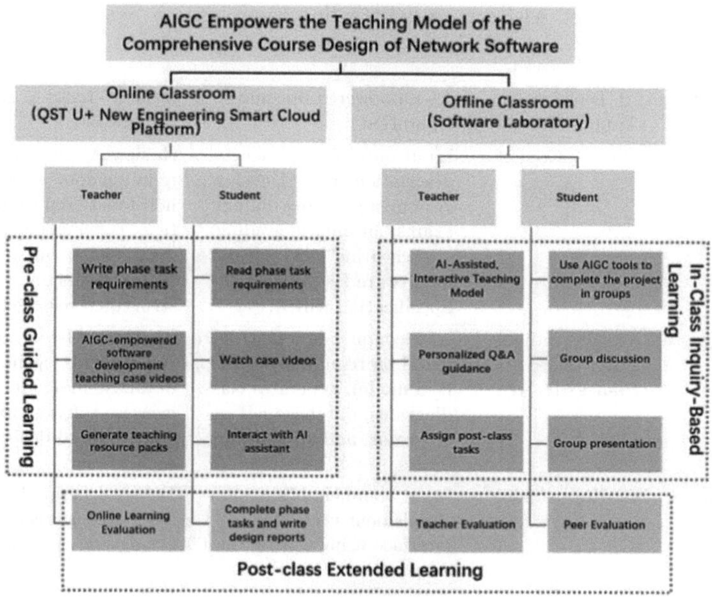

Fig. 2. "Dual-Line Integration, Three-Stage Progression" AI-Empowered Teaching Mode.

3.2 Teaching Evaluation Innovation

To mobilize and stimulate students' learning motivation, this course implements whole-process assessment and innovatively constructs a "Three-Dimensional, Six-Metric" course evaluation model. The assessment of student learning effectiveness is achieved through multi-dimensional data fusion, as shown in Table 3. This model includes three core dimensions: The Process dimension uses dynamic data such as Git commit frequency and AI tool usage logs to quantify students' engineering practice participation and AI collaboration proficiency; The Outcome dimension integrates objective indicators such as SonarQube code quality scores and test coverage; The Developmental dimension uses peer assessment and AI-assisted innovation evaluation, focusing on system design novelty and creative problem-solving. The six evaluation metrics (Participation, Proficiency, Standardization, Completeness, Collaboration, Innovation) correspond to the core ability requirements for software engineering talent. Through machine learning algorithms for weighted analysis of multi-source data, an ability matrix and student evaluation results are ultimately generated. Based on the student evaluation results, personalized learning suggestions are provided. This teaching evaluation meets the needs of formative assessment and also provides data support for teaching improvement.

Example: Multi-source evaluation data collection for a certain student is shown in Table 4.

Table 2. Case Study of AI-Empowered "Online Examination System" Development Process

Development Stage	AI Tool & Application	AI-Empowered Specific Operation	Student Tasks & Ability Cultivation
Requirements Analysis	GitHub Copilot	Input natural language description (e.g., "Develop a system supporting online exams, automatic grading, anti-cheating"), AI generates a Software Requirements Specification (SRS).	Review AI-generated requirements, supplement non-functional requirements (e.g., concurrency support for 1000 users), cultivate requirements analysis and structured expression ability.
System Design	Visual Studio IntelliCode/ PlantUML AI	AI recommends architecture based on requirements (e.g., B/S mode), generates class diagrams, database ER diagrams, and API design drafts.	Evaluate AI-recommended architecture, optimize database index design, exercise software architecture trade-off and decision-making ability.
Code Generation	GitHub Copilot	Input comments (e.g., "Implement user login interface using Spring Boot"), AI generates Controller, Service layer code.	Debug generated code, add JWT token verification logic, strengthen code debugging and secure coding ability.
Code Recommendation	GitHub Copilot	When writing "random test paper generation algorithm", AI recommends code snippets based on genetic algorithms.	Compare the efficiency of AI recommendation vs. manual implementation, learn algorithm optimization and code reuse skills.
Defect Detection	SonarQube	AI scans code, flags potential vulnerabilities (e.g., SQL injection risk) and provides repair suggestions.	Verify vulnerabilities and manually repair them (e.g., switch to PreparedStatement), master defensive programming and security audit ability.
Automated Testing	Testim.io/ Selenium IDE	AI generates test cases (e.g., simulate 100 users concurrently submitting exams), outputs performance test reports.	Supplement boundary tests (e.g., handling timeout submissions), cultivate test scenario design and performance optimization ability.
Document Generation	Swagger AI/Doxygen	AI parses code to generate API documentation (e.g., input/output description for /api/submit-exam).	Correct ambiguous descriptions in the documentation (e.g., clarify "error code 400" as "request parameter missing"), improve technical documentation standardization ability.
Assisted Decision-Making	Jira AI/ClickUp	AI analyzes task progress, warns of "automatic grading module delay", suggests adjusting development priority.	Reassign tasks based on AI suggestions, coordinate team division of labor, exercise agile management and risk response ability.

Table 3. "Three-Dimensional, Six-Metric" Course Evaluation Model

Evaluation Dimension	Evaluation Metric	Data Source
Process Evaluation (50%)	Participation (60%), Proficiency (40%)	Git commit record analysis, AI tool usage logs
Outcome Evaluation (40%)	Standardization (70%), Completeness (30%)	SonarQube code quality detection, Requirements Traceability Matrix test coverage
Developmental Eval. (10%)	Collaboration (40%), Innovation (60%)	Peer assessment, AI-assisted innovation solution review

Table 4. Multi-source Evaluation Data for a Student

Evaluation Dimension	Evaluation Metric	Data Indicator	Raw Data
Process	Participation	Git commit count	58 times
	Proficiency	AI tool usage accuracy rate	82%
Outcome	Standardization	Code quality score	87/100
	Completeness	Unit test coverage	76%
Developmental	Collaboration	Peer assessment score	8.5/10
	Innovation	Innovation solution score	4.2/5

Based on the evaluation data, an ability evaluation matrix is obtained with the help of AI tools, as shown in Table 5.

Through the ability evaluation matrix, and according to the evaluation indicator weights in Table 3, the student evaluation result is obtained. Based on the student evaluation result, personalized learning suggestions are given to the student.

(1) Strengthen Advantages: Outstanding innovative thinking ability (exceeding 98% of peers), recommended to participate in AI innovation projects.
(2) Improvement Direction: Test coverage (76%) is below the course average (82%), need to strengthen boundary test training.
(3) Recommended Resources: LeetCode testing special topic library.

4 Analysis of Teaching Effectiveness

This course underwent AI-empowered teaching reform in the Spring 2025 semester. Teaching practice verification showed significant results compared to

Table 5. Ability Evaluation Matrix for a Student

Evaluation Metric	Score	Key Finding
Participation	85	Submission frequency higher than 90% of peers
Proficiency	82	Fewer Copilot prompt optimization attempts
Standardization	88	Code comment coverage reached 95%
Completeness	76	Module completion 100%, testing needs strengthening
Collaboration	85	Completed 5 effective code reviews
Innovation	95	Proposed 3 innovative solutions adopted by the team

the traditional teaching method in 2024. In terms of quantitative indicators, students' project development efficiency, excellent code quality rate, and unit test coverage have significantly improved. In the ability development dimension, based on the evaluation of the "Three-Dimensional, Six-Metric" model, 87% of students reached a proficient application level of AI tools, and innovative thinking ability increased by an average of 29%. According to questionnaire feedback, 91% of students believe they have formed a sustainable "human-machine collaboration" work mode in software development. These empirical data fully verify the significant advantages of this teaching mode in enhancing students' engineering practice ability and cultivating innovative software talent.

Of course, we cannot ignore that introducing AI-assisted programming tools into the course also carries potential risks [10]. For example, some students may become overly dependent on AI, leading to degradation of basic programming skills and weakening of core skills such as algorithm design and debugging; AI tools may replicate defect patterns present in the training data (e.g., SQL injection logic), requiring manual audit; sometimes batch-generated code lacks innovation, inhibiting students' original thinking in solving complex problems. Subsequent teaching designs such as "AI code review defense" and "manually rewriting key modules" are used to mitigate risks and balance efficiency with ability cultivation.

5 Conclusion

This study confirms that the AIGC-empowered teaching mode for the comprehensive course design of network software significantly enhances students' engineering practice ability and innovation capability. Verified by the "Three-Dimensional, Six-Metric" intelligent evaluation model, this model has made breakthrough progress in quantitative indicators such as development efficiency and code quality, as well as ability dimensions such as AI tool application and innovative thinking. Future research can further explore the deep integration of multimodal AIGC tools in teaching and the embedding of AI ethics education in the curriculum. This model provides an important reference for the reform of practical software development courses in the context of new-generation information technologies.

References

1. Zhang, B., Lü, Y., Zhang, Y., Yao, G., Qin, X.: GAI empowers software development: exploration and practice of a comprehensive course design teaching model. China Comput. Commun. 2025(12) (2025)
2. Siyuan, H., Zinan, G., Jia, L.: From knowledge learning to thinking cultivation: educational transformation in the era of ChatGPT. J. Soochow Univ. (Educ. Sci. Ed.) **11**(03), 63–72 (2023)
3. Zhang, J.: The transformation of software development by artificial intelligence technology. Software 2025(05) (2025)
4. Duan, J.: Automatically generated code in the era of large AI models: a new trend in software development. In: China Building Metal Structure Magazine Co., Ltd., Proceedings of the 2024 Forum on Smart Construction and Economic Development from the Perspective of New Quality Productivity (Volume III). COSCO Shipping Technology (Beijing) Co. Ltd., pp. 18–19 (2024)
5. Liu, K., Fang, J., Zhu, Z.: Case-based teaching design and practice of programming courses in information technology under the background of strengthening military new engineering. Comput. Educ. (02), 81–84+89 (2024)
6. Fengguang, X., Zhiyan, J., Jianhua, Z., et al.: Reform of the programming curriculum system for "Learning by Doing". Comput. Educ. **08**, 103–108 (2024)
7. Zanhong, Z.: Practice of three-dimensional teaching and evaluation of advanced programming language based on OBE. Comput. Educ. **04**, 194–198 (2024)
8. Jiang, C., Duan, Y.: Preliminary exploration of computer practical course reform in the context of ChatGPT. Exp. Technol. Manag. **40**(12), 1–7+23 (2023)
9. Zhicong, C.: AI technology empowers computer software development. Smart China **03**, 36–37 (2025)
10. Xiang, D., Lijun, G.: Ways, risks and countermeasures of ChatGPT's intervention in higher education. Higher Educ. Expl. **05**, 12–17 (2023)

Data Management and Security

Practice of Teaching Reform in Data Structure and Algorithm Course Based on 'BOPPPS+4E' Model

Hong Yu(✉), Han Liu, Linlin Zong, and Xiaotong Zhang

School of Software, Dalian University of Technology, Dalian, China
{hongyu,hanliu,llzong,zhangxt}@dlut.edu.cn

Abstract. In response to the disconnect between traditional content in the Data Structure and Algorithm curriculum and current industry developments, along with insufficient training in students' comprehensive abilities and a lack of learning initiative, a teaching reform based on the 'BOPPPS+4E' model has been implemented to meet the talent demands of the software industry. The reform utilizes a blended teaching approach, combining online SPOCs, large-class lectures, laboratory sessions, and small-group flipped classrooms, thus integrating the BOPPPS model with 4E teaching methods (hEuristic, projEct-based, discovEry-oriented, and rEsearch-based) and enabling continuous assessment. Specifically, the model refines the course objectives into three dimensions—knowledge, skills, and qualities. This helps students consolidate professional knowledge foundations while improving autonomous learning abilities, computational thinking, and innovation capabilities. It also cultivates students' scientific, pragmatic, and rigorous learning and professional attitudes, as well as their sense of innovation, teamwork spirit, and dedication to independent software development.

Keywords: BOPPPS · Online-offline hybrid teaching · Flipped classroom model

1 Introduction

With the rapid development of information technology, Data Structure and Algorithm has become a core course in computer science, holding a crucial position in disciplines such as computer science, software engineering, and network engineering. The course primarily covers six parts: introduction, linear lists, trees and binary trees, graphs, searching, and sorting. Its highly abstract content imposes stringent demands on students' logical thinking and programming skills. As most students are in the first semester of their sophomore year with only basic coding abilities, they face significant challenges during the learning process.

Traditional teaching of Data Structure and Algorithm course has exposed numerous problems. In terms of content, there is an overemphasis on fundamental theory that is seriously out of touch with new industrial applications.

J. Chi et al. (Eds.): CNETCNED 2025, CCIS 2809, pp. 105–119, 2026.
https://doi.org/10.1007/978-981-95-7124-6_10

Although the curriculum covers a wide range of topics, it lacks depth in research, innovation, and comprehensiveness, thereby failing to meet students' needs for cutting-edge knowledge and hindering the cultivation of their innovative thinking and comprehensive application abilities. In the practical component of the course, students exhibit a marked deficiency in training their ability to apply acquired knowledge to solve complex problems. Traditional instruction tends to overemphasize repetitive exercises for consolidation while neglecting the development of overall student abilities, leaving many students ill-equipped when confronted with real-world challenges. Additionally, from a pedagogical standpoint, student initiative is not adequately fostered—they passively absorb a vast quantity of trivial and abstract information during lectures, often understanding the material in theory, yet being unable to articulate or apply it effectively, severely undermines both learning outcomes and interest. These issues require urgent reforms of teaching to improve educational quality and cultivate high-caliber talents who can meet contemporary demands.

Numerous institutions have already embarked on teaching reforms for Data Structure and Algorithm course [1–4]. For instance, Carnegie Mellon University has maintained its focus on foundational computer science courses while actively incorporating courses on AI principles and practical applications. In its teaching laboratories, students are even allowed to use AI programming assistants in introductory courses, emphasizing the development of skills for critically evaluating the readability and maintainability of AI-generated code in order to foster critical thinking. Similarly, Stanford University, adhering to the concept of "human-machine collaboration", emphasizes AI-assisted programming, encouraging students to use AI tools to improve development efficiency while also focusing on higher-order competencies such as teamwork and system design. Some universities have optimized their curriculum by integrating cutting-edge industry knowledge and creating a series of innovative project case studies to improve students' practical and creative abilities; other institutions have adopted blended teaching models that combine online platforms with interactive offline classes to enrich resources and improve student engagement. However, there remains room for improvement in effectively integrating multiple teaching methodologies to holistically enhance students' skills.

In contrast to previous studies, this paper presents a novel teaching framework based on the 'BOPPPS+4E' model. By organically integrating the six key stages of the BOPPPS model [5–7] with four teaching approaches: heuristic, project-based, discovery-oriented, and research-based, this framework not only emphasizes the acquisition of knowledge, but also actively promotes student participation and skill development. Through differentiated instruction and diversified teaching methods, it addresses the varied learning needs of students, thereby improving their overall competence and quality.

This study aims to undertake a comprehensive reform of Data Structure and Algorithm course based on the 'BOPPPS + 4E' instructional model. The goal is to overcome the shortcomings of traditional teaching methods, improve instructional quality, and cultivate overall student competencies. Specifically, by introducing the 'BOPPPS + 4E' teaching model, the course objectives are refined into three dimensions: knowledge, skills, and qualities, enabling students to build upon a solid foundation of professional knowledge while developing autonomous learning abilities, computational thinking, and innovation capabilities. In addition, the model fosters a scientific, pragmatic and rigorous approach to both learning and professional conduct, nurturing a sense of innovation, teamwork, and a commitment to independent software development. This reform may also serve as a valuable reference for similar instructional innovations in other related subjects, thereby promoting the general advancement and innovation of the educational system.

2 'BOPPPS+4E' Teaching Model Analysis

2.1 Overview of the BOPPPS Teaching Model

As shown in Fig. 1, the BOPPPS teaching model is an instructional design framework that offers educators a systematic, student-centered approach [7–9]. This model emphasizes active student participation and moves away from traditional teacher-centered instruction. By structuring the class into six key stages that foster interaction and feedback, the model creates a closed-loop teaching process capable of enhancing instructional effectiveness and promoting deep learning.

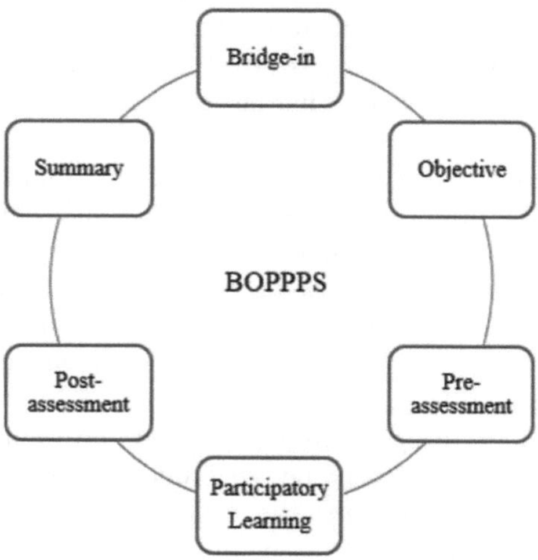

Fig. 1. Six stages of BOPPPS model.

These six stages are: Bridge-in, Objective, Pre-assessment, Participatory Learning, Post-assessment, and Summary. The Bridge-in stage serves as the lesson's opening, aiming to capture students' attention, stimulate interest, and create a connection between prior knowledge and new content. For instance, in Data

Structure and Algorithm course, an instructor might highlight real-life cases closely related to data structures—such as route planning in map navigation (involving graph shortest path algorithms) or product searches on e-commerce platforms (involving search algorithms)—to spark curiosity and enhance classroom engagement.

In the Objective stage, the instructor clearly communicates what students are expected to learn, setting specific, measurable, and achievable goals. This clarity in learning direction not only facilitates subsequent evaluation but also helps students understand the value of the lesson, thereby boosting motivation. For example, when discussing sorting algorithms, the teacher might explicitly state that students need to mastery the principles, implementation steps, and time complexity analysis of algorithms such as bubble sort, insertion sort, and quick sort.

The Pre-assessment stage is used to evaluate students' baseline knowledge and understand their learning needs. This assessment helps instructors identify learning gaps and adjust their teaching plans accordingly, ensuring that the instruction meets the actual needs of the students. Additionally, it prompts students to reflect on their current knowledge, thereby fostering self-directed learning. Methods such as brief questionnaires, brainstorming sessions, rapid questioning, or group discussions can be employed for this purpose.

Participatory Learning, the core of the BOPPPS model, centers on active student engagement. Through interactive discussions, practical applications, and reflective exercises, students apply theoretical knowledge to real-world situations, deepening their understanding and internalizing the material. Educators can facilitate this process by organizing group discussions, case studies, role-plays, or hands-on activities—experiences that cultivate critical thinking and problem-solving skills.

The Post-assessment stage evaluates whether the learning objectives have been achieved, thereby providing a measure of teaching effectiveness. It allows teachers to identify areas where students may have misunderstandings or deficiencies and to adjust future instruction accordingly. Immediate feedback is provided to help students gauge their learning progress. Common techniques in this stage include short quizzes, project presentations, problem-solving activities, and reflective journals.

Finally, the Summary stage involves reviewing and reinforcing key concepts to consolidate learning outcomes and lay the foundation for future study. Instructors can guide students in revisiting the main points of the lesson, organizing their knowledge, and strengthening their understanding and memory of critical concepts.

In the context of Data structure and Algorithm course, implementing the BOPPPS teaching model can significantly boost students' interest and engagement. By linking abstract concepts with practical examples through an engaging introduction, clearly defining learning objectives, fostering active participation, and providing timely assessments and summaries, the model enhances both student involvement and overall learning effectiveness.

2.2 The Connotations of the 4E Teaching Method

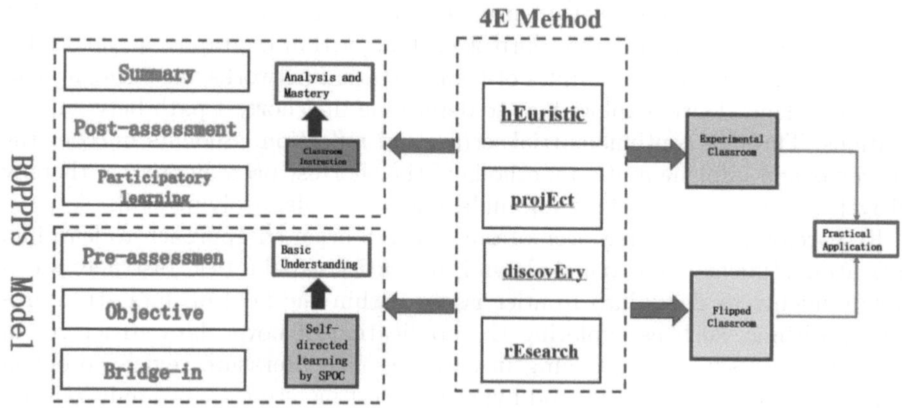

Fig. 2. Overview of 'BOPPPS+4E' model.

As shown in Fig. 2, the 'BOPPPS+4E' model integrates four approaches-hEuristic, projEct-based, discovEry-based, and rEsearch-based teaching—with the aim of comprehensively enhancing students' learning abilities and overall competence.

Heuristic teaching emphasizes engaging students' cognitive processes and, by adhering to the objective laws of learning, maximizes the stimulation of their thinking and motivation. In courses, instructors can pose thought-provoking questions to guide students toward active thinking. For instance, when explaining binary tree traversal algorithms, an instructor might ask, "How can we visit each node of a binary tree in a specific order to meet various application needs?" This encourages students to explore solutions through discussion and reflection, fostering a deep understanding of the principles and applications of traversal algorithms. Such an approach not only sparks interest and active participation but also provides opportunities for self-exploration, self-reflection, and self-expression, thereby helping to establish a democratic and harmonious teacher-student relationship.

Project-based teaching [12,13] centers around the completion of specific projects, allowing students to learn and apply knowledge in a practical context. Instructors might design real-world projects related to data structures and algorithms, such as developing a simple library management system that requires the application of concepts like linear lists and search algorithms to implement functionalities such as adding, deleting, and querying books. Through collaborative group work—from requirement analysis and algorithm design to coding, testing, and debugging—students comprehensively enhance their practical skills, teamwork, and understanding of the subject matter.

Discovery-based teaching focuses on encouraging students' autonomous inquiry. Here, instructors provide only key facts and questions when introducing concepts and principles, prompting students to actively think, independently explore, and discover the relevant principles and conclusions on their own. For example, when introducing the shortest path algorithm in graphs, an instructor might present real-world examples of transportation networks, encouraging students to independently explore how to determine the shortest path between two locations. Through continuous trial, error, and reflection, students uncover the core ideas and implementation methods of the shortest path algorithm, thereby cultivating innovative thinking and independent problem-solving skills.

Research-based teaching promotes a research-oriented approach to learning, cultivating students' research skills and innovative capabilities. Instructors can guide students to delve into frontier issues within the field of data structures and algorithms, such as exploring the application of novel data structures in big data processing. By engaging in activities like literature review, problem analysis, experimental design, and hypothesis testing, students not only gain in-depth professional knowledge but also learn the processes of scientific research, which lays a solid foundation for their future academic and professional pursuits.

Together, these four teaching methods are mutually complementary: heuristic teaching stimulates cognitive engagement; project-based teaching enhances practical skills; discovery-based teaching fosters autonomous inquiry; and research-based teaching develops research competencies, collectively contributing to the comprehensive improvement of students' abilities.

2.3 Advantages of the 'BOPPPS+4E' Integration

The integration of the 'BOPPPS+4E' teaching model brings significant benefits to the instruction of data structures and algorithms, exerting a positive and long-lasting impact on both teaching effectiveness and the cultivation of students' comprehensive capabilities.

The structured design of the 'BOPPPS+4E' model provides a clear framework for educational activities, while the 4E teaching principles infuse each instructional stage with a variety of pedagogical strategies and methods, complementing one another effectively. During the initiation phase, heuristic teaching methods pose thought-provoking questions that quickly capture students' attention, stimulate their interest, and encourage more active engagement in subsequent learning. For example, when explaining the hash table as a data structure, an instructor might ask, "In scenarios involving massive data storage and retrieval, how can target data be quickly located?" This question prompts students to think deeply and paves the way for the introduction of the hash table concept. In the participatory learning phase, project-based, inquiry-based, and research-based teaching methods are fully employed. Project-based learning enables students to apply their knowledge of data structures and algorithms in practice by completing real-world projects, thereby deepening their understanding and enhancing practical skills as well as teamwork. For instance, in the "High-speed Railway Route Planning" project, students must use graph data structure and the shortest path algorithm to design an efficient high-speed rail network. Collaborating in groups allows them to master the relevant knowledge and skills more effectively. Inquiry-based teaching encourages autonomous exploration, fostering innovative thinking and the ability to solve problems independently. In experimental or flipped classroom settings, instructors can guide students to discover solutions for specific challenges—for example, prompting them to explore various string matching algorithms and analyze their respective strengths and weaknesses. Research-based learning provides opportunities for in-depth study, cultivating students' research acumen and innovative capacity, and enabling them to explore cutting-edge issues in Data Structure and Algorithm, such as optimizing data structures within quantum computing environments.

The post-assessment phase employs diverse evaluation methods to comprehensively assess students' mastery of the material and the enhancement of their abilities, thereby offering a foundation for instructional improvement. The consolidation phase helps students refine their knowledge systems, reinforce key concepts, and solidify their learning achievements. Through the integrated application of the 'BOPPPS+4E' teaching model, students not only systematically grasp the knowledge of data structures and algorithms but also achieve holistic improvements in cognitive, practical, innovative, and research skills, thereby laying a solid foundation for future professional development and academic research.

3 Based on the 'BOPPPS+4E' Teaching Reform Practice

3.1 Optimization of Teaching Objectives

In the teaching reform practice based on the 'BOPPPS+4E' model, teaching objectives have been comprehensively and thoroughly optimized to better meet the talent cultivation demands of the new era. On the cognitive level, students are not only expected to master traditional knowledge in data structures and algorithms but are also guided to understand the underlying principles and mechanisms of these concepts in practical applications. For instance, when explaining hash tables, students are introduced not only to the fundamental concepts and operations but also to a detailed analysis of their application principles in fields such as blockchain and database indexing, enabling them to deeply comprehend the role of hash tables in addressing real-world issues.

On the skill level, the focus is on cultivating students' ability to engage in autonomous learning and solve complex problems using the 'BOPPPS+4E' model. Through heuristic teaching methods, students are encouraged to think proactively, thereby enhancing their innovative thinking abilities. In project-based teaching, students improve their practical skills and teamwork abilities by working on real projects. For example, in the "High-Speed Rail Route Planning" project, students are required to apply graph data structure and the shortest path algorithm collaboratively to plan routes, which not only hones their programming skills but also develops their team communication and coordination capabilities.

On the quality level, the 'BOPPPS+4E' teaching process reinforces the students' scientific spirit and innovative consciousness. Both discovery-based and research-oriented teaching approaches encourage students to explore the unknown and cultivate their research competence and innovation capabilities. During research-oriented teaching, students are guided to investigate cutting-edge issues in the field of data structures and algorithms, such as optimizing data structures in quantum computing environments, which fosters their innovative thinking and practical abilities. Through these optimizations, students achieve comprehensive improvement in their knowledge, skills, and overall quality, thereby laying a solid foundation for their future career development and academic research.

3.2 Upgrading and Optimizing Teaching Content

Integration of Industry and Disciplinary Frontiers. In order to closely align the teaching content with the evolving needs of the industry, 18 cutting-edge topics related to data structures—such as blockchain, maximum flow, frequent pattern tree, and graph community—have been actively introduced and incorporated into the new edition of the textbook. When teaching blockchain technology, its core data structures are explained in detail, including the Merkle tree and the chain structure. The Merkle tree performs hash calculations on a large volume of transaction data, progressively merging the computed values through several layers to ultimately produce a root hash. This mechanism enables rapid verification of data integrity and consistency and is widely used in blockchain to detect any tampering of transaction data. In contrast, the chain structure links individual blocks in chronological order, with each block containing the hash value of the preceding block together with its own data and hash. This design ensures the immutability and security of the blockchain. By introducing these advanced topics, students gain insight into the practical applications of data structures in emerging technologies, thereby broadening their knowledge base and stimulating their interest in learning.

Construction of a Project Case Collection. A carefully curated set of practical projects has been designed, including 16 extended practice projects that are closely aligned with real-world applications—such as high-speed railway route planning and spell checking—and 6 innovative projects that integrate scientific research, such as Weibo user relationship analysis and Web community discovery. For example, in the high-speed railway route planning project, students are required to use graph data structure and shortest path algorithms to design the optimal high-speed rail route by comprehensively considering factors like the geographical locations of multiple cities, passenger flow, and construction costs. Through this process, students not only consolidate their knowledge of data structures and algorithms but also learn how to apply theoretical concepts to practical problems, thereby enhancing their analytical and problem-solving skills. Similarly, the Weibo user relationship analysis project tasks students with employing graph-related concepts to model and analyze relationships among

Weibo users—such as following and interactions—in order to uncover characteristics and behavioral patterns within user groups, thus fostering innovative thinking and research capabilities.

Establishment of Integrated Teaching Resources. In terms of textbook development, provincial-level "12th Five-Year Plan" textbooks and innovative new-format textbooks have been published. These resources, with their rich content and rational structure, not only cover traditional data structures and algorithms but also integrate cutting-edge industry content and real-world application cases to provide students with comprehensive learning materials. Additionally, algorithm dynamic visualization software has been developed to represent abstract algorithms in an intuitive graphical format, aiding students in understanding the processes and principles underlying algorithm execution. Moreover, 37 micro-course videos—each focusing on a key knowledge point and of short duration—have been produced to facilitate learning anytime and anywhere. A problem bank featuring nearly a thousand questions, including multiple-choice questions, fill-in-the-blank items, and programming problems, has been established to meet the diverse learning needs of students. Furthermore, an automated code assessment and tracking analysis platform built on Huawei Cloud has been introduced; it automatically evaluates students' programming assignments, provides timely feedback on their learning progress, and tracks their learning processes to help instructors adjust teaching strategies accordingly. In addition, thirteen semesters of MOOC courses and six semesters of SPOC courses have been offered on the China University MOOC platform, thereby expanding students' access to a wealth of online learning resources.

Table 1. Different classroom model for different Class Type

Class type	Classroom model
Flipped classroom	students present, the audience asks questions, and the teacher evaluates
Laboratory session	students practice, and teachers and students evaluate
Large-class	the teacher-centered lecture model
SPOC self-learning phase	self-directed learning

3.3 Innovation in Teaching Organization

Online-Offline Hybrid Teaching Environment. Based on the Chinese University MOOC platform, an online-offline hybrid teaching environment has been established as shown in Table 1. It encompasses four distinct instructional settings: online SPOC, large classroom, laboratory session, and small-group flipped classroom. In the online SPOC self-learning phase, instructors release guiding questions and learning objectives in advance, enabling students to independently complete the essential knowledge acquisition, testing, and reinforcement exercises. For instance, while studying the chapter on linear lists, students watch instructional videos on the online SPOC platform to learn the concepts, storage structures, and basic operations of linear lists, and then complete the platform's quizzes and practice exercises to assess their learning outcomes. Additionally, students conduct industry application research to gain insight into the practical application scenarios of linear lists, thereby initiating the process of knowledge construction. The large classroom primarily focuses on knowledge delivery, supplemented by student discussion and analysis. In such sessions, instructors systematically explain the key and challenging aspects of the curriculum, guiding students toward comprehensive understanding. When explaining sorting algorithms, for example, the instructor details the principles and implementation steps of various sorting methods and then organizes discussions among students to analyze the advantages, disadvantages, and applicable scenarios of these algorithms. Laboratory sessions emphasize the completion of various practical projects, thereby reinforcing students' ability to apply knowledge. In these sessions, students undertake practical projects such as planning high-speed rail routes and performing spell checks, applying the data structures and algorithmic knowledge they have acquired to real-world projects, which in turn enhances their practical skills. The small-group flipped classroom focuses on student presentations and interactive discussions, cultivating students' ability to identify, analyze, and solve problems. In this setting, students showcase the results of their laboratory work or project practices, engage in exchanges with peers and instructors, and discuss the challenges encountered in their learning process, collaboratively exploring solutions.

Functions and Roles of Different Teaching Environments. The online SPOC environment provides students with a space for independent learning, allowing them to study at their own pace and develop autonomous learning skills. Students can repeatedly view instructional videos after class to deepen their understanding of the material, and also communicate with peers and instructors in online discussion forums to resolve encountered issues. The large classroom setting ensures that students systematically master the knowledge, as the instructor's explanations help them to build a comprehensive knowledge framework. Through vivid lectures and case analyses, instructors assist students in grasping abstract concepts and complex algorithms, while also guiding them to think critically and engage in discussions, thereby stimulating their interest in learning. Laboratory sessions enable students to consolidate and apply their knowledge through hands-on practice, enhancing their capability to solve practical problems. By completing project-based tasks, students can integrate theoretical knowledge with practical application, fostering innovative thinking and teamwork skills. The small-group flipped classroom [10,11], on the other hand, promotes intellectual exchange among students, nurturing critical thinking and expressive abilities. In these sessions, by presenting their work and engaging in discussions, students are able to approach problems from various perspectives, thereby improving their analytical and problem-solving skills. The interplay of different teaching environments forms an integrated whole, providing comprehensive support for students' learning and development.

3.4 Implementation of the 'BOPPPS+4E' Teaching Method.

Implementation of Each Stage in the BOPPPS Model. In the implementation of the teaching method based on 'BOPPPS+4E', each stage of the BOPPPS model is meticulously arranged and effectively executed. In the orientation stage, industry-related application problems are presented to introduce the learning content and stimulate students' interest and curiosity. When explaining the shortest path algorithm for graphs, the instructor displays a case study of route planning in map navigation and raises the issue of how to quickly find the shortest path between two points, thereby prompting student reflection and naturally introducing the learning of the shortest path algorithm. In the objective stage, the learning objectives for the lesson are clearly communicated so that students understand the direction of their study. For example, when explaining sorting algorithms, the instructor explicitly informs students that they need to master the principles, implementation steps, and time complexity analyses of algorithms such as bubble sort, insertion sort, and quick sort, thus setting clear expectations for the learning content. The pre-test stage is shifted to the SPOC online learning phase, where online tests and questionnaire surveys are used to assess students' existing knowledge and learning needs, providing a basis for subsequent instruction. Based on the pre-test results, the instructor can adjust the teaching content and methods to meet the varying learning needs of different students. During the participatory learning segment in large class settings, the instructor employs multiple teaching approaches to guide students in the gradual analysis, design, and implementation of various algorithms. When explaining the algorithms, the teacher facilitates small group discussions, encouraging students to share their viewpoints and collaboratively explore the ideas behind algorithm implementation. The post-test stage, conducted through quizzes and project presentations, evaluates students' mastery of knowledge and improvement in skills. Based on the post-test results, the instructor promptly provides feedback and evaluations to help students identify their shortcomings and promote further learning. Finally, in the conclusion stage at the end of the course, the instructor guides students in reviewing the key points of the lesson, organizing the knowledge framework, and deepening their understanding and retention of the content.

Integration of the 4E Teaching Approach. Heuristic teaching runs throughout the entire instructional process. The instructor poses thought-provoking questions to encourage students to think actively. For instance, when explaining the traversal algorithm of binary trees, the teacher asks, "If we need to visit the nodes of a binary tree in a different order, how should we design the algorithm?" This stimulates students' thinking and leads them to explore methods of implementing the traversal algorithm. Project-based learning is fully utilized in laboratory and flipped classrooms by involving practical projects such as high-speed rail route planning and Weibo user network analysis, allowing students to learn and apply knowledge in the process of project completion. In the high-speed rail route planning project, students are required to use data structures and shortest path algorithms to solve real-world route planning problems, thereby enhancing their practical ability and teamwork skills. Discovery-based learning encourages students to independently explore problems. In laboratory settings, the instructor provides practical problems and relevant resources, allowing students to investigate and develop their own solutions. For example, when addressing string-matching problems, the instructor guides students to experiment with different matching algorithms and analyze their pros and cons, thereby cultivating innovative thinking and the ability to solve problems independently. Research-based teaching guides students in exploring cutting-edge issues in the field, fostering their research literacy. The instructor can propose frontier research topics in data structures and algorithms—for example, the application of new data structures in big data processing—prompting students to review literature, conduct research, and write research reports, thus enhancing their research and innovation capabilities.

Correspondence between Teaching Content Types and Instructional Implementation. The teaching content for each chapter is categorized into three types: fundamental understanding, analytical mastery, and practical application, which are implemented respectively through SPOC online learning, large-class lectures, and flipped classroom combined with laboratory sessions. Fundamental understanding content, such as the basic concepts of data structures and the fundamental principles of algorithms, is delivered via SPOC online learning to enable self-study; students can initially grasp this basic knowledge by watching instructional videos and reading electronic textbooks. Analytical mastery content, such as performance analysis of algorithms and the examination of application scenarios for data structures, is delivered in large-class lectures where instructors provide in-depth explanations and analyses to guide students toward a comprehensive understanding and mastery. For example, when analyzing the time complexity of sorting algorithms, the instructor employs detailed derivations and case studies to help students master the methods and techniques for time complexity calculation and analysis. Practical application content, such as the development of actual projects and problem-solving, is carried out in flipped classrooms and laboratory sessions, where students apply the learned knowledge in practice by completing projects, presenting outcomes, and engaging in discussions to enhance their practical skills and problem-solving abilities.

4 Teaching Reform Outcomes

4.1 Student and Expert Evaluations

The blended online-offline instructional approach has received high recognition from both students and experts. Students have reported that "classroom learning is engaging" and that "practical projects are challenging," indicating that the teaching reform has successfully stimulated their interest and motivated them to explore actively and enhance their skills through demanding hands-on experiences. For five consecutive years, the average student evaluation scores for all instructors have exceeded 98 points, which not only reflects high student satisfaction with the reform but also demonstrates significant improvements in the overall learning experience. Expert evaluators from the supervisory team described the classroom teaching as having "a clear structure, engaging activities, attractive content, and effective teaching methods." Their professional endorsement confirms both the scientific basis and effectiveness of the teaching reform, recognizing its positive impact in optimizing course content and innovating teaching methods, and thereby providing strong support for further promotion and deepening of the reform measures.

4.2 Application of Teaching Resources

The comprehensive teaching resources developed during the reform process have been widely utilized. To date, four sessions of the course have been offered on the China University MOOC website, attracting over 15,000 learners. These resources include provincial "12th Five-Year Plan" textbooks, new-format textbooks, dynamic algorithm visualization software, micro-course videos, extensive exercise banks, and an automated coding assessment and tracking analysis platform. The diversity and richness of these materials provide learners with multiple pathways and abundant resources, not only meeting the needs of students but also benefiting a broader audience interested in data structures and algorithms. This widespread application has expanded the course's influence, improved the utilization efficiency of teaching resources, and promoted the sharing of high-quality educational content.

4.3 Student Capability Enhancement

Throughout the course, students have shown gradual improvement in their competencies. More than 80% of them have demonstrated the ability to independently identify problem prototypes from practical projects, and to design and implement effective solutions. This indicates that, after acquiring solid theoretical knowledge, their practical skills and problem-solving abilities have significantly advanced, enabling them to apply what they have learned to real-world projects flexibly. After completing the course, many students actively participated in related research projects and published papers at top-tier conferences, further evidencing their growth in research and innovation capabilities. Such academic achievements not only lay a strong foundation for their future scholarly endeavors but also bring honor to the institution and the discipline, reflecting the success of the teaching reform in cultivating comprehensive competencies and innovative potential.

5 Conclusion

This study conducted a comprehensive reform of Data Structure and Algorithm course based on the 'BOPPPS + 4E' teaching model. By optimizing learning objectives, innovating course content, reorganizing instructional methods, implementing the 'BOPPPS + 4E' approach, and reforming the course evaluation system, significant teaching outcomes were achieved. Students' enthusiasm and initiative were greatly enhanced, leading to noticeable improvements in the acquisition of knowledge, skill development, and overall competence. Moreover, the teaching resources have been widely disseminated, providing high-quality study materials to a broader range of learners and thereby expanding the course's impact. The successful integration of ideological and political education within the curriculum has achieved an organic unity between knowledge transfer and value guidance. With the continuous advancement of educational technology, the 'BOPPPS + 4E' teaching model must also be persistently innovated and refined. Future developments can further leverage artificial intelligence, virtual reality, and other emerging technologies to enrich instructional methods and resources, thereby providing students with a more immersive and personalized learning experience. By utilizing AI for intelligent analysis and individualized guidance—tailoring learning content and recommendations based on each student's progress and characteristics—the process of mastering knowledge and enhancing skills can be significantly improved. Through ongoing exploration and practice, the 'BOPPPS + 4E' teaching model is expected to play an increasingly influential role in education, contributing to the cultivation of high-caliber talent tailored to the needs of the modern era.

References

1. D. Zhang, X. Ma, F. Hu, J. Wang and D. Zhao.:Innovative Practice of Data Structure Teaching by Knowledge Graph+AI Q&A+Visualization. 2025 7th International Conference on Computer Science and Technologies in Education (CSTE), Wuhan, China, 2025, pp. 822-826, https://doi.org/10.1109/CSTE64638.2025.11092126
2. Yucheng Song, Shaoli Jin.: Research on Teaching Content Reform of Data Structure for Data Science and Big data Technology Major. 2023 13th International Conference on Information Technology in Medicine and Education (ITME), Wuyishan, China, 2023, pp. 55-57, https://doi.org/10.1109/ITME60234.2023.00022
3. Dingying Tan, Pingping Chen, Wenyi Xie, Huiling Liu.: Al-enabled "One Centre and Four Integration" Teaching Practice for Data Structures and Algorithms. 2024 International Conference on Informatics Education and Computer Technology Applications (IECA), Beijing, China, 2024, pp. 152-159, https://doi.org/10.1109/IECA62822.2024.00036
4. Xuejing Ding.: Teaching Reform and Exploration of Data Structure Course Based on Artificial Intelligence. 2024 International Conference on Artificial Intelligence and Digital Libraries (AIDL). Nanjing, China, 2024, pp. 18-21, https://doi.org/10.1109/AIDL66202.2024.00011

5. En Yuan, Weiwei Chen, Rui Wang, Yanqin Tang, Yongfen Wu, Wenyu Zhang.: Teaching Practice of Data Structure Based on Rain Classroom and BOPPPS Model. 2021 IEEE 3rd International Conference on Computer Science and Educational Informatization (CSEI). Xinxiang, China, 2021, pp. 144-147, https://doi.org/10.1109/CSEI51395.2021.9477727
6. P. A. Hatwalne, S. S. Chaudhary, S. V. Prayagi, R. V. Adkane, Sonali Vairagade.:Comparative Investigation of BOPPPS–AI Integrated Flipped Classroom Method and Conventional Teaching Method in Mechanical Engineering Education.2024 2nd DMIHER International Conference on Artificial Intelligence in Healthcare, Education and Industry.Wardha, India, 2024, pp. 1-5, https://doi.org/10.1109/IDICAIEI61867.2024.10842710
7. Yan Sun.: On Designing Experiment Teaching for Undergraduates' Effective Learning of Logistics Distribution Center Planning and Management Course Based on PBL and BOPPPS.2020 International Conference on Information Science and Education (ICISE-IE).Sanya, China, 2020, pp. 612-616, https://doi.org/10.1109/ICISE51755.2020.00137
8. Li-hua Qi, Dong-qiu Xing, Li Wen, Jing-na Cui.: Research on the Teaching Strategy of BOPPPS in the Intelligent Environment of Smart Classroom. 2021 2nd International Conference on Information Science and Education (ICISE-IE). Chongqing, China, 2021, pp. 197-200, https://doi.org/10.1109/ICISE-IE53922.2021.00053
9. Min Wu, Lu Zhang, Huan Sun.: Design of Blended Teaching Model Based on BOPPPS Model. 2023 5th International Conference on Computer Science and Technologies in Education (CSTE).Xi'an, China, 2023, pp. 101-105, https://doi.org/10.1109/CSTE59648.2023.00025
10. Lianghua Gong.: Construction of flipped classroom teaching model based on mobile learning platform. 2021 2nd International Conference on Information Science and Education (ICISE-IE). Chongqing, China, 2021, pp. 1265-1268, https://doi.org/10.1109/ICISE-IE53922.2021.00283
11. Jiang Jin-gang, Zhang Jia-wei, Du Hai-yan, Wang Kai-rui, Dai Ye, Tang Dedong.:Application of Flipped Classroom Teaching Method in the Single-Chip Microcomputer Course. 2024 13th International Conference on Educational and Information Technology (ICEIT).Chengdu, China, 2024, pp. 184-188, https://doi.org/10.1109/ICEIT61397.2024.10540809
12. Luran Wang, Abel Nyamapfene.: Student Experiences of PBL During Remote Learning: A Case Study: IEEE Global Engineering Education Conference (EDUCON). Tunis, Tunisia **2022**, 1822–1823 (2022). https://doi.org/10.1109/EDUCON52537.2022.9766776
13. Wenhua Bai, Lihua Su, Renpeng Zhang, Jianwen Chen.: Classroom Practical Teaching Based On Intelligent Data. 2022 8th Annual International Conference on Network and Information Systems for Computers (ICNISC).Hangzhou, China, 2022, pp. 727-730, https://doi.org/10.1109/ICNISC57059.2022.00146

Communications and Networking Technologies

Big Data-Driven Framework for University Asset Management and Auditing

Pan Chang[1,2] and Gang Xu[3(✉)]

[1] Shanghai New York University Constructional Working Group, East China Normal University, Shanghai 200062, China
pchang@ecnu.edu.cn
[2] Information Technology Department, Shanghai New York University, Shanghai 200124, China
[3] Informatization Governance Office, East China Normal University, Shanghai 200062, China
gxu@admin.ecnu.edu.cn

Abstract. With the deep integration of information technology and Internet of Things (IoT) technology in the field of higher education, asset management in universities faces severe challenges posed by diverse asset types, widespread distribution, and dynamic changes. Traditional manual inventory methods and partial automation solutions are increasingly unable to meet the management demands of modern smart campuses in terms of efficiency, accuracy, and cost. This paper proposes and implements an automatic asset auditing and management method based on the Splunk big data analytics platform, specifically tailored for university scenarios. This method constructs a real-time digital profile of assets by uniformly collecting multi-source heterogeneous data generated by network devices, servers, classroom terminals, audio-visual systems, and various IoT devices. At the methodological level, this paper designs an automatic asset status confirmation framework based on identifier correlation, a physical location anomaly detection mechanism derived from network topology, and cross-validation rules for data integrity. Experimental results in a university environment demonstrate that this method can increase the automation coverage of asset inventory to over 95%, reduce auditing time by 92%, and achieve an accuracy rate of up to 99%. This not only significantly lowers labor costs and operational complexity but also enhances the security and compliance of teaching and research assets through real-time anomaly alerts, providing an efficient and reliable intelligent solution for large-scale, dynamic university asset management.

Keywords: Big Data Analytics · University Asset Management · Automated Auditing · Data Fusion · Splunk · Asset Security

J. Chi et al. (Eds.): CNETCNED 2025, CCIS 2809, pp. 123–135, 2026.
https://doi.org/10.1007/978-981-95-7124-6_11

1 Introduction

1.1 Background

In the wave of global digital transformation, the operating models of higher education institutions are undergoing fundamental changes. The construction of smart campuses has driven the deep popularization of the Internet of Things (IoT), cloud computing, and various teaching applications, collectively weaving a complex digital network covering teaching, scientific research, and daily life. Against this backdrop, the boundaries of IT Asset Management (ITAM) in universities have been thoroughly broken. Its managed objects have rapidly expanded from data center servers and office computers to include audio-visual equipment in smart classrooms, precision instruments in laboratories, public terminals in libraries, and various self-service terminals distributed across the campus. This trend of "asset ubiquitousness" has made university IT asset auditing unprecedented in terms of scale, heterogeneity, and transience. Meanwhile, network security threats are escalating, and any asset within a university network can become a target. An undiscovered, unmanaged, or misconfigured teaching or research device can become a weak link in the entire campus network defense system, posing a serious security risk [1]. Therefore, comprehensive, real-time, and accurate identification and monitoring of all assets are no longer merely issues of management efficiency, but strategic imperatives directly related to the continuity of teaching and research activities, the security of core data, and the compliance of educational assets. The traditional ITAM model, relying on periodic manual auditing and isolated tools, has proven inadequate in this highly dynamic university environment [2].

1.2 Problem Statement and Research Motivation

A core issue prevalent in university asset management practices is the chasm between the dynamic nature of assets and the static, lagging management methods. Assets are distributed across various areas like academic buildings, libraries, laboratories, and administrative offices. The high mobility of users (faculty, staff, and visitors) and frequent asset changes (e.g., semester transitions, project launches, classroom function renovations) lead to severe data silo issues, making it impossible to effectively integrate asset data from various departments, functional units, and third-party service providers. When using traditional ITAM methods, infrequent auditing result in outdated information that fails to reflect the true state of assets, while frequent auditing consumes significant human and material resources. This unmanageable "out-of-focus" and "distortion" directly leads to a series of problems such as unclear counts of teaching equipment, high risks of asset loss, and suboptimal resource allocation. Therefore, the motivation behind this research is to bridge this gap. We believe the key to solving this problem lies in transforming the paradigm of asset management, shifting from "passive recording" to "active perception." By systematically utilizing the massive, multi-source, heterogeneous machine data generated by assets during their operation, we aim to construct an intelligent management framework capable of continuous self-auditing and self-improvement. This will enable high-frequency, fully automated auditing without wasting human and material resources.

1.3 Research Objectives and Main Contributions

This paper aims to design and implement a unified, data-driven, intelligent asset auditing framework. This framework leverages big data analytics to integrate fragmented asset data into a comprehensive, real-time, and trustworthy panoramic view of assets, enabling multi-dimensional, automated, continuous auditing. The main contributions of this paper can be summarized as follows:

Proposed a Layered General Auditing Framework: We introduce a four-layer theoretical architecture encompassing data collection, data processing and fusion, intelligent analytics and auditing, and application and presentation. This provides a systematic methodology for integrating heterogeneous asset data within a university environment and achieving automated auditing.

Defined an Auditing Mechanism Based on Multi-source Data Fusion: We detail how to fuse data from various sources including network protocols, system and application logs, API data, campus network topology information, and existing asset management systems to perform cross-validation and in-depth auditing across five dimensions: existence, consistency, physical location, operational status, and compliance.

2 Literature Review

This chapter aims to systematically review the technologies related to automated asset auditing, providing an in-depth evaluation of their capabilities and limitations, in order to clarify the technical positioning and innovative value of this research.

2.1 Traditional Asset Auditing Techniques

Traditional asset Auditing techniques have evolved from purely manual to semi-automated methods. Manual Auditing, as the most primitive approach, is still used in most university settings today. Its advantage is the lack of technological investment, but its drawbacks are equally obvious: it's labor-intensive, inefficient, prone to errors, and performed at very low frequencies, leading to severely outdated and inaccurate asset information. To improve efficiency, barcode and QR code technologies were introduced. By scanning instead of manual entry, these methods reduced data recording error rates. However, they didn't change the core "one-by-one processing" model and required "line-of-sight" operation. For large-scale, widely distributed asset auditing across campus, the efficiency gains were limited [3]. Radio Frequency Identification (RFID) technology marked a significant leap in this field. It allows for non-contact, non-line-of-sight, long-distance batch reading of tags, greatly enhancing Auditing speed [4]. However, the large-scale application of RFID in universities is still constrained by several factors: first, the relatively high cost of tags and readers; second, signal interference from environmental factors like classroom walls and metal cabinets; finally, RFID primarily solves the "existence" problem but cannot provide in-depth information such as precise operational status, software configurations, or network connections, leading to a relatively singular data dimension [4,5].

2.2 Network Protocol-Based Asset Discovery

With the advancement of network technology, using network management protocols to discover assets has become a mainstream approach. Simple Network Management Protocol (SNMP) is widely used to poll and monitor network devices, servers, and other assets that support this protocol [6]. SNMP can retrieve rich operational data such as device models, interface statuses, and CPU load. Its limitation lies in being a "whitelist" mechanism; it can only monitor devices that have been pre-configured and managed, failing to actively discover unknown or "shadow IT assets" within the network. Moreover, when using SNMP to monitor some mid- to low-end devices, the high CPU usage caused by SNMP may prevent these devices from having sufficient performance to carry out their primary tasks effectively. Link Layer Discovery Protocols (LLDP/CDP), on the other hand, compensate for SNMP's shortcomings in network topology discovery. These protocols can identify directly connected neighbor devices at the data link layer, which is crucial for mapping accurate L2 network topologies and pinpointing the physical connection ports of assets [7]. However, their scope of action is limited to this; they cannot provide an end-to-end view across routers, nor can they delve into the internal configurations and status details of assets.

2.3 IT Operations Analytics Based on Big Data Platforms

The rise of IT Operations Analytics (ITOA) marks a new phase in asset monitoring. Big data platforms like Splunk, with their powerful capabilities for collecting, indexing, and analyzing machine data (logs, metrics, traces), enable deep insights into the operational status of IT systems [8]. In practice, ITOA is often applied in areas such as Application Performance Monitoring (APM) and Security Information and Event Management (SIEM), for instance, by correlating and analyzing logs to troubleshoot faults or detect security threats. However, there's a significant gap in existing research and applications: while ITOA platforms possess the most comprehensive and real-time operational data for assets, very few studies systematically restructure and apply this data to the core purpose of asset auditing. Most applications remain confined to domain-specific analyses, lacking a high-level framework to integrate and cross-validate this operational data with authoritative sources like Configuration Management Databases (CMDBs) and network topologies proactively and periodically. This integration is crucial for answering fundamental asset management questions such as "What do we own?", "Where are they located?", "What is their status?", and "Are they compliant?".

2.4 Application of Internet of Things in Physical Asset Tracking

For highly mobile physical assets or those unable to connect to traditional networks, Internet of Things (IoT) technologies offer new tracking methods, such as Bluetooth Low Energy (BLE) beacons, Lora WAN, and GPS. These technologies are used in logistics, healthcare, manufacturing, and other sectors to track high-value equipment, tools, or goods, providing real-time location information [9]. However, these IoT tracking systems are often specialized, vertical solutions, and the data they generate is separate from IT operational data (such as network logs and system performance data), creating new "data silos."

2.5 Summary of Literature Review and Research Gaps

In summary, current asset auditing technologies are notably fragmented and limited in their scope. RFID and IoT primarily focus on physical "existence" and "location"; network protocols emphasize "connectivity"; and ITOA platforms excel at capturing operational "status". Each of these technologies operates in isolation, meaning no single method can provide a complete picture of an asset. This data and functional disconnect is the fundamental reason behind the widespread inefficiency and inaccuracy in current asset management. Presently, there's a significant lack of a top-level framework capable of effectively integrating these diverse, heterogeneous data sources and conducting continuous analysis with a unified auditing logic. The innovation of this research lies precisely in proposing such a framework. It aggregates data collected from multiple dimensions, using a big data analytics platform as a "furnace" to smelt different "ores" (data) into high-value, actionable "alloys" (asset insights). This approach enables truly comprehensive, real-time, and intelligent asset auditing across the entire domain.

3 System Design and Implementation

3.1 System Architecture and Design Rationale

We've developed an intelligent auditing framework that transforms asset auditing from fragmented engineering practices into a systematic scientific method, see Fig. 1 for details. This framework operates on a four-layer structure, built around a core idea: any asset operating on a network leaves digital footprints. By systematically capturing, integrating, and analyzing these traces, we can achieve precise asset profiling and status tracking. In this framework, we've formalized the core idea. Let $A = a_1, a_2, ..., a_n$ be the set of all assets under management. For any $a \in A$, its state at time t can be described by a Unified Asset Record (UAR), represented as an attribute tuple. The essence of automated auditing is to define a series of logical predicates $P(a)$ about the asset's state, which are Boolean functions returning true if and only if asset a's state satisfies predefined conditions. We specifically elaborate on two core predicates: Location Consistency Predicate $P_{loc}(a)$: This predicate verifies if an asset's physical location aligns with its registered information. Its evaluation process involves multi-source data fusion:

$$P_{loc}(a) = (\pi_{loc}(f_{topo}(\pi_{port}(f_{mac}(a.id_{mac})))) = a.attr_{loc\_cmdb}) \quad (1)$$

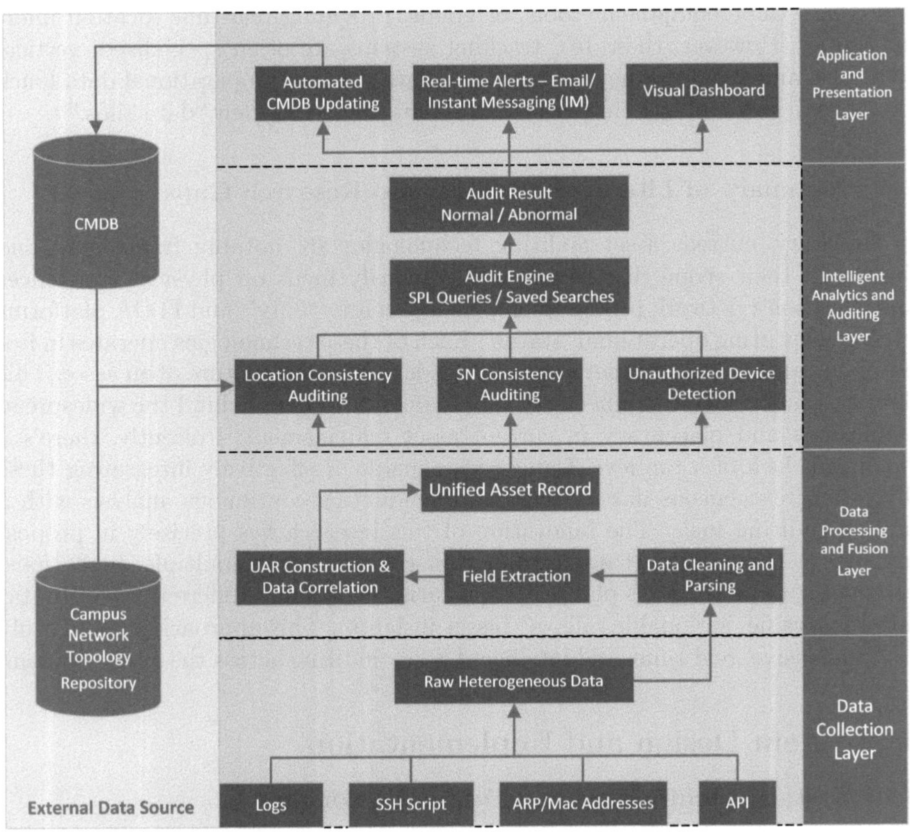

Fig. 1. Architecture Diagram of the Intelligent Asset Auditing Framework

Here, $a.id_{mac}$ is the asset's MAC address, and f_{mac} is a function that uses switch logs to find the port ($a.port$) to which this MAC address is connected. f_{topo} then queries the network topology database to map the port to a physical room ($a.loc_{inf}$). Finally, π represents a projection operation, extracting the relevant attribute. The essence of this formula is to determine if the "location inferred in real-time from network connections" equals the "static location recorded in the CMDB." In practice, this corresponds to a join query that correlates the switch's

MAC address table, network port wiring diagrams, and the asset management database to verify if the asset's physical location has changed without authorization. Serial Number(SN) Consistency Predicate $P_{sn}(a)$: This predicate is used to verify if a device has been replaced. It compares the dynamically collected SN with the authoritative record in the CMDB:

$$P_{sn}(a) = (\pi_{sn}(f_{dyn}(a.id)) = a.attr_{sn\_cmdb}) \tag{2}$$

Here, $a.id$ is the asset's unique identifier (such as IP or hostname), and f_{dyn} is a function that dynamically obtains the device's actual SN ($a.sn_{dyn}$) through methods like SSH, APIs, or management system logs. The truth value of this predicate directly reflects the consistency between the physical device and its digital identity, making it a critical audit point for preventing malicious asset replacement or information discrepancies. Overall, the core objective of the framework is to compute the set $a \in A | \neg P_{loc}(a) \vee \neg P_{sn}(a) \vee ...$ within each audit cycle. This means identifying any asset for which any predicate returns false, and outputting it as an anomaly event.

3.2 Core Process Implementation

Our framework's implementation grounds the theoretical model in engineering practice, leveraging a big data platform. The data acquisition layer serves as the system's foundational sensing component, with its primary challenge being the coverage of diverse and heterogeneous data sources across the network. We utilize the Splunk big data processing platform to comprehensively capture the "digital footprints" of assets from multiple dimensions, including network, system and application logs, and asset databases, then process and integrate the captured data. To illustrate the core process more clearly, let's consider a networked microphone charging bay in a smart classroom as an example device. At the network level, we periodically execute scripts to obtain the ARP tables and MAC address tables from core and access switches. This provides real-time insights into the actual network connection status of devices. For instance, here's an example of network access data for our instance device:

```
# Data Parsed from Access Switch MAC Address Table
2025-07-05 17:01:03,switch=10.13.3.49,mac=00:0e:dd:a1:d5:fa,
    intf=Gi0/5,vlan=120
# Data Parsed from Core Switch ARP Table
2025-07-05 17:01:06,core=10.13.5.24,mac=00:0e:dd:a1:d5:fa,ip
    =10.21.4.151,vlan=120
```

At the system and application level, we gather inherent SN identifiers for devices through methods like SSH, APIs, and management system logs. This provides crucial information for verifying the authenticity and identity of assets, moving beyond just network presence. For our example device, the networked microphone charging bay, here's how the SN data might appear, generated from a controller's logs:

```
time="05/Jul/2025:17:00:08 +0800" client_ip="10.14.17.3"
    x_forwarded_for="-" user="-" site="_" server_port="80"
    request="GET ?module=sn&sn=TU221410113&model=Shure&ip
    =10.21.4.151&room=EB111 HTTP/1.1" http_referer="-"
    http_user_agent="GuzzleHttp/7" cookie="-" status="200"
    body_bytes_sent="100" bytes_sent="337"
    response_time_seconds="0.000"
```

The various data collected immediately flow into the data processing and fusion layer. The core task of this layer is to build an analyzable UAR for each asset through data cleaning, parsing, and correlation. This process is essentially about creating a high-fidelity "digital twin" for the assets in the physical world. Splunk's powerful field extraction capabilities can automatically parse key information from unstructured logs. For instance, it can extract the instance device's SN from the logs mentioned previously. Once extracted, this data is correlated with other collected information to form the UAR's attribute tuple, like this:

```
mac=00:0e:dd:a1:d5:fa,switch_intf=10.13.3.49:Gi0/5,ip
    =10.21.4.151,room=EB111,sn=TU221410113
```

The most crucial step in this layer is data fusion. We correlate the dynamically collected operational data with two core, authoritative data sources: the CMDB and the Campus Network Topology Database. This process transforms isolated data points into a rich, interconnected information network, forming the bedrock for subsequent intelligent analysis. To enhance fusion performance within Splunk, we use periodic scripts to export the complete information from these authoritative data sources into CSV files. For instance, here's the asset and network topology library information for our example device:

```
#Data Synchronized from Campus Topology Database (Accurate to
    Access Switch Port)
switch_intf,switch,switch_name,switch_location,int,label,
    location,patch_panel
10.13.3.49:Gi0/5,10.13.3.49,SW1EA-SHQT,QT-E-01F-R1,Gi0/5,E02-
    D115,EB111,E01-R01-P01:1
#Data Synchronized from Asset Management System
asset_barcode,asset_name,cost_center_name,serial_number,
    category,wired_mac_address,wired_ip_address,status,remark,
    location,ip_manageable,visible_to,building,last_audit_time
    ,last_audit_by
43301510, Shure Charging bay SBC220,Information Technology,
    TU221410113,charging bay,00:0e:dd:a1:d5:fa,10.210.4.151,In
     Use, on the podium,EB111,1,['Classroom AV Asset'],Qiantan
     Academic Building,2025-07-04 19:57:06,app:c0000121
```

After processing and fusion, the UARs are fed into the framework's central intelligence âĂŞ the intelligent analysis and auditing layer. All auditing logic is implemented using Splunk Search Processing Language (SPL) and executed periodically as "saved searches."

The auditing at this stage involves multi-dimensional cross-validation. For instance, location consistency auditing is specifically realized through an SPL query that performs a real-time comparison between the *inferred_location* attribute within the UAR and the *cmdb_location* (registered location) attribute. Any discrepancy is identified as an anomaly and triggers an alert. Similarly, SN consistency auditing is achieved by comparing the dynamically collected SN with the authoritative record in the CMDB. This dual verification of a device's physical and digital identity effectively prevents assets from being maliciously replaced. For our instance device, the following SPL query can be executed to compare the data:

```
| inputlookup csv_lookup_assets
| eval cmdb_sn=serial_number , cmdb_location=location , mac=
  wired_mac_address
| join type=left mac
    [ search index=network sourcetype IN (device:arp, device:
        mac) earliest=-5m
    | stats values(switch) as switch , values(core) as core ,
        values(ip) as ip,values(intf) as intf by mac
    | eval switch_intf=switch.":".intf]
| join type=left ip
    [ search index=classroom sourcetype=nginx:device:sn
        earliest=-5m
    | eval inferred_sn=sn ]
| join type=left switch_intf
    [| inputlookup csv_lookup_network_access
    | eval inferred_location=location ]
| table mac, ip, asset_name, inferred_sn, cmdb_sn,
  inferred_location, cmdb_location
```

Furthermore, by performing set operations between the IP address management system and the list of active network IPs, we can accurately detect unauthorized devices accessing the campus network, as well as offline network devices.

Finally, in the application and presentation layer, audit results are transformed into actionable insights. For all assets that successfully pass the audit, the system automatically updates the *last_audit_time* field in the CMDB via API calling, forming a closed management loop and indicating that the asset has successfully undergone automated auditing. For any asset deemed anomalous by an audit rule, the system triggers real-time alerts. These alerts, containing asset details, anomaly type, and relevant context (such as last known location and time), are pushed to administrators via email or enterprise instant messaging. Concurrently, we've created a series of visualization dashboards that graphically display the overall health of campus assets (e.g., online status, online rate, failure rate), anomaly trends, and key metrics in real-time. This provides intuitive data support for management decision-making.

4 Experimental Validation and Results Analysis

To empirically validate the effectiveness of our proposed theoretical framework and quantify its superiority over traditional methods, we conducted an experiment using all IT equipment within the NYU Shanghai Qiantan campus. This allowed us to test the robustness and practical efficacy of our theoretical model in handling the complexity and dynamism of a real-world university campus environment, thereby providing objective evidence for the framework's practical value.

4.1 Experimental Design and Evaluation

Our experiment was deployed across a university campus environment, comprising four distinct buildings and a total of approximately 4,000 heterogeneous assets. This diverse asset pool typically included: servers, routers, and switches located in data centers and intermediate distribution frames (IDFs); computers in public laboratories; office network devices, IP phones, and wireless access points (APs); and various audio-visual equipment integrated within smart classrooms. It is important to note that roughly 800 of these assets, such as speakers, power sources, and other analog apparatus, lack network connectivity and thus require manual verification.

We leveraged Splunk Enterprise as the core analytical engine, developing script programs to collect all relevant machine data. To comprehensively evaluate the framework's performance, we defined multi-dimensional metrics covering efficiency, accuracy, and security insights. We then compared the experimental results against traditional manual auditing methods and mainstream RFID solutions. Key evaluation metrics included:

Automation Rate: The proportion of total assets automatically audited.

Auditing Time: The human-hours required to complete one full auditing cycle.

Accuracy Rate: The consistency between the digital information and physical reality.

Security Insights: The framework's ability to identify security-related incidents or vulnerabilities.

4.2 Results Analysis and Performance Validation

The experimental results strongly demonstrate the superior performance of our framework in the specific context of a university campus. On core metrics, our framework achieved an automation rate exceeding 95% and an impressive accuracy rate of 99%. Furthermore, the human-hour cost to complete a full auditing cycle was drastically reduced from approximately 700 person-hours to less than 56 person-hours, representing a remarkable 92% increase in efficiency. Table 1 visually presents its comparative advantages over traditional solutions:

Table 1. Comparison of Auditing Approaches: Big Data-Driven, Manual, and RFID-Based Solutions

Evaluation Metric	Big Data-Driven	Traditional Manual Auditing	RFID Solution (Sample Reference)
Automation Rate	> 95%	0%	∼ 80% (Limited by metal assets)
Auditing Time (Person-Hours)	< 56	∼ 700	∼ 200
Accuracy Rate	∼ 99%	∼ 85% (Prone to errors, information lag)	∼ 90% (Affected by tag damage/loss, metal shielding, distance)
Security Insights	High (Detects compliance/security events)	NA	NA

More importantly, the value of this framework extends beyond mere efficiency and accuracy improvements; it significantly enhances our proactive security and risk insight capabilities. During its deployment, the system successfully identified multiple instances of abnormal asset locations and detected 5–6 critical device offline events daily. For example, a high-performance graphics workstation, officially registered to a laboratory in the school of arts and sciences, was detected connecting to a network port in a business school office. The framework immediately triggered an alert. Upon verification, IT administrators confirmed this was an unauthorized asset reallocation, allowing for timely mitigation of potential data security risks. Furthermore, smart classroom support personnel now rely on the dashboard and receive instant message alerts daily. This enables them to stay informed about any offline computers, projectors, central control systems, or amplifiers within classrooms, ensuring the smooth progression of teaching activities. These cases irrefutably demonstrate that this framework is not just an efficient "asset auditing tool", but also an intelligent "campus asset security sentinel" and a valuable aid in improving service quality.

5 Discussion

The remarkable success achieved by our research framework in practical application is fundamentally driven by a systematic methodology that transforms multi-dimensional, heterogeneous data into trustworthy and actionable asset insights. The framework's triumph isn't attributed to a breakthrough in a single technology, but rather to the organic combination of comprehensive fusion of disparate data sources and near real-time intelligent analysis capabilities. The former, by cross-validating data from multiple sources including network, system and application logs, and business databases builds a much more reliable asset identity profile than any single data source could. This robust data integration is the cornerstone for achieving an impressive 99% accuracy rate. The latter transforms asset management from a static, lagging inventory activity into a dynamic, continuous monitoring process, which is key to the revolutionary leap in efficiency. Therefore, the core theoretical contribution of this paper lies in proposing a systematic, multi-layered auditing solution that transcends the perspective of any single technology. Unlike fragmented existing solutions, this framework defines a universal methodology for connecting data silos into a valuable network. Its practical value in a university setting is multi-faceted: it not only significantly boosts the operational efficiency of logistics and IT departments through automation, but more importantly, it acts as a proactive "asset sentinel", It can timely detect incidents such as the misappropriation of teaching and research equipment, unauthorized devices accessing the campus network, and critical equipment failures. This strengthens IT asset security, meets the compliance audit requirements of educational departments, and provides precise data support for optimizing teaching resource allocation. However, we must also acknowledge the framework's limitations. Its effectiveness is highly dependent on the quality of authoritative data sources like the CMDB and network topology. Additionally, initial deployment presents a certain level of technical complexity. Furthermore, covering completely non-networked assets still requires manual intervention within a hybrid auditing module.

6 Conclusion and Future Work

This paper successfully designed, implemented, and validated a systematic, data-driven framework for automated asset auditing, specifically addressing the dynamism, complexity, and security challenges faced by modern universities. Through a layered architecture, the framework effectively integrates heterogeneous data from multiple dimensions, including campus networks, teaching systems, and the Internet of Things. Experimental results strongly demonstrate that, compared to traditional methods, this framework achieves breakthrough advancements in asset auditing automation rate (>95%), efficiency (92% time reduction), and accuracy ($\sim$ 99%). It also significantly enhances the security of teaching and research assets through real-time anomaly detection. The core contribution of this research lies in providing the higher education sector with both a theoretical model and a practical paradigm for transforming fragmented asset data into holistic, actionable insights.

Building upon the achievements and limitations of this research, future work can delve into several directions to evolve the framework towards more advanced intelligence and broader application scenarios.

Firstly, a primary direction for evolution is to enhance the framework's cognitive depth, moving from current post-event auditing and real-time monitoring towards predictive maintenance. This will require introducing machine learning models into the "Intelligent Analytics and Auditing Layer". By performing time-series analysis on long-term accumulated asset performance and error logs, we can develop the capability to issue warnings before hardware failures occur.

Secondly, to improve the framework's sensing precision, future efforts can focus on integrating high-precision indoor positioning technologies, such as Wi-Fi fingerprinting or Bluetooth beacons, into the "Data Collection Layer". This will overcome the current limitation of relying solely on network ports for location auditing.

Finally, the theoretical model of this framework possesses excellent generality. Its cross-domain application migration to areas like Industrial Internet of Things or smart healthcare represents an important avenue for exploring and maximizing its theoretical and practical value.

References

1. Tchao, E.T., et al.: Barrier free internet access: Evaluating the cyber security risk posed by the adoption of bring your own devices to e-learning network infrastructure. arXiv preprint arXiv:1710.08795. (2017)
2. Jebril, I., et al.: The impact of strategic intelligence and asset management on enhancing competitive advantage: The mediating role of cybersecurity. Uncertain Supply Chain Manage. **11**(3), 1041–1046 (2023)
3. Kato, H., Tan, K.T.: Pervasive 2D barcodes for camera phone applications. IEEE Pervasive Comput. **6**(4), 76–85 (2007)
4. Weinstein, R.: RFID: a technical overview and its application to the enterprise. IT Professional **7**(3), 27–33 (2005)
5. Ton, N.T.N., et al.: Inventory management system using RFID and barcode-a modeling and simulation approach. In: 2024 7th International Conference on Green Technology and Sustainable Development (GTSD), pp. 362–367 (2024)
6. Mauro, D., Schmidt, K.: Essential SNMP: help for system and network administrators (2005)
7. Clemm, A.: Network management fundamentals (2006)
8. Chang, P., Xu, G.: Practical Big Data Analytics with Splunk (2025)
9. Li, S., et al.: The internet of things: a survey. Inf. Syst. Front. **17**(2), 243–259 (2015)

From Rule-Based Defense to Machine Learning: A Comparative Study on SQL Injection Detection

Li Yaxing(✉) and Han Yu

Dalian University of Technology, Dalian, China
yhan@dlut.edu.cn

Abstract. Traditional rule-based SQL injection detection methods are increasingly ineffective against modern obfuscation techniques. This work explores the shift from static rules to machine learning–based dynamic detection through a comprehensive comparative study. Using the CSIC-2010 dataset (over 36,000 normal and 12,500 malicious requests), we evaluate five models—Logistic Regression, Decision Tree, Support Vector Machine (SVM), Random Forest, and Gradient Boosting—employing character-level TF-IDF features and MaxAbsScaler normalization. A full detection pipeline is constructed, integrating preprocessing, model training, and API encapsulation for deployment. Experimental results show that ensemble models outperform traditional approaches in accuracy and recall, while SVM and Logistic Regression achieve competitive performance with lower complexity. These findings highlight the limitations of rule-based defenses and validate machine learning as a technically superior and practical paradigm for real-time SQL injection detection.

Keywords: SQL injection detection · Anomalous traffic · Machine learning · Dynamic security · Real-time threat detection

1 Introduction

Against the backdrop of a digital economy exceeding $50 trillion in scale, web applications have become the foundational infrastructure for global commerce. However, the security threats they face are growing exponentially. Among these, SQL injection attacks represent one of the oldest (first publicly disclosed in 1998) and most persistent web security threats. According to Akamai's 2023 statistics, the global average web application suffers 1,200 SQL injection attack attempts per month. The 2017 Equifax data breach occurred precisely because an unpatched known SQL injection vulnerability led to the exposure of 143 million user records, resulting in direct economic losses exceeding $700 million. Furthermore, attackers can leverage time-based blind injection techniques to silently probe database structures. The harm extends beyond mere data theft, escalating to systemic security collapse risks.

J. Chi et al. (Eds.): CNETCNED 2025, CCIS 2809, pp. 136–160, 2026.
https://doi.org/10.1007/978-981-95-7124-6_12

Existing research (e.g., OWASP ZAP, SQLMap) typically employs rule-based detection methods for SQL injection. The core of this approach is a rule-matching mechanism that uses techniques like regular expressions to perform pattern matching against predefined rules and patterns on preprocessed input data. Naturally, before pattern matching, researchers must compile a library of predefined attack patterns based on historical attack cases and feedback from the security community. Typically, this predefined attack pattern library relies heavily on in-depth analysis of known SQL injection attack patterns and the extraction of characteristic information from them. This includes common SQL keywords (e.g., SELECT, UNION, DROP), special characters (e.g., single quotes, double quotes, semicolons), and typical injection patterns (e.g., `' OR '1'='1`).

By comparing input data against specific patterns defined in the pattern library, the system can effectively identify potential SQL injection risks and possible malicious activities. Some researchers further enhance detection accuracy by constructing query trees from inputs using SQL syntax and semantic analysis methods. However, due to the persistent evolution of SQL injection techniques—which have advanced from simple statement concatenation to highly organized technical systems—the update and maintenance of predefined attack pattern libraries become ongoing tasks. This ensures that novel or variant attack patterns can be promptly covered and identified.

According to statistics, approximately 36% of current SQL injection payloads employ complex techniques such as hexadecimal encoding and Unicode obfuscation to circumvent rule-based detection methods. For instance, attackers can effectively evade up to 80% of traditional detection mechanisms by converting `UNION SELECT` into its hexadecimal form: `%55%4e%49%4f%4e%20%53%45%4c%45 %43%54`.

More insidiously, through second-order injection—specifically stored attacks—to persistently embed payloads within systems, creating ongoing security vulnerabilities for web applications.

Machine learning-based dynamic detection technology offers a new paradigm to address this challenge [1]. By learning from vast datasets of legitimate and malicious SQL statements, machine learning methods can automatically analyze normal user behavior and SQL query patterns to identify anomalous or malicious inputs. Recent research demonstrates that compared to traditional rule-based approaches, machine learning models possess the adaptive capability to learn new attack patterns, significantly enhancing detection accuracy and timeliness [2].

Taking a model based on Bidirectional Long Short-Term Memory (BiLSTM) and Attention Mechanism as an example, SQL injection detection models equipped with machine learning-based dynamic detection technology can automatically learn the sequential characteristics of SQL queries and focus on potential attack patterns, significantly improving detection performance [6]. Experiments demonstrate that this SQL injection detection model achieves superior detection precision and recall rates on large-scale datasets compared to traditional rule-based methods, with an accuracy rate reaching 99.72%.

However, new challenges emerge. Despite the significant advantages of machine learning-based dynamic detection in SQL injection detection, considerable academic debate persists regarding the selection of optimal detection models [5]. Different machine learning models exhibit distinct characteristics in feature extraction, pattern recognition, and anomaly detection. For instance, Support Vector Machines (SVM) demonstrate strong classification performance in high-dimensional spaces and are well-suited for small-scale datasets; decision tree models employ tree structures for decision-making, offering strong interpretability [4]; random forests enhance detection accuracy by integrating multiple decision trees; logistic regression excels in handling linear relationships; the k-nearest neighbors (kNN) algorithm relies on distance metrics between samples for classification; Bayesian classifiers make decisions based on probability theory, demonstrating advantages when processing features with statistical characteristics [7]. Different models exhibit varying strengths in feature extraction, pattern recognition, and anomaly detection. Therefore, there is an urgent need for systematic performance comparisons and comprehensive evaluations to clarify the advantages and disadvantages of different models, thereby providing more reliable detection solutions for practical applications [3].

To address this issue, this study benchmarks five mainstream binary classification models (logistic regression, decision trees, SVM, random forests, gradient boosting) using the authoritative CSIC-2010 dataset (containing over 36,000 normal requests and 12,500 malicious requests). Through this comparative experiment, we aim to provide more effective model selection criteria for SQL injection detection and advance the application of machine learning-based SQL injection defense technologies.

2 Model Overview

2.1 Logistic Regression Model

Logistic Regression is a statistical method for binary classification problems, where the response variable is a categorical variable with two possible outcomes, typically labeled 0 and 1. Despite its name, it is not a regression model but an algorithm designed for classification tasks. Unlike linear regression, which directly outputs numerical values, logistic regression employs the sigmoid function to map linearly combined input features into probability values between 0 and 1, thereby enabling classification.

In practical applications, logistic regression is commonly used to estimate the probability of an event occurring. Examples include the probability of a user purchasing a product, a patient having a specific disease, or an advertisement being clicked.

In logistic regression, we perform a weighted sum of input features using a linear model and feed the result into the sigmoid function to obtain a probability value. Specifically, the output of a logistic regression model can be expressed as:

$$\hat{y} = \sigma(w^T x + b) \tag{1}$$

where $\hat{y}$ is the predicted probability value representing the probability that the sample belongs to class 1, w is the weight vector, x is the input feature vector, b is the bias term, and $\sigma(z)$ is the logistic function (Sigmoid function).

The sigmoid function is defined as:

$$\sigma(z) = \frac{1}{1 + e^{-z}} \tag{2}$$

The objective of logistic regression is to optimize the model parameters by minimizing the loss function. Log loss is commonly used to evaluate the model's predictive performance. The log loss function is defined as:

$$L(w, b) = -\frac{1}{N}\sum_{i=1}^{N}[y_i \log(\hat{y}_i) + (1 - y_i)\log(1 - \hat{y}_i)] \tag{3}$$

where N is the number of samples, y_i is the true label of the sample (0 or 1), and $\hat{y}_i$ is the model's predicted probability.

For clarity, the pseudocode of the logistic regression training algorithm is given below:

Algorithm 1: Logistic Regression Training Algorithm

Data: Training set $D = \{(x_1, y_1), \ldots, (x_N, y_N)\}$, Learning rate α, Maximum iterations T

Result: Optimized parameters w^*, b^*

```
Initialize w ← 0, b ← 0 ;            // Random or zero initialization
for t = 1 to T do
    for i = 1 to N do
        Compute prediction: ŷ_i = σ(w^T x_i + b);
    end
    Compute loss: L = -(1/N) Σ_{i=1}^N [y_i log(ŷ_i) + (1 - y_i) log(1 - ŷ_i)];
    Compute gradients:;
    ∂L/∂w = (1/N) Σ_{i=1}^N (ŷ_i - y_i) x_i;
    ∂L/∂b = (1/N) Σ_{i=1}^N (ŷ_i - y_i);
    Update parameters:;
    w ← w - α ∂L/∂w;
    b ← b - α ∂L/∂b;
    if convergence criterion met then
        break;
    end
end
return w, b;
```

2.2 Decision Tree Model

The Decision Tree is a widely used model in data analysis and prediction. It represents a mapping relationship between object attributes and object values.

Each node in the tree represents an object, each branch path represents a possible attribute value, and each leaf node corresponds to the value of the object along the path from the root node to that leaf node. Decision tree models can perform both classification analysis (predicting categorical variable values) and regression analysis (predicting continuous variable values). The corresponding models are the Decision Tree Classifier and the Decision Tree Regressor. In this experiment, we use the classification decision tree model (Decision Tree Classifier).

In the field of data mining, decision tree technology is frequently employed for data analysis and prediction tasks. Through decision tree learning algorithms, models can be automatically generated from data to help identify patterns and regularities. The construction process typically adopts a recursive splitting method, starting from the root node and selecting the optimal feature to partition the data until a stopping condition is met.

Decision tree models are among the most widely applied machine learning models due to their simple feature preprocessing, ease of integration with ensemble learning, strong fitting capabilities, and interpretability. The generation process of decision trees typically employs the CART (Classification and Regression Trees) algorithm, which is formally described in Algorithm 2.

Algorithm 2: CART Decision Tree Algorithm

Data: Training set $D = \{(x_1, y_1), (x_2, y_2), \ldots, (x_N, y_N)\}$
Result: Decision Tree T

```
BuildTree(D);
begin
    if termination criteria met then
        return leaf node with majority class;
    end
    f* ← SelectOptimalFeature(D) using Gini Index;
    (D_left, D_right) ← SplitDataset(D, f*);
    T_left ← BuildTree(D_left);
    T_right ← BuildTree(D_right);
    return decision node with feature f*, left subtree T_left, right subtree
      T_right;
end
Apply pruning techniques to prevent overfitting;
return T;
```

In this experiment, the optimal feature selection in the CART algorithm is based on the Gini Index. The Gini Index is a metric measuring dataset impurity or unevenness, widely used in decision tree algorithms to select optimal features for data splitting. A lower Gini Index indicates higher dataset purity, meaning samples are more likely to belong to the same category.

For a dataset D with K categories, the Gini Index is calculated as:

$$Gini(D) = 1 - \sum_{k=1}^{K} p_k^2 \tag{4}$$

where p_k represents the proportion of samples in the k-th category, i.e., the number of samples belonging to category k divided by the total number of samples.

2.3 Support Vector Machine (SVM) Model

Support Vector Machine (SVM) is a supervised learning model developed based on statistical learning theory. It emphasizes constructing models with strong generalization capabilities under limited sample conditions, making it widely applied in classification and regression analysis. Its core idea is to construct an optimal hyperplane in feature space to effectively separate samples of different categories.

In classification tasks, SVMs use kernel functions to map raw low-dimensional data into higher-dimensional feature spaces, enabling linear separability in the elevated dimensions. Kernel functions serve as mathematical tools for calculating similarity between data points, indirectly achieving high-dimensional mapping through inner product operations while avoiding explicit dimensionality transformation. Common kernel functions include the Linear Kernel, Polynomial Kernel, Radial Basis Function (RBF), and Sigmoid Kernel. Equipped with these kernels, SVM can handle not only linearly separable problems but also effectively solve non-linearly separable problems through non-linear mappings.

After kernel processing, training instances are transformed into points in the feature space. The subsequent training objective is to find a hyperplane that separates points representing positive class samples from those representing negative class samples. This hyperplane is represented by a weight vector $\mathbf{w}$ and a bias term b, expressed as:

$$f(x) = w^T x + b \tag{5}$$

where $\mathbf{x}$ represents the feature vector of the sample, w represents the weight vector (which is also the normal vector of the hyperplane, determining its direction), b is the bias term indicating the position of the hyperplane, and $f(x)$ is the decision function of the Support Vector Machine, acting as a linear classifier and representing the distance from the sample $\mathbf{x}$ to the hyperplane.

To ensure each sample is correctly classified and maximize the margin between the classification hyperplane and both positive and negative samples, for a given training sample $\{(x_i, y_i)\}_{i=1}^{N}$ where $y_i \in \{-1, +1\}$, the support vector machine imposes the following constraint:

$$y_i(w^T x_i + b) \geq 1, \quad \forall i = 1, 2, \ldots, N \tag{6}$$

where y_i is the true label of sample x_i, taking values of $+1$ or -1 (representing positive or negative classes, respectively). When $y_i = +1$, the SVM requires that the sample must lie on the positive side of the hyperplane, i.e., $(w^T x_i + b) \geq 1$. When $y_i = -1$, the SVM requires the sample to lie on the negative side of the hyperplane, i.e., $w^T x_i + b \leq -1$.

To achieve this goal, the SVM aims to maximize the geometric margin between positive and negative samples. Therefore, the SVM optimizes the minimization of the norm of its weight vector. That is, its objective function is:

$$\min_{\mathbf{w},b} \frac{1}{2}||\mathbf{w}||^2 \tag{7}$$

In most practical applications, certain samples in the dataset cannot be perfectly separated by a linear hyperplane. Therefore, researchers introduced slack variables. The role of slack variables is to provide an allowable error margin for each sample. If a sample cannot fully satisfy the classification criteria, the slack variable records these "errors" and permits their existence.

Here is an overall description for the whole process:

Algorithm 3: Support Vector Machine Training Algorithm

Data: Training set $D = \{(x_1, y_1), \ldots, (x_N, y_N)\}$, Regularization parameter C, Kernel function $K(x_i, x_j)$
Result: Support Vector Machine Model with parameters α^*, b^*
Transform data to feature space using kernel function $K(x_i, x_j)$;
Formulate the dual optimization problem:;
$\max_\alpha \sum_{i=1}^N \alpha_i - \frac{1}{2}\sum_{i=1}^N \sum_{j=1}^N \alpha_i\alpha_j y_i y_j K(x_i, x_j)$;
Subject to constraints:;
$0 \leq \alpha_i \leq C, \quad \forall i = 1, \ldots, N$;
$\sum_{i=1}^N \alpha_i y_i = 0$;
Solve the quadratic programming problem to obtain $\alpha^* = \{\alpha_1^*, \ldots, \alpha_N^*\}$;
Identify support vectors: $S = \{i : \alpha_i^* > 0\}$;
Compute bias term:;
$b^* = \frac{1}{|S|}\sum_{i\in S}\left(y_i - \sum_{j=1}^N \alpha_j^* y_j K(x_i, x_j)\right)$;
return SVM model with parameters $\{\alpha^*, b^*, \text{support vectors}\}$;

The final decision function for classification is:

$$f(x) = \text{sign}\left(\sum_{i\in S} \alpha_i^* y_i K(x_i, x) + b^*\right) \tag{8}$$

where S represents the set of support vector indices, and $K(x_i, x)$ is the kernel function.

2.4 Random Forest Model

Random Forest is an ensemble learning method that enhances model accuracy and stability by constructing multiple decision trees and combining their outputs for prediction. It determines final predictions through voting or averaging mechanisms, finding broad application in both classification and regression problems. Its core principle involves reducing overfitting and improving generalization capabilities by integrating multiple weak learners (i.e., decision trees).

In a random forest, each decision tree is trained on a randomly selected training subset. These training subsets are randomly sampled from the original training data using bootstrap sampling, ensuring data diversity. For each tree's training, the random forest randomly selects feature subsets at each node split, thereby reducing model variance and preventing overfitting. Suppose we have a training set $\{(x_1, y_1), (x_2, y_2), \ldots, (x_N, y_N)\}$, where x_i represents the input feature vector, y_i denotes the corresponding label in a classification problem, and $y_i \in \{1, 2, \ldots, K\}$. Then the training process of a random forest can be described as follows:

Algorithm 4: Random Forest Algorithm

Data: Training set $D = \{(x_1, y_1), \ldots, (x_N, y_N)\}$, Number of trees T
Result: Random Forest Model F
Initialize empty forest $F = \{\}$;
for $t = 1$ **to** T **do**
  $D_t \leftarrow$ `BootstrapSample(`D`)` ; `// Sample with replacement`
  for *each node split in tree construction* **do**
    $\mathcal{F}_t \leftarrow$ `SelectRandomFeatures(`$\mathcal{F}$`)` ; `// Random feature subset`
    Select optimal feature $f^* \in \mathcal{F}_t$ using splitting criterion;
  end
  $T_t \leftarrow$ `BuildDecisionTree(`D_t`, `$\mathcal{F}_t$`)`;
  $F \leftarrow F \cup \{T_t\}$;
end
return F;

Finally, the forest's prediction is the weighted average (for regression) or majority vote (for classification) of all trees' predictions:

$$f(x) = \frac{1}{T} \sum_{i=1}^{T} f_i(x) \tag{9}$$

where T is the number of decision trees, and $f_i(x)$ is the prediction value of the i-th tree.

2.5 Gradient Boosting Model

Gradient Boosting is an ensemble learning method commonly used for regression and classification tasks. It progressively optimizes model performance by constructing a sequence of weak learners (typically decision trees). Unlike conventional machine learning algorithms, including the Random Forest learning algorithm, Gradient Boosting is an iterative learning process. Each training step trains a new base learner based on the prediction error of the current model, progressively correcting the model's error to enhance overall performance.

The objective of each training round is to optimize the model by learning from its residuals (i.e., prediction errors). In each iteration, the newly added base learner is adjusted based on the error from the previous round, enabling the final model to better fit the data.

The core idea of Gradient Boosting is to use an additive model to progressively reduce the residuals of the target loss function. In each iteration, the new decision tree learns from the prediction error (i.e., residuals) and optimizes itself through gradient descent, progressively reducing the overall model's loss function, just as the pseudocode below illustrates:

Algorithm 5: Gradient Boosting Algorithm

Data: Training set $D = \{(x_1, y_1), \ldots, (x_N, y_N)\}$, Number of iterations M, Learning rate γ

Result: Gradient Boosting Model $F_M(x)$

Initialize $F_0(x) = \arg\min_\gamma \sum_{i=1}^{N} L(y_i, \gamma)$; `// Initial prediction`

for $m = 1$ **to** M **do**

  Compute residuals: $r_{i,m} = -\left[\frac{\partial L(y_i, F(x_i))}{\partial F(x_i)}\right]_{F=F_{m-1}}$ for $i = 1, \ldots, N$;

  Fit weak learner $h_m(x)$ to residuals:

   $h_m = \arg\min_h \sum_{i=1}^{N} (r_{i,m} - h(x_i))^2$;

  Update model: $F_m(x) = F_{m-1}(x) + \gamma h_m(x)$;

end

return $F_M(x)$;

Mathematically, the additive model can be expressed as:

$$F_m(x) = F_{m-1}(x) + \gamma h_m(x) \tag{10}$$

where $F_m(x)$ is the model at iteration m, $F_{m-1}(x)$ is the model from the previous iteration, $h_m(x)$ is the newly learned weak learner (typically a decision tree) in this iteration, and γ is the learning rate, which controls the contribution size of the new tree.

In each iteration, the additive model calculates residuals based on the current model's predictions and trains a new model to fit these residuals. The output of each new model is then added to the previous model's prediction, progressively approximating the goal of minimizing the loss function.

2.6 Term Frequency-Inverse Document Frequency (TF-IDF) Algorithm

Among algorithms for vectorizing text data, the Bag of Words (BoW) model, Term Frequency-Inverse Document Frequency (TF-IDF), and word embedding (Word Embedding) are three common techniques. Among these, the TF-IDF algorithm is employed in this experiment.

TF-IDF (Term Frequency-Inverse Document Frequency) is a widely used weighting technique in text retrieval and text mining. It is a statistical method for evaluating the importance of a word within a document relative to a document collection or corpus. A word's importance increases proportionally with its frequency within a document, but decreases inversely with its overall frequency across the corpus. This calculation effectively mitigates the influence of common words on keywords, enhancing the relevance between keywords and documents.

TF-IDF consists of two components: Term Frequency (TF) and Inverse Document Frequency (IDF).

Term Frequency (TF) represents how often a term appears in the text. Typically, to eliminate the influence of document length, term frequency is normalized by dividing the number of times a term appears by the total number of words in the document. Its formula is expressed as:

$$\mathrm{TF}(w) = \frac{\text{Number of times term } w \text{ appears in document}}{\text{Total number of words in document}} \tag{11}$$

Inverse Document Frequency (IDF) measures the prevalence of a keyword. It quantifies how common a term is across the entire corpus. If a term appears in many documents, its IDF value will be low, indicating weak discriminative power. Conversely, if a term appears only in a few documents, its IDF value will be high, indicating strong discriminative power. Its formula is expressed as:

$$\mathrm{IDF}(w) = \log\left(\frac{\text{Total number of documents in corpus}}{\text{Number of documents containing term } w + 1}\right) \tag{12}$$

TF-IDF is the weight value obtained by multiplying TF and IDF. A higher TF-IDF value indicates greater importance of the term within the document. It is expressed as follows:

$$\text{TF-IDF}(w) = \mathrm{TF}(w) \times \mathrm{IDF}(w) \tag{13}$$

3 Experimental Process

3.1 Experimental Environment

This experiment was conducted on a Windows system. The primary programming language used was Python 3.8.10, relying on multiple core libraries. Specifically, scikit-learn was employed for training and evaluating machine learning models, Flask for building web applications, and SQLAlchemy for database operations. Additionally, the hardware environment for running the experiment included an Intel Core i7-12700H processor, NVIDIA GeForce RTX 3060 discrete graphics card, 16GB DDR4 memory, and 512GB NVMe SSD storage, ensuring high computational power and data processing efficiency.

3.2 Training Dataset

The dataset used in this experiment is the CSIC-2010 dataset. This dataset was released as an appendix in the paper "Application of the Generic Feature Selection Measure in Detection of Web Attacks" by the Spanish National Research Council (CSIC). It originates from a simulation of network traffic targeting e-commerce applications. The CSIC-2010 dataset contains 36,000 normal requests and over 25,000 attack requests, encompassing attack samples such as SQL injection, file traversal, CRLF injection, XSS, and SSI.

To train and evaluate the model, we first partitioned the data into an 80% training set and a 20% test set. The training set comprises 28,800 normal requests and 10,000 abnormal requests, while the test set contains 7,200 normal requests and 2,500 abnormal requests. This partitioning ensures balanced distributions between training and testing sets, enabling the model to learn effectively and generalize to new request data.

3.3 Data Preprocessing

During the data preprocessing phase, raw HTTP request logs undergo parsing and normalization to convert them into a structured, standardized format. This ensures data consistency and removes potential noise.

HTTP request logs typically contain extensive header information and metadata, such as User-Agent, Content-Type, URL, query parameters, and other fields. In common attack scenarios like SQL injection and cross-site scripting (XSS), malicious intent is often concealed within maliciously crafted URLs or query parameters. While information like User-Agent and Content-Type plays a crucial role in standard web interactions, its practical value for SQL injection detection is low. Such data may even interfere with the model's ability to identify key features (Fig. 1).

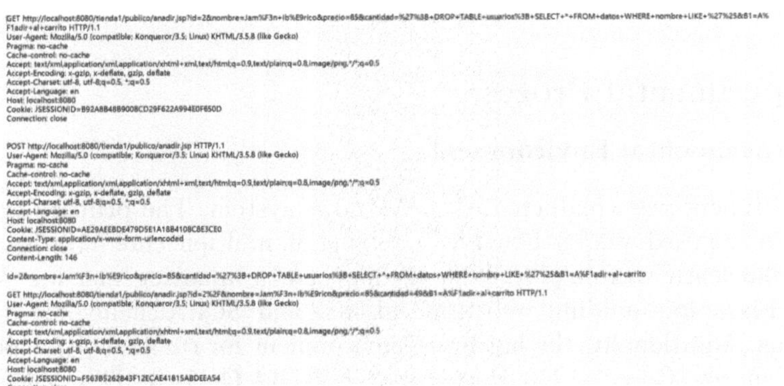

```
GET http://localhost:8080/tienda1/publico/anadir.jsp?id=2&nombre=Jam%F3n+Ib%E9rico&precio=85&cantidad=%27%3B+DROP+TABLE+usuarios%3B+SELECT+*+FROM+datos+WHERE+nombre+LIKE+%27%25&B1=A%
F1adir+al+carrito HTTP/1.1
User-Agent: Mozilla/5.0 (compatible; Konqueror/3.5; Linux) KHTML/3.5.8 (like Gecko)
Pragma: no-cache
Cache-control: no-cache
Accept: text/xml,application/xml,application/xhtml+xml,text/html;q=0.9,text/plain;q=0.8,image/png,*/*;q=0.5
Accept-Encoding: x-gzip, x-deflate, gzip, deflate
Accept-Charset: utf-8, utf-8;q=0.5, *;q=0.5
Accept-Language: en
Host: localhost:8080
Cookie: JSESSIONID=B92A8B48B9008CD29F622A994E0F650D
Connection: close

POST http://localhost:8080/tienda1/publico/anadir.jsp HTTP/1.1
User-Agent: Mozilla/5.0 (compatible; Konqueror/3.5; Linux) KHTML/3.5.8 (like Gecko)
Pragma: no-cache
Cache-control: no-cache
Accept: text/xml,application/xml,application/xhtml+xml,text/html;q=0.9,text/plain;q=0.8,image/png,*/*;q=0.5
Accept-Encoding: x-gzip, x-deflate, gzip, deflate
Accept-Charset: utf-8, utf-8;q=0.5, *;q=0.5
Accept-Language: en
Host: localhost:8080
Cookie: JSESSIONID=AE29AEEBDE479D5E1A18B4108C8E3CE0
Content-Type: application/x-www-form-urlencoded
Connection: close
Content-Length: 146

id=2&nombre=Jam%F3n+Ib%E9rico&precio=85&cantidad=%27%3B+DROP+TABLE+usuarios%3B+SELECT+*+FROM+datos+WHERE+nombre+LIKE+%27%25&B1=A%F1adir+al+carrito

GET http://localhost:8080/tienda1/publico/anadir.jsp?id=2%2F&nombre=Jam%F3n+Ib%E9rico&precio=85&cantidad=49&B1=A%F1adir+al+carrito HTTP/1.1
User-Agent: Mozilla/5.0 (compatible; Konqueror/3.5; Linux) KHTML/3.5.8 (like Gecko)
Pragma: no-cache
Cache-control: no-cache
Accept: text/xml,application/xml,application/xhtml+xml,text/html;q=0.9,text/plain;q=0.8,image/png,*/*;q=0.5
Accept-Encoding: x-gzip, x-deflate, gzip, deflate
Accept-Charset: utf-8, utf-8;q=0.5, *;q=0.5
Accept-Language: en
Host: localhost:8080
Cookie: JSESSIONID=F563B5262843F12ECAE41815ABDEEA54
```

Fig. 1. Original Request Dataset.

Therefore, to highlight the most discriminative parts of requests and reduce data dimensionality, this study introduces a URL format conversion method. This simplifies complex log data into a structured representation centered on URLs and query parameters. The specific process is as follows:

First, the system reads HTTP requests stored in raw data files. These files contain two categories of data: normal requests and malicious requests. After processing, the system reads HTTP request logs from the raw data files. Following preliminary processing, requests of different types are written into two new files, respectively used for subsequent feature extraction and model training.

Next, for GET requests, the system extracts the URL portion, removing the protocol header (e.g., "http://" or "https://") to retain only the path and parameter segments. Similar processing applies to POST and PUT requests, where the system extracts the request method and URL, combining them into a new string. After extracting the URL, the system searches for the POST and PUT request body data (i.e., the data content within the request) and appends it as query parameters to the URL. For instance, if request data exists, the final format becomes "POST /path?data" or "PUT /path?data". This approach not only preserves all information from POST and PUT requests but also converts them into a format identical to GET requests, facilitating subsequent processing.

After extracting the URL and parameters, the system uniformly decodes all URLs and converts them to lowercase. This prevents feature confusion and data inconsistencies caused by case differences. Additionally, before parsed request data is written to new files, all line breaks are removed. This ensures each request is presented as a single complete line.

3.4 Model Training

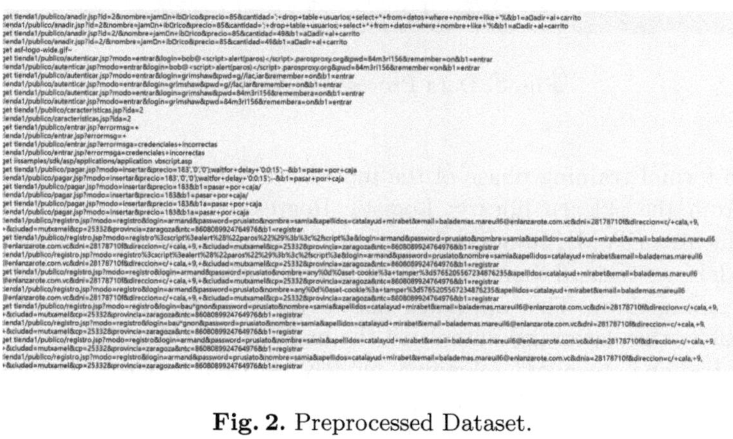

Fig. 2. Preprocessed Dataset.

After preprocessing raw requests into standardized URLs and query parameters, the next step involves vectorizing this textual data to transform it into feature vectors that machine learning models can understand and process (Fig. 2).

In this process, we used the TfidfVectorizer from the sklearn library to vectorize the request data. TfidfVectorizer is a vectorization tool based on the Term Frequency-Inverse Document Frequency (TF-IDF) algorithm, effectively converting text into feature vectors. During vectorization, we employed character-level n-grams (ranging from 2 to 4) to capture local features within the request data, enabling better detection of character-level correlations.

However, simple vectorization alone does not guarantee good training results. Due to the nature of text data, the resulting vectors are typically sparse. The vocabulary in text is finite, and relative to the entire possible vocabulary, the vast majority of words do not appear in every request. Consequently, most elements in the feature matrix may be zero, with only a small number of non-zero elements.

To ensure the machine learning model can effectively process this sparse data, we applied MaxAbsScaler for normalization after vectorization. Unlike other common normalization methods, MaxAbsScaler offers the significant advantage of being directly applicable to sparse matrices without requiring conversion to dense matrices. This avoids the additional computational and memory overhead associated with sparse-to-dense conversion, thereby improving computational efficiency and optimizing memory usage.

Next, we called the train_test_split function from the sklearn.model_selection module to partition the dataset into training and test sets. Following standard practice, 80% of the data was allocated for training, while 20% was reserved for subsequent testing (Fig. 3).

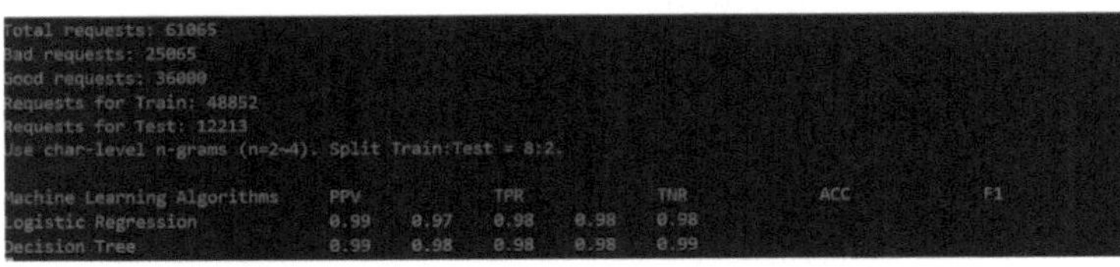

Fig. 3. Data Processing Workflow.

In the formal training phase of the model, we defined five machine learning models from the sklearn library: Logistic Regression, Decision Tree, Support Vector Machine (SVM), Random Forest, and Gradient Boosting. After defining these models, we trained them using the training dataset, with each model fitting to the training data. This approach allows us to compare their performance against each other later and determine the most suitable classifier.

After training, to avoid reloading models for each request, we saved each trained model using the pickle module from Python's standard library. Additionally, the vectorizer and standardizer were saved as separate files for easy loading and reuse. This allows models, vectorizers, and standardizers to be loaded and used directly across different environments without retraining.

3.5 Model Evaluation

During the model evaluation phase, we assessed the performance of the trained models using the test set. Evaluation metrics included the confusion matrix, precision (PPV), recall (TPR), specificity (TNR), accuracy (ACC), and F1 score (Fig. 4).

Fig. 4. Saved pickle files.

The confusion matrix is a tool for evaluating classification model performance, displaying the comparison between model predictions and actual outcomes, including true positives, false positives, true negatives, and false negatives. Precision (PPV) measures the proportion of samples correctly predicted as positive among all samples predicted as positive. Recall (TPR) measures the proportion of samples correctly predicted as positive among all actual positive samples. Specificity (TNR) reflects the proportion of samples correctly predicted as negative among all actual negative samples. Accuracy (ACC) represents the proportion of correctly predicted samples out of all samples, indicating the model's overall predictive capability. The F1 score is the harmonic mean of precision and recall, providing a balanced evaluation of the model's performance between these two metrics, particularly useful for imbalanced datasets.

The evaluation results cover all models we trained, including five models: Logistic Regression, Decision Tree, Support Vector Machine, Random Forest, and Gradient Boosting. Each model's evaluation results provide its prediction performance data on the test set. Through this prediction performance data, we can effectively determine which model performs most excellently in detecting SQL injection attacks.

3.6 Model Interface Encapsulation

After training the machine learning models and validating their accuracy, the next step is to integrate the trained models into the application interface for real-time classification and prediction of web requests. To achieve this, we designed a concise request processing and anomaly detection interface comprising two core functions: `preprocess_request(req)` and `predict_anomaly(request_text, model_name)`. The `preprocess_request(req)` function handles parsing and standardizing HTTP requests to conform to the model's input format. Meanwhile, `predict_anomaly(request_text, model_name)` employs the trained machine learning model to detect parsed and normalized HTTP requests, returning the probability of attacks such as SQL injection.

This interface contains two core functions. `preprocess_request(req)` handles parsing and standardizing HTTP requests, converting them into a format acceptable to the model. `predict_anomaly(request_text, model_name)` employs a trained machine learning model to detect anomalies in the request and returns the probability of attacks like SQL injection.

The parameter `req` in `preprocess_request()` represents the HTTP request object, typically a Flask request object, containing information like the request method (GET, POST, etc.), URL path, query string, and request body. Similar to the preprocessing function in the experimental model training phase, this function automatically extracts the URL path, query parameters, or request body data from the request and preprocesses them. If the request method is POST or PUT, the request body data is appended to the URL to ensure consistent formatting. Additionally, the protocol (e.g., http:// or https://) and the domain name are stripped, retaining only the path and query parameters. Finally, all URL paths and query parameters are decoded and converted to lowercase, forming a standardized request text for model processing.

The preprocessed request text is then passed as input to the anomaly detection request interface. In this experiment, this functionality is encapsulated within the `predict_anomaly()` function. The preprocessed request text is fed into `predict_anomaly(request_text, model_name="logistic_regression")`, which loads the specified machine learning model and returns the probability that the request belongs to an anomaly category such as SQL injection. The parameter `request_text` represents the standardized request text, i.e., the string processed by `preprocess_request(req)`, containing the URL path, query parameters, and possible request body content; while `model_name` specifies the machine learning model used for anomaly detection, including five pre-trained models: "logistic_regression," "decision_tree," "svm," "random_forest," and "gradient_boosting." The default value is set to "logistic_regression," meaning that if model_name is not specified, the logistic regression model is used by default.

During the model training phase, we stored the pre-trained text vectorizer, normalizer, and model files using the pickle module. Therefore, in this interface, we only need to load these saved files one by one. First, we use the TF-IDF vectorizer saved during training (`vectorizer.pkl`) to convert the request text into vectors. Next, we use the scaler (`scaler.pkl`) to standardize the converted vectors, ensuring the data distribution aligns with the training phase. Subsequently, we select the model pickle file to load based on the model_name parameter and invoke the `predict_proba()` method to calculate the probability that the request belongs to an abnormal category (e.g., SQL injection attacks). Subsequently, we only need to compare this probability value with a predefined threshold to promptly identify abnormal requests and implement corresponding security measures, such as blocking, logging, or sending alerts.

Through this encapsulation, we significantly enhance the reusability and maintainability of our code. It also ensures the efficiency and flexibility of the anomaly detection process. Each functional component can be optimized and replaced independently. This way, when we wish to incorporate more advanced machine learning models or new preprocessing methods in the future, we can easily make replacements without needing to refactor the entire system.

3.7 Interface Deployment

After completing the interface encapsulation, the next step is to integrate the encapsulated model processing interface into a web application to test its ability to detect SQL injection requests in real time.

We selected the popular and flexible Flask framework to build the experimental web application. Flask is not only lightweight and easily extensible but also works efficiently with other modules, ensuring the system can respond to potential SQL injection attacks in real-time within actual environments. Below are the specific implementation details of the web application used in this experiment:

Flask Web Application Architecture. The entire Flask application employs strict modularization across its components, with the overall architecture as follows:

- **Flask Main Application Module:** Responsible for initializing the Flask application, processing requests, managing routing, and interacts with other modules.
- **Request Preprocessing Module:** Extracts and cleans text data from HTTP requests, removes potential malicious inputs, and converts data into a format understandable by machine learning models.
- **Anomaly Detection Module:** Uses pre-trained machine learning models to detect SQL injection in processed requests, predicting whether each request contains SQL injection risks.
- **Database Management Module:** Interacts with the SQLite database to store user request data, detection results, and logs.
- **API Interface Module:** Provides multiple API interfaces for simulating and defending against SQL injection attacks, enabling interaction with frontend systems and developers.
- **Model Management Module:** Enables users to dynamically switch between different SQL injection detection models to test their effectiveness and performance.

The Request Preprocessing Module and Anomaly Detection Module directly utilize our previously encapsulated `preprocess_request` and `predict_anomaly` interfaces. Each module collaborates to collectively simulate SQL injection detection and defense.

Database Design. This application utilizes SQLite as its database. The database contains three tables:

User Table: Stores user login credentials, including usernames and passwords, primarily for simulating login and registration processes to test the module's detection capabilities for POST requests (Table 1).

Table 1. Structure of the User Table

Column Name	Type	Description
username	TEXT	Username
password	TEXT	Password (unencrypted)

Product Table: This table stores product information, including product name, price, and description. It is primarily used to simulate product queries and test the module's ability to handle GET requests (Table 2).

Table 2. Structure of the Product Table

Column Name	Type	Description
product_id	INTEGER	Product ID
name	TEXT	Product Name
price	REAL	Product Price
description	TEXT	Product Description

Request Table: This table stores detailed information for each request, including request text, request method, request URL, SQL injection probability, and the ID of the currently invoked model. As the system's core, it records the processing status of all requests for subsequent analysis and evaluation (Table 3).

Table 3. Structure of the Request Table

Column Name	Type	Description
request_text	TEXT	Original text of the request
method	TEXT	Request method (GET/POST)
url	TEXT	Request URL
sql_injection_probability	REAL	SQL Injection Probability
model_id	INTEGER	Current model ID being called

API Interface Design. The system provides multiple API interfaces, listed as follows:

/**login:** This interface handles user login and supports POST requests. Users can enter their password and username to log in. This interface intentionally incorporates an SQL injection vulnerability. Users may attempt SQL injection attacks to test whether the system can successfully detect and intercept abnormal requests (Figs. 5 and 5).

/**register:** This interface handles user registration and, like /login, supports POST requests. New users can enter a password and username to complete account creation. This interface also incorporates an SQL injection vulnerability. Attackers may attempt injection attacks using special characters or malicious SQL statements (Fig. 6).

/**product:** This interface is used to query product information and supports GET requests. Here, users can retrieve detailed product information by providing

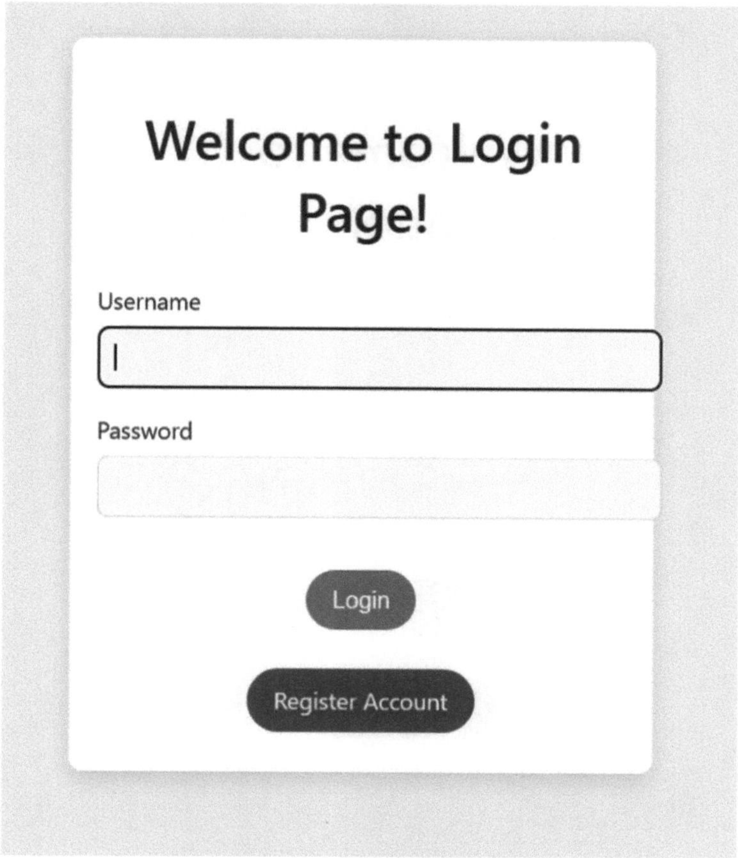

Fig. 5. /login Route Interface.

the product ID. This interface involves database query operations and is another critical endpoint for our SQL injection testing (Fig. 7).

/request: This interface is a request query endpoint that retrieves all requests stored by the system, supporting the retrieval of all records related to SQL injection requests (Fig. 8).

/export_requests: This interface exports request data. It allows users to export all request data to CSV format for subsequent analysis. The exported data includes detailed information for each request and the probability of SQL injection (Fig 9).

/clear_requests: This interface clears all stored request records, used for system reset or data cleanup.

/change_model: This interface allows users to dynamically change the model ID to select different machine learning models for SQL injection detection. Supported models include logistic regression, decision trees, support vec-

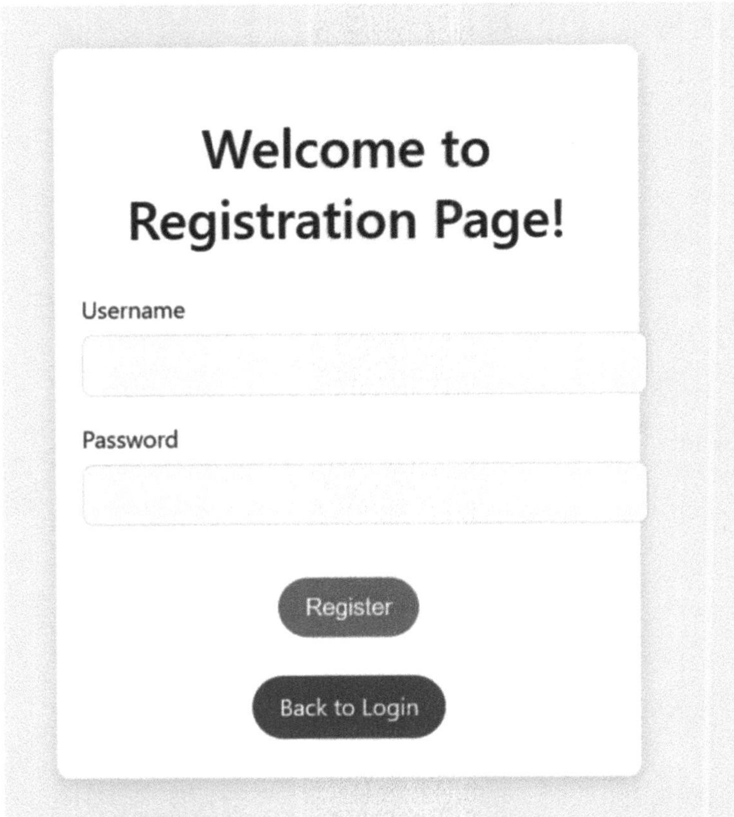

Fig. 6. /register Route Interface.

tor machines (SVM), Random Forest, and Gradient Boosting. Users can switch between models as needed to test their effectiveness in detecting SQL injection.

The interface is deployed via Flask's `@app.before_request` hook function. Whenever the server receives an HTTP request directed at `/login`, `/register`, or `/product`, the `before_request` hook is triggered, invoking the `filter_request` function to preprocess the request and perform anomaly detection.

The `filter_request` function handles each HTTP request and assesses its SQL injection risk. First, it extracts the request's text content and calls the `preprocess_request` function imported from the interface to preprocess it. Subsequently, the preprocessed request text is passed to the `predict_anomaly` function imported from the interface to calculate the probability of SQL injection.

If the model predicts an SQL injection probability exceeding the set threshold (e.g., 0.8), the request is flagged as abnormal. The system returns a 403 Forbidden error, halting further processing regardless of the request's validity. Regardless of abnormality, all request details—including the raw request text,

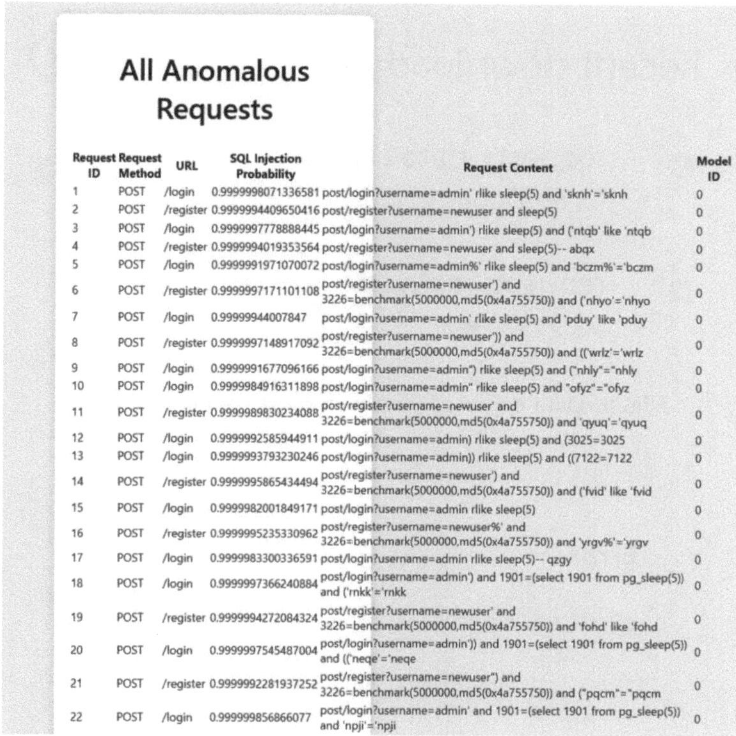

All Anomalous Requests

Request ID	Request Method	URL	SQL Injection Probability	Request Content	Model ID
1	POST	/login	0.9999998071336581	post/login?username=admin' rlike sleep(5) and 'sknh'='sknh	0
2	POST	/register	0.9999994409650416	post/register?username=newuser and sleep(5)	0
3	POST	/login	0.9999997778888445	post/login?username=admin') rlike sleep(5) and ('ntqb' like 'ntqb	0
4	POST	/register	0.9999994019353564	post/register?username=newuser and sleep(5)-- abqx	0
5	POST	/login	0.9999991971070072	post/login?username=admin%' rlike sleep(5) and 'bczm%'='bczm	0
6	POST	/register	0.9999997171101108	post/register?username=newuser') and 3226=benchmark(5000000,md5(0x4a755750)) and ('nhyo'='nhyo	0
7	POST	/login	0.99999944007847	post/login?username=admin' rlike sleep(5) and 'pduy' like 'pduy	0
8	POST	/register	0.9999997148917092	post/register?username=newuser')) and 3226=benchmark(5000000,md5(0x4a755750)) and (('wrlz'='wrlz	0
9	POST	/login	0.9999991677096166	post/login?username=admin") rlike sleep(5) and ("nhly"="nhly	0
10	POST	/login	0.9999984916311898	post/login?username=admin" rlike sleep(5) and "ofyz"="ofyz	0
11	POST	/register	0.9999989830234088	post/register?username=newuser' and 3226=benchmark(5000000,md5(0x4a755750)) and 'qyuq'='qyuq	0
12	POST	/login	0.9999992585944911	post/login?username=admin) rlike sleep(5) and (3025=3025	0
13	POST	/login	0.9999993793230246	post/login?username=admin)) rlike sleep(5) and ((7122=7122	0
14	POST	/register	0.9999995865434494	post/register?username=newuser') and 3226=benchmark(5000000,md5(0x4a755750)) and ('fvid' like 'fvid	0
15	POST	/login	0.9999982001849171	post/login?username=admin rlike sleep(5)	0
16	POST	/register	0.9999995235330962	post/register?username=newuser%' and 3226=benchmark(5000000,md5(0x4a755750)) and 'yrgv%'='yrgv	0
17	POST	/login	0.9999983300336591	post/login?username=admin rlike sleep(5)-- qzgy	0
18	POST	/login	0.9999997366240884	post/login?username=admin') and 1901=(select 1901 from pg_sleep(5)) and ('rnkk'='rnkk	0
19	POST	/register	0.9999994272084324	post/register?username=newuser' and 3226=benchmark(5000000,md5(0x4a755750)) and 'fohd' like 'fohd	0
20	POST	/login	0.9999997545487004	post/login?username=admin')) and 1901=(select 1901 from pg_sleep(5)) and (('neqe'='neqe	0
21	POST	/register	0.9999992281937252	post/register?username=newuser") and 3226=benchmark(5000000,md5(0x4a755750)) and ("pqcm"="pqcm	0
22	POST	/login	0.999999856866077	post/login?username=admin' and 1901=(select 1901 from pg_sleep(5)) and 'npji'='npji	0

Fig. 7. /product Route Interface

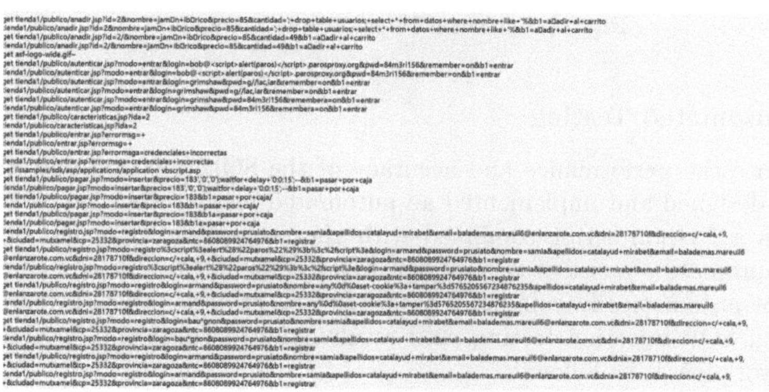

Fig. 8. /request Route Interface.

request method, request URL, and SQL injection probability—are stored in an SQLite database. This provides essential data support for subsequent data analysis and model evaluation (Fig. 10).

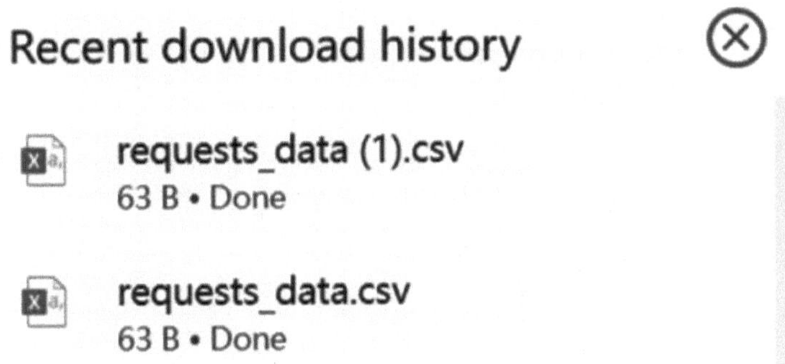

Fig. 9. Data exported via the /export_requests route.

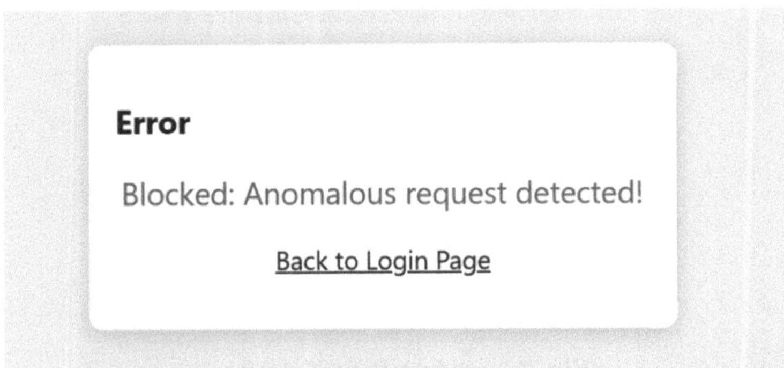

Fig. 10. Interface for intercepted requests.

3.8 Automated Testing

To validate the performance and accuracy of the SQL injection detection system, we designed and implemented an automated testing workflow. This workflow uses a Python script combined with the requests library and SQLMAP tool to automate a series of tasks. By invoking different routes and commands, the script automatically completes tasks such as request table cleanup, model switching, SQL injection testing, and result export. The complete automated testing workflow is as follows:

Cleaning the Data Environment. Before each test run, the script calls the Flask application's `/clear_requests` route to delete all request records from the database. This ensures testing occurs in a clean data environment, preventing interference from historical data.

Selecting the Test Model. The script dynamically switches models by calling the `/change_model` route. Model IDs from 0 to 4 correspond to Logistic Regression, Decision Tree, Support Vector Machine, Random Forest, and Gradient Boosting models, respectively. This enables sequential testing of SQL injection detection using different models.

Execute SQL Injection Testing. The script automatically invokes the SQLMAP tool via Python's `subprocess.run()` function to perform automated SQL injection attack testing on the target interface.

For this test, we configured several critical SQLMAP parameters. Setting `-level=2` and `-risk=2` increases testing depth and risk level, helping uncover vulnerabilities that routine tests might miss. `-threads=4` specifies the number of concurrent threads for SQLMAP execution, significantly boosting the testing speed. Through parallel processing, the script can cover multiple interfaces and various attack methods, accelerating the testing process and avoiding delays caused by sequential testing. The `-timeout=10` setting established a request timeout, ensuring that no single request would consume excessive time during testing due to slow or unresponsive server replies.

During testing, the script sequentially simulates SQL injection attacks against the `/login`, `/register`, and `/product` interfaces. Each simulated attack lasts five minutes, with a total testing duration of 15 min per model (Fig. 11).

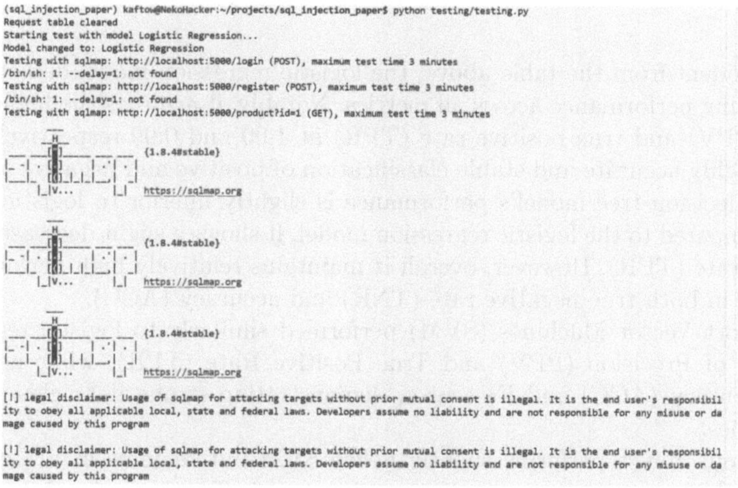

Fig. 11. SQLMAP Testing Process.

Upon completion of this step, the process returns to Step 2) to select another test model until all models have been tested.

Export Test Results. After all models are tested, the system exports all recorded request data to a CSV file via the `/export_requests` route and saves it locally. The CSV file includes raw request text, request method, URL, and SQL injection probability, enabling verification of automated test outcomes.

4 Experiment Results Analysis

4.1 Training Outcomes

After completing the experiment, we evaluated five distinct machine learning models. Each model's performance was measured using multiple evaluation metrics, including Precision (PPV), True Positive Rate (TPR), True Negative Rate (TNR), Accuracy (ACC), and F1 Score. For easy comparison, detailed performance results for each model are provided below (Table 4):

Table 4. Training Performance Metrics for Machine Learning Models

Model	Precision (PPV)	TPR	TNR	Accuracy (ACC)	F1 Score
Logistic Regression	1.00	0.99	1.00	0.99	0.99
Decision Tree	0.98	0.98	0.99	0.98	0.98
Support Vector Machine (SVM, linear kernel)	0.99	0.99	1.00	0.99	0.99
Random Forest (Number of Trees = 50)	0.98	0.97	0.99	0.98	0.97
Gradient Boosting (Number of Trees = 100)	0.97	0.90	0.98	0.95	0.93

As evident from the table above, the logistic regression model demonstrates outstanding performance across all metrics. Notably, it achieves the highest precision (PPV) and true positive rate (TPR) at 1.00 and 0.99 respectively, indicating highly accurate and stable classification of positive and negative samples.

The decision tree model's performance is slightly inferior to logistic regression. Compared to the logistic regression model, it shows a slight decrease in true positive rate (TPR). However, overall it maintains relatively high performance, excelling in both true negative rate (TNR) and accuracy (ACC).

Support Vector Machines (SVM) performed similarly to logistic regression in terms of Precision (PPV) and True Positive Rate (TPR), while achieving high Accuracy (ACC) and F1 scores, demonstrating strong data classification capabilities.

Random Forest performs slightly below SVM but remains at a high level, particularly demonstrating a significant advantage in True Negative Rate (TNR). It is well-suited for classification tasks in imbalanced datasets.

Among all models, Gradient Boosting performed worst on True Positive Rate (TPR) at only 0.90, meaning it had the lowest ability to identify positive samples. However, it still performed well on True Negative Rate (TNR), demonstrating acceptable ability to identify negative samples. It may find better application in scenarios favoring negative samples.

Overall, the Logistic Regression model and Support Vector Machine (SVM) are the most outstanding models. They perform excellently in terms of precision, recall, specificity, accuracy, and F1 score, making them particularly suitable for tasks requiring high precision. While decision trees and random forests perform well, they fall slightly short in recall, potentially underperforming in tasks demanding high recall rates. Gradient Boosting models retain some utility for identifying negative samples, but their low recall and overall accuracy issues make them unsuitable for high-risk scenarios.

4.2 Automated Testing Results

In this automated testing, we evaluated the performance of five different models—decision trees, support vector machines (SVM), gradient boosting, logistic regression, and random forests—in SQL injection detection tasks. By simulating SQL injection attacks using the SQLMAP tool and assessing model performance based on their response to anomalous requests, we obtained the following results (Figs. 12 and 13):

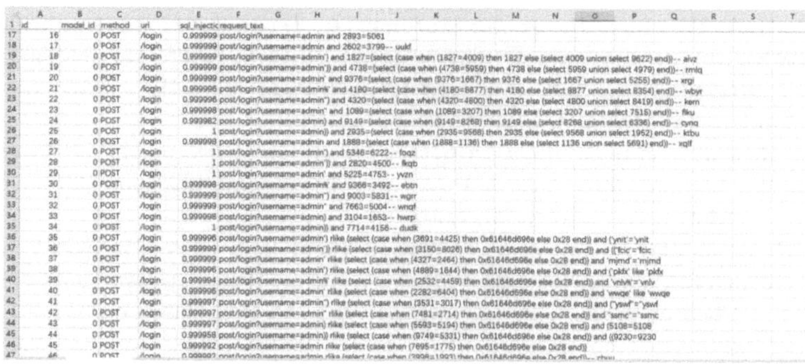

	A	B	C	D	E	F
1	id	model_id	method	url	sql_injectic	request_text
17	16	0	POST	/login	0.999999	post/login?username=admin and 2893=5061
18	17	0	POST	/login	0.999999	post/login?username=admin and 2602=3799-- uukf
19	18	0	POST	/login	0.999999	post/login?username=admin') and 1827=(select (case when (1827=4009) then 1827 else (select 4009 union select 9622) end))-- aivz
20	19	0	POST	/login	0.999999	post/login?username=admin')) and 4738=(select (case when (4738=5959) then 4738 else (select 5959 union select 4979) end))-- rmlq
21	20	0	POST	/login	0.999999	post/login?username=admin' and 9376=(select (case when (9376=1667) then 9376 else (select 1667 union select 5255) end))-- xrgi
22	21	0	POST	/login	0.999996	post/login?username=admin%' and 4180=(select (case when (4180=8877) then 4180 else (select 8877 union select 8354) end))-- wbyr
23	22	0	POST	/login	0.999996	post/login?username=admin") and 4320=(select (case when (4320=4800) then 4320 else (select 4800 union select 8419) end))-- kern
24	23	0	POST	/login	0.999998	post/login?username=admin" and 1089=(select (case when (1089=3207) then 1089 else (select 3207 union select 7515) end))-- flku
25	24	0	POST	/login	0.999982	post/login?username=admin) and 9149=(select (case when (9149=8268) then 9149 else (select 8268 union select 6336) end))-- cynq
26	25	0	POST	/login	1	post/login?username=admin)) and 2935=(select (case when (2935=9568) then 2935 else (select 9568 union select 1952) end))-- ktbu
27	26	0	POST	/login	0.999998	post/login?username=admin and 1888=(select (case when (1888=1136) then 1888 else (select 1136 union select 5691) end))-- xqlf
28	27	0	POST	/login	1	post/login?username=admin') and 5346=6222-- foqz
29	28	0	POST	/login	1	post/login?username=admin')) and 2820=4500-- fkqb
30	29	0	POST	/login	1	post/login?username=admin' and 5225=4753-- yvzn
31	30	0	POST	/login	0.999998	post/login?username=admin%' and 9366=3492-- ebtn
32	31	0	POST	/login	0.999999	post/login?username=admin") and 9003=5831-- wgrr
33	32	0	POST	/login	0.999999	post/login?username=admin" and 7663=5004-- wnqf
34	33	0	POST	/login	0.999998	post/login?username=admin) and 3104=1653-- hwrp
35	34	0	POST	/login	1	post/login?username=admin)) and 7714=4156-- dudk
36	35	0	POST	/login	0.999996	post/login?username=admin') rlike (select (case when (3691=4425) then 0x61646d696e else 0x28 end)) and ('ynit'='ynit
37	36	0	POST	/login	0.999999	post/login?username=admin')) rlike (select (case when (3150=8026) then 0x61646d696e else 0x28 end)) and (('fcic'='fcic
38	37	0	POST	/login	0.999999	post/login?username=admin' rlike (select (case when (4327=2464) then 0x61646d696e else 0x28 end)) and 'mjmd'='mjmd
39	38	0	POST	/login	0.999996	post/login?username=admin") rlike (select (case when (4889=1844) then 0x61646d696e else 0x28 end)) and ("pkfx" like "pkfx
40	39	0	POST	/login	0.999994	post/login?username=admin%' rlike (select (case when (2532=4459) then 0x61646d696e else 0x28 end)) and 'vnlv%'='vnlv
41	40	0	POST	/login	0.999996	post/login?username=admin' rlike (select (case when (2282=6404) then 0x61646d696e else 0x28 end)) and 'wwqe' like 'wwqe
42	41	0	POST	/login	0.999997	post/login?username=admin") rlike (select (case when (3531=3017) then 0x61646d696e else 0x28 end)) and ("yswf"="yswf
43	42	0	POST	/login	0.999997	post/login?username=admin" rlike (select (case when (7481=2714) then 0x61646d696e else 0x28 end)) and "ssmc"="ssmc
44	43	0	POST	/login	0.999997	post/login?username=admin) rlike (select (case when (5593=5194) then 0x61646d696e else 0x28 end)) and (5108=5108
45	44	0	POST	/login	0.999958	post/login?username=admin)) rlike (select (case when (9749=5331) then 0x61646d696e else 0x28 end)) and ((9230=9230
46	45	0	POST	/login	0.999992	post/login?username=admin rlike (select (case when (7695=1775) then 0x61646d696e else 0x28 end))
47	46	0	POST	/login	0.999992	post/login?username=admin rlike (select (case when (3998=1993) then 0x61646d696e else 0x28 end))-- [illegible]

Fig. 12. Automated Testing Results.

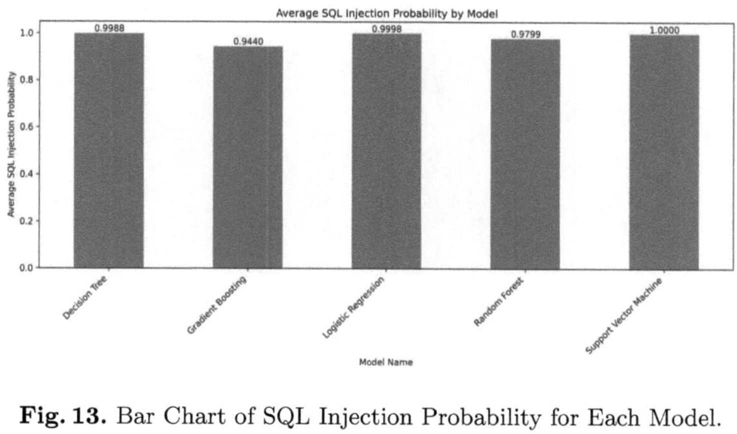

Fig. 13. Bar Chart of SQL Injection Probability for Each Model.

The test results indicate that Support Vector Machines (SVM) demonstrated the strongest performance in SQL injection detection, achieving 100% detection accuracy. Concurrently, Decision Trees and Logistic Regression also exhibited robust capabilities, achieving scores close to 1. In contrast, Gradient Boosting and Random Forest showed slightly weaker performance. Therefore, in practical applications, it is recommended to prioritize support vector machines as the SQL injection detection model. Of course, logistic regression or decision trees are also viable options.

References

1. Zheng, H.: Research on Machine Learning-Based Detection Techniques for SQL Injection and XSS Attacks. Master's thesis, Nanchang University (2022). https://doi.org/10.27232/d.cnki.gnchu.2022.002909
2. Su, L., Liu, X., Chen, F., et al.: SQL injection detection method based on N-Gram and TFIDF. Comput. Digital Eng. **49**(06), 1177–1181 (2021)
3. Guo, J., Liu, W., Luo, F., et al.: Automation Technology and Application, 1–6 (2025-03-31). http://kns.cnki.net/kcms/detail/23.1474.TP.20241113.0850.018.html
4. Chen, Y.: Research on SQL injection identification algorithm based on random forest. Modern Inf. Technol. **3**(15), 146–149 (2019)
5. Zhu, Z.: Research on SQL Injection Attack Detection Based on HTTP Traffic. Master's thesis, Beijing University of Posts and Telecommunications (2021). https://doi.org/10.26969/d.cnki.gbydu.2021.002518
6. Li, C.: Research on SQL Injection Detection Technology Based on Naive Bayes and LSTM Recurrent Neural Networks. Master's thesis, Hunan University (2018)
7. Zhang, S.: Research on SQL Injection Payload Detection Based on Machine Learning. Master's thesis, Guangxi Minzu University (2023). https://doi.org/10.27035/d.cnki.ggxmc.2023.001212

Novel Power Allocation Grouping Scheme for Multi-user VLC NOMA Systems

Yang Tu[1](✉), Chuan Li[1], Runyu Liu[2], Tianci Jiang[1], and Jiancheng Chi[3]

[1] Chongqing College of International Business and Economics, Chongqing, China
michael_tu79@hotmail.com
[2] Japan Advanced Institute of Science and Technology, Nomi City, Japan
[3] Dalian University of Technology, Dalian, China

Abstract. This paper proposes a novel power allocation grouping scheme for multi-user Visible Light Communication (VLC) Non-Orthogonal Multiple Access (NOMA) systems to overcome the limited modulation bandwidth of commercial white LEDs. Specifically, users are partitioned into groups of four based on the proposed Minimizing Channel Gain Average Difference (MCGAD) algorithm, which pairs two high-gain and two low-gain users. Within each group, we employ an asymmetrically clipped and DC-biased optical OFDM (ADO-OFDM) NOMA approach on two sub-pairs, and introduce an optimal power allocation algorithm to determine both inter-pair and intra-pair power ratios. Simulation results demonstrate that our power allocation grouping strategy significantly enhances system performance, achieving higher spectral efficiency and energy efficiency compared to conventional methods. This work lays the foundation for scalable, high-throughput, and energy-efficient VLC networks in multi-user scenarios.

Keywords: VLC · MCGAD NOMA · ADO-OFDM · Grouping · Spectral Efficiency · Energy Efficiency

1 Introduction

Visible light communication (VLC) utilizing LEDs for both indoor illumination and data transmission is expected to play an important role in future wireless communication networks. Using white light-emitting diodes (LEDs) for both illumination and data transmission, VLC offers the potential for efficient and high-capacity communication in densely populated indoor environments [1]. However, the limited modulation bandwidth of commercially available LEDs often constrains the achievable data rate, especially when multiple users must be served concurrently, creating a significant bottleneck [10].

Non-Orthogonal Multiple Access (NOMA) has been extensively investigated in RF systems to boost spectral efficiency and user capacity through power-domain multiplexing and successive interference cancellation (SIC) [7]. Despite

J. Chi et al. (Eds.): CNETCNED 2025, CCIS 2809, pp. 161–171, 2026.
https://doi.org/10.1007/978-981-95-7124-6_13

its success in RF, directly integrating NOMA into VLC faces additional challenges due to the intensity modulation and direct detection (IM/DD) requirement, which mandates the transmitted signals remain real and unipolar [4]. Furthermore, heterogeneous user channel gains caused by variations in user positions can lead to severe performance imbalance between near and far users, underscoring the need for novel grouping strategies and power allocation algorithms specifically tailored to VLC scenarios [8].

To address these constraints, a hybrid scheme known as ADO-OFDM was adopted [3], wherein asymmetrically clipped optical OFDM (ACO-OFDM) signals occupy the odd subcarriers, while DC-biased optical OFDM (DCO-OFDM) signals occupy the even subcarriers [5,6]. This approach aims to balance power utilization and spectral efficiency within the VLC framework, making it well-suited to support NOMA-based multi-user scenarios.

Recent work on multi-user VLC NOMA has focused on two main areas: power allocation and user grouping. Adaptive power allocation schemes have been proposed in several studies to optimize the performance of visible light communication (VLC) systems. These schemes aim to dynamically adjust the transmission power based on channel conditions, ensuring efficient data transfer and maximizing the system's reliability [9]. While these approaches enhance throughput, their computational complexity often increases with the number of users, reducing practicality in larger networks. Moreover, reliance on ascending or descending channel gain sorting can lead to suboptimal group formation in environments with diverse user locations [11]. Against this backdrop, the primary aim of this work is to tackle the user grouping and power allocation problem in multi-user VLC NOMA systems to improve system throughput and user fairness without incurring prohibitive computational costs [12].

To achieve these goals, we propose a novel joint grouping strategy MCGAD, and a power allocation scheme tailored to the unique challenges of VLC. Using channel gain disparities of users, the framework adaptively forms clusters and distributes transmission power among user groups efficiently. Our approach not only reduces overhead, but also improves fairness, as demonstrated through both theoretical analysis and simulation. Numerical results confirm that the new method significantly enhances overall system throughput and user satisfaction compared to existing algorithms designed for multi-user VLC NOMA.

The remainder of this paper is organized as follows. Section 2 describes the system model and outlines the problem formulation of user grouping and power allocation, including optimization objectives and constraints. Section 3 elaborates on the proposed grouping scheme and associated power allocation algorithm, emphasizing its operational principles and complexity. Section 4 evaluates the solution via simulations, comparing its performance with that of existing methods in terms of spectral efficiency, fairness, and scalability. Finally, Sect. 5 concludes the paper and discusses potential avenues for future research.

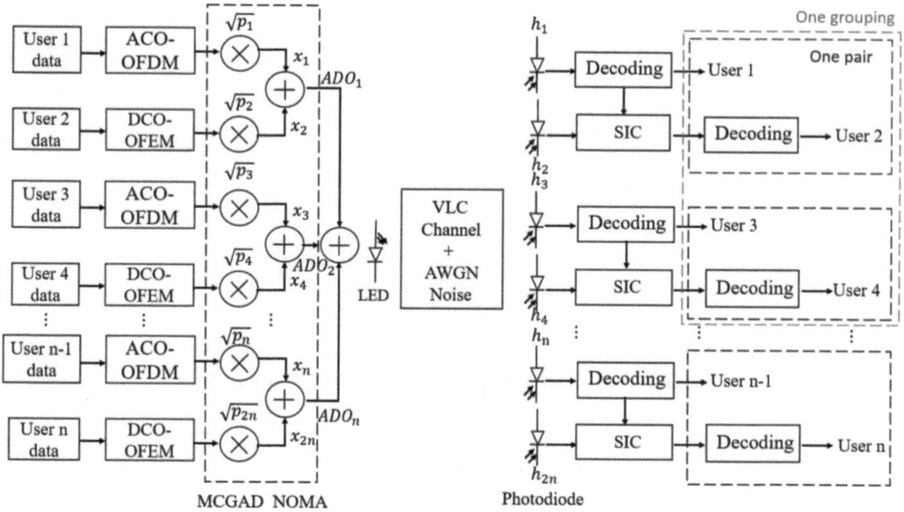

Fig. 1. Proposed MCGAD NOMA for Multi-user VLC

2 System Model

2.1 Channel Model

In this paper, the optical channel gain between the transmitter and receiver is model using

$$h = \frac{(m+1)A}{2\pi d^2} \cos^m \phi \cos \varphi \tag{1}$$

where d is the distance between the LED and the photodiode, m is the Lambertian order of the LED luminaire, ϕ is the emergence angle of the light, φ is the incident angle of the light and A is the area of the photodiode [2]. Consequently, the received signal on the user side is given by

$$y(t) = hx_{\mathrm{ADO}}(t) + n(t) \tag{2}$$

where $n(t)$ is the noise component, which is usually caused by the ambient light as well as the thermal noise within the receiver circuit, and it can be well modeled as Gaussian noise.

2.2 ADO-OFDM Transmitter and Receiver Model

Figure 2 and 3, respectively, illustrate the transmitter and receiver structures for a two-user ADO-OFDM NOMA system [3]. As shown in Fig. 2, the data intended for User 1 (located relatively far from the LED transmitter) is modulated into the asymmetrically clipped optical OFDM signal component (ACO-OFDM), which occupies only the odd subcarriers. After ensuring Hermitian symmetry for real-valued outputs, the time-domain ACO-OFDM sequence is clipped at the zero

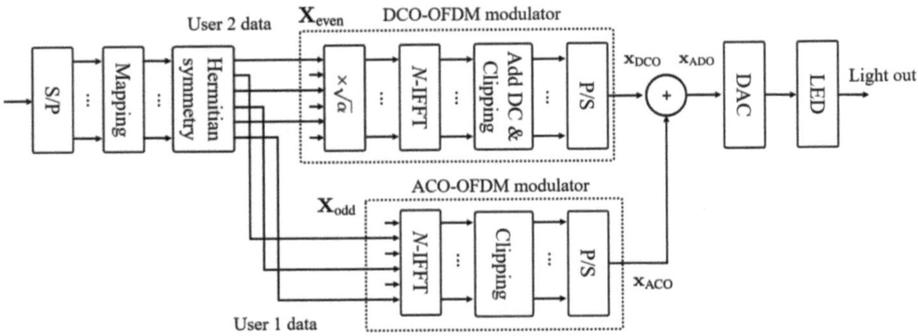

Fig. 2. Proposed ADO-OFDM NOMA Transmitter

level to enforce unipolarity suitable for IM/DD. Meanwhile, User 2's data (closer to the LED transmitter) is carried by the DC-biased optical OFDM (DCO-OFDM) component on the even subcarriers. A power allocation coefficient, α, is introduced to balance the power ratio between these two components, followed by a DC bias added to shift the DCO-OFDM waveform above zero. The two OFDM signals are then superimposed in the time domain to form $x_{\text{ADO},n}$, which is subsequently converted by a digital-to-analog converter (DAC) into an electrical signal, $x_{\text{ADO}}(t)$, used to drive the LED.

On the receiver side (Fig. 3), both users receive the same ADO-OFDM signal, albeit under different channel conditions. User 1 (the far user) performs conventional OFDM demodulation on the odd subcarriers after channel equalization to retrieve its QAM symbols directly. In contrast, User 2 (the near user) employs successive interference cancellation (SIC). First, it estimates and reconstructs the far user's ACO–OFDM component including the clipping noise that falls on the even subcarriers then subtracts this interference from its received signal. The residual signal is finally demodulated on the even subcarriers, thus recovering User 2's data. This ADO-OFDM NOMA framework strikes a balance between spectral efficiency and power utilization, allowing two users with distinct channel conditions to be served concurrently by a single LED transmitter.

2.3 MCGAD NOMA

In practice, VLC networks often encounter varying traffic demands and changing user activity. To address these dynamics, we propose an integrated MCGAD NOMA framework that extends two-user ADO-OFDM NOMA to larger multi-user systems. As illustrated in Fig. 1, multiple users are partitioned into pairs, each forming a two-user ADO block, and these blocks are then superimposed in the power domain.

Let $n \geq 4$ be the total number of users, with $k \geq 2$ such that $n = 2k$. Hence, k two-user ADO blocks coexist. If $S^{\text{ado}}_{(n,k)}(t)$ represents the aggregated multi-user

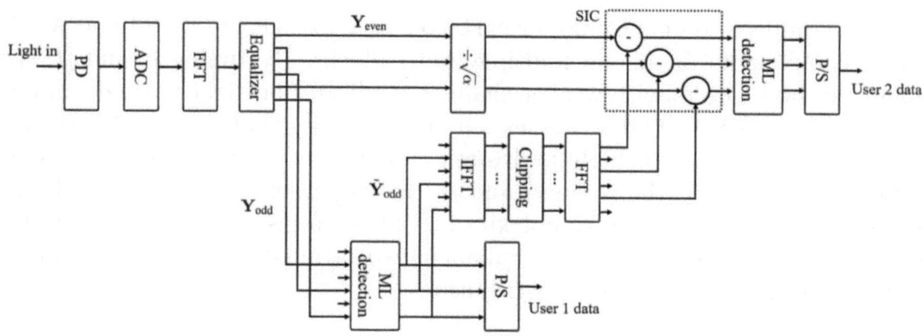

Fig. 3. Proposed ADO-OFDM NOMA Receiver

ADO signal, then one possible form is

$$S_{(n,k)}^{\text{ado}}(t) = \sqrt{\frac{p_{n-3}}{p_{n-2}}}\, x_{k-1}^{\text{ado}}(t) + \sqrt{\frac{p_{n-1}}{p_n}}\, x_k^{\text{ado}}(t), \tag{3}$$

where p_i are power-allocation coefficients for User i, and $x_j^{\text{ado}}(t)$ is the ADO waveform of the j-th two-user pair. For $n = 4$, $k = 2$, as an example:

$$S_{(4,2)}^{\text{ado}}(t) = \sqrt{\frac{p_1}{p_2}}\, x_1^{\text{ado}}(t) + \sqrt{\frac{p_3}{p_4}}\, x_2^{\text{ado}}(t). \tag{4}$$

Each two-user block itself consists of:

$$x_{(n-k)}^{\text{ado}}(t) = \sqrt{p_{n-1}}\, x_{n-1}(t) + \sqrt{p_n}\, x_n(t), \tag{5}$$

where $x_{n-1}(t)$ and $x_n(t)$ denote the baseband signals for Users $n-1$ and n. For instance, $x_2^{\text{ado}}(t)$ in the four-user case would combine $x_3(t)$ and $x_4(t)$ as

$$x_2^{\text{ado}}(t) = \sqrt{p_3}\, x_3(t) + \sqrt{p_4}\, x_4(t). \tag{6}$$

Meanwhile, the total power assigned to each ADO block can be written as

$$p_T = \sum_{i=1}^{k} p_i^{\text{ado}}, \tag{7}$$

where p_i^{ado} is the aggregate power for the i-th ADO pair. For example,

$$s_1^{\text{ado}}(t) = \sqrt{p_1}\, x_1(t) + \sqrt{p_2}\, x_2(t), \quad s_2^{\text{ado}}(t) = \sqrt{p_3}\, x_3(t) + \sqrt{p_4}\, x_4(t), \tag{8}$$

indicates two superposed ADO signals when $n = 4$.

To maintain flexibility, additional ratios such as

$$\alpha = \frac{p_n}{p_{n-1}}, \quad \beta = \frac{p_k^{\text{ado}}}{p_{k-1}^{\text{ado}}},$$

may be introduced to manage power partitioning across DCO-OFDM and ACO-OFDM components or among multiple ADO blocks. By tuning α and β, the system can boost users with weaker channel conditions or higher rate demands.

Overall, MCGAD NOMA enables a hybrid strategy that links multiple two-user ADO pairs into a scalable multi-user design. Through appropriate power coefficients $\{p_i^{\text{ado}}\}$ and the ratios α and β, this approach balances throughput, fairness, and implementation complexity in VLC systems. As a result, MCGAD NOMA offers a unified solution for enhancing spectral efficiency while adapting to various traffic loads and user distributions.

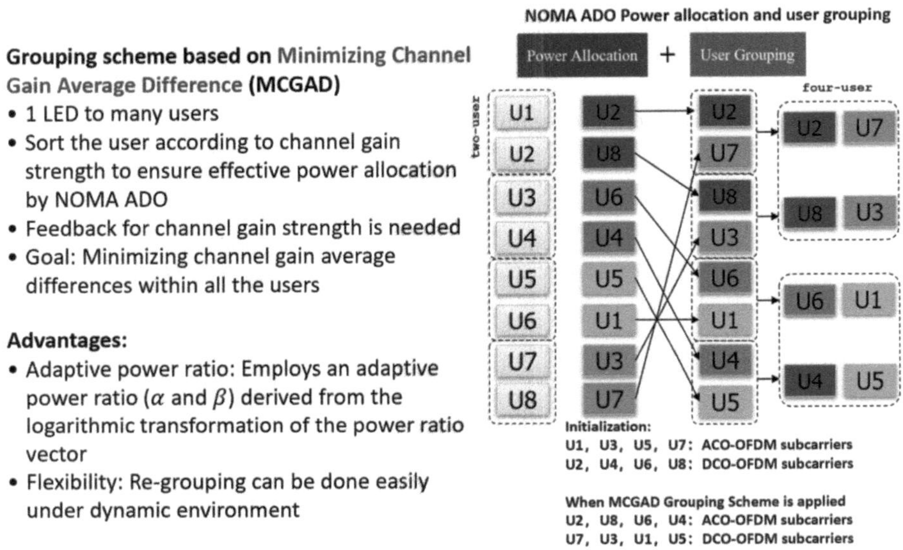

Fig. 4. Proposed grouping scheme for MCGAD NOMA for multi-user VLC

2.4 Grouping Scheme

As shown in Fig. 4, our MCGAD-based grouping scheme for multi-user VLC networks begins by collecting user parameters such as their line-of-sight channel gains (h_{LOS}) and the total available power (P_{total}). Each user is sorted by channel gain, and an initial assignment places them on either ACO- or DCO-OFDM subcarriers according to relative channel strength. A threshold Δ_{avg} is defined to gauge how evenly channel gains are distributed across the network. Next, an iterative procedure refines two adjustable power ratios, (α, β), so that users with weaker channels receive enough power to maintain acceptable performance, while stronger users avoid unnecessary over-allocation. After each update, the algorithm checks whether the average channel-gain difference remains above or below the threshold. If room for improvement is detected, users may be re-paired or shifted between ACO and DCO layers; otherwise, the final grouping and power allocation are determined and the algorithm concludes.

This process effectively captures the logic previously illustrated by a more detailed flow diagram: first, user information is gathered and sorted, then a targeted optimization of power distribution is carried out. If the outcome meets the desired fairness or throughput objectives, no further refinement is needed. Otherwise, additional checks and reassignments continue until the system converges. By employing this adaptive mechanism, MCGAD NOMA is able to accommodate evolving user positions or traffic loads, ensuring robust performance in large number of users VLC.

3 Simulation Parameters

In our simulations, we consider a 5 m × 5 m × 3 m indoor environment, where an LED luminaire is centrally positioned on the ceiling at a height of 2.5 m above the floor. User devices are placed on a plane 0.75 m above the floor, leaving a vertical separation of 1.75 m between the LED and the users. The LED is assumed to have a Lambertian order of 1, providing broad coverage, as verified by its radiation pattern depicted in Fig. 5. According to the simulated results, the greatest light intensity and thus the highest channel gain occur near the center of the room, while these values decrease toward the room's corners. In this setup, the channel gain is on the order of 10^{-7}.

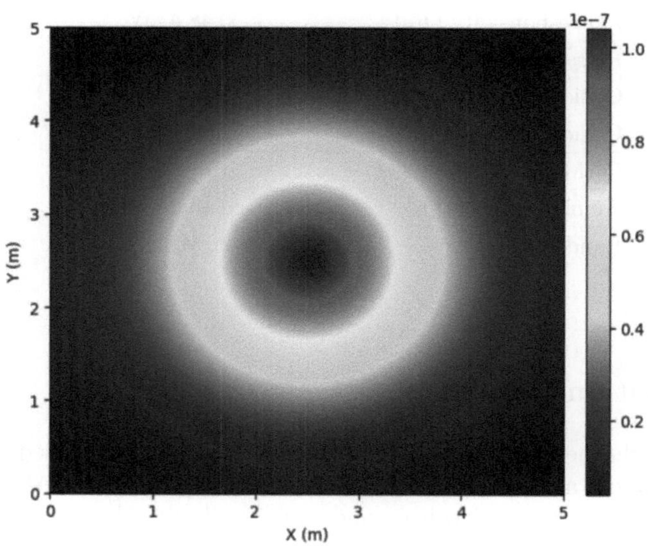

Fig. 5. Channel gain (Lambertian order = 1)

To evaluate the performance of the proposed MCGAD NOMA system, we consider a representative configuration of user positions, as illustrated in Fig. 4.

In the simulation, we use 8 users as an example. These 8 users are first ranked based on their channel conditions. For instance, User 2 has the highest channel gain, while User 7 has the lowest channel gain. The users are then grouped into pairs according to the grouping strategy shown in the figure. Specifically, Users 2, 7, 8, and 3 are within one group. Within this group, User 2 and User 7 form one pair, while User 8 and User 3 form another pair.

For each pair, ADO-OFDM NOMA is applied. Two ADO-OFDM signals are generated for the group, where each signal carries the data intended for all four users. These two ADO-OFDM signals are then superimposed, resulting in a single signal capable of carrying the data for the entire group.

The detailed simulation parameters are summarized in Table 1.

Table 1. Simulation Parameters and Settings

Parameter	Value
Room size	5.0 m, 5.0 m, 3.0 m
Position of the LED	2.5 m, 2.5 m, 2.5 m
Light emission height of the LED	2.5 m
LED half-power angle ($\phi_{1/2}$)	60°
Lambertian order (m)	1
PD field-of-view angle (ψ_{FOV})	45°
Physical area of size PD	0.5 mm × 0.5 mm
PD responsivity (R_p)	0.48 A/W
Refractive index of concentrator (n)	1.5
Optical filter gain (T_s)	1
Optical power of LED	1 W
QAM constellation size	16
Number of users (n)	4 to 20
Bandwidth	20 MHz

4 Simulation Results

To evaluate the performance of the proposed ADO-OFDM-based NOMA system, we analyze a multi-user VLC scenario using the MCGAD (Minimized Channel-Gain Disparity) algorithm and compare it with the conventional ADO-OFDM NOMA and MCGD (Maximizing Channel Gain Difference) algorithms. MCGD groups users by maximizing channel gain differences within subsets, while MCGAD clusters users with similar channel conditions to minimize power disparity and iteratively adjusts power allocation parameters α and β.

Simulation results demonstrate that the proposed MCGAD algorithm consistently outperforms conventional ADO-OFDM NOMA and MCGD in terms

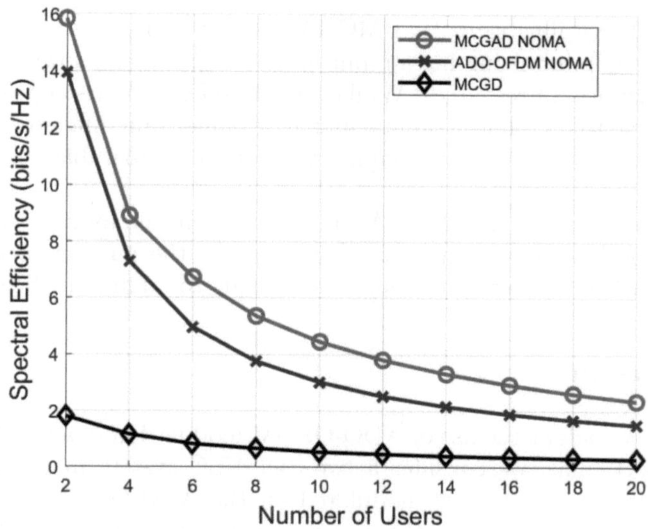

Fig. 6. Performance of spectral efficiency for multi-user VLC scenario

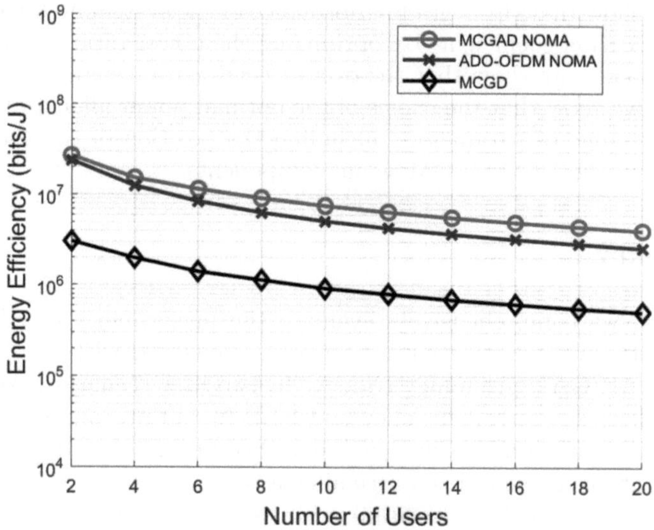

Fig. 7. Performance of energy efficiency for multi-user VLC scenario

of both spectral efficiency (SE) and energy efficiency (EE) across varying numbers of users. As shown in Fig. 7, MCGAD maintains higher energy efficiency compared to the other methods, even as the number of users increases. This highlights its ability to mitigate power losses and maintain energy-efficient operation under multi-user scenarios.

Similarly, Fig. 6 illustrates that MCGAD achieves significantly better spectral efficiency by minimizing intra-group power disparities, allowing for a more balanced utilization of resources. While MCGD suffers from steep performance degradation due to its reliance on maximizing channel gain differences, MCGAD ensures stable performance by grouping users with comparable channel conditions.

These results confirm that MCGAD is a robust solution for improving SE and EE in dynamic VLC environments, particularly as the number of users scales beyond four, where conventional methods struggle to maintain efficiency.

5 Conclusion

In this paper, we adapt the use of ADO-OFDM modulation in a multi-user VLC system. In particular, we consider a two-user VLC system in which the data transmitted for the far user is modulated on the ACO-OFDM signal component, and the data intended for the near user is modulated on the DCO-OFDM component. Considering similar methodologies used in NOMA, the signal components intended for different users are assigned different power levels. Our simulation results show that the overall performance of the system highly depends on the power allocation coefficient. By optimizing the power ratio between the two signal components, we show that the overall BER can be significantly reduced. Additionally, we show that the choice of the optimal power allocation coefficient depends on a range of parameters, including the position of the users and the clipping level in the DCO-OFDM signal components.

6 Summary

In this paper, we comprehensively evaluate the performance of ADO-OFDM NOMA in both two-user and multi-user VLC scenarios, with an emphasis on the proposed MCGAD grouping strategy. In two-user scenarios, ADO-OFDM effectively balances spectral efficiency and BER by optimizing power allocation through the α parameter. However, as the user count increases, multi-user interference necessitates advanced resource allocation.

The proposed MCGAD algorithm addresses this challenge by minimizing channel gain disparities within groups and adaptively adjusting parameters α and β. Simulation results demonstrate that MCGAD achieves higher throughput, better fairness, and more stable BER compared to conventional MCGD and ADO-OFDM baselines. These gains make MCGAD particularly effective in high-load environments, such as indoor VLC systems with many users.

Overall, the results confirm the potential of combining ADO-OFDM's modulation efficiency with advanced NOMA scheduling strategies like MCGAD, providing a pathway for scalable and robust VLC networks with enhanced performance in diverse channel conditions.

Acknowledgements. This work was supported by the 2025–2026 Key Research Project of Chongqing College of International Business and Economics (Grant No. KYZK2025004).

References

1. Chi, N., Zhou, Y., Wei, Y., Hu, F.: Visible light communication in 6G: advances, challenges, and prospects. IEEE Veh. Technol. Mag. **15**(4), 93–102 (2020)
2. He, C., Wang, T.Q., Armstrong, J.: Performance of optical receivers using photodetectors with different fields of view in a MIMO ACO-OFDM system. J. Lightwave Technol. **33**(23), 4957–4967 (2015)
3. Tu, Y., He, C., Lim, Y., Tan, Y.: Performance of asymmetrically clipped dc biased optical OFDM in a NOMA-based visible light communication system. IEICE Tech. Rep. **124**(107), 7–11 (2024)
4. Ohnai, K.: Basic technology of optical wireless OFDM system. WBS Res. Group Proposal **13**(1), 38–46 (2019)
5. Armstrong, J., Lowery, A.J.: Power efficient optical OFDM. Electron. Lett. **42**(6), 370–372 (2006)
6. Dissanayake, S.D., Armstrong, J.: Comparison of ACO-OFDM, DCO-OFDM and ADO-OFDM in IM/DD systems. J. Lightwave Technol. **31**(7), 1063–1072 (2013)
7. He, C., Armstrong, J.: Clipping noise mitigation in optical OFDM systems. IEEE Commun. Lett. **21**(3), 548–551 (2016)
8. Armstrong, J.: OFDM for optical communications. J. Lightwave Technol. **27**(3), 189–204 (2009)
9. OK, H.S., Sah, A.K.: Multi-user grouping for NOMA enabled VLC system. IEEE Commun. Lett.**28**(5), 1072–1076 (2024)
10. Chi, J., Qiu, T., Xiao, F., Zhou, X.: ATOM: adaptive task offloading with two-stage hybrid matching in MEC-enabled industrial IoT. IEEE Trans. Mob. Comput. **23**(5), 4861–4877 (2024)
11. Chi, J., Zhou, X., Xiao, F., Qiu, T., Chen, C.L.P.: Enhancing adaptability and efficiency of task offloading by broad learning in industrial IoT. IEEE Trans. Netw. Sci. Eng. **12**(1), 263–276 (2025)
12. Chi, J., Zhou, X., Xiao, F., Lim, Y., Qiu, T.: Task offloading via prioritized experience-based double dueling DQN in edge-assisted IIoT. IEEE Trans. Mob. Comput. **23**(12), 14575–14591 (2024)

Educational Technology and Emerging DomainsTeaching

Teaching Framework for UAV-Related Courses in Low-Altitude Economy Based on PDCA Cycle and DRL

Yunchong Guan[1,2,3](✉), Liang Zhao[1], Xiguang Li[1], Junling Shi[1], Qian Wang[2,4], Haibo Yang[2,4], Ammar Hawbani[1], Hongkun Qiu[1], Yipeng Cao[1], Yanju Dong[1], Guiying Meng[1], Na Lin[1], Yunhe Sun[1], and Cunqian Yu[1]

[1] Shenyang Aerospace University, Shenyang 110136, China
[2] Shenyang Fengchi Software Co. Ltd., Shenyang 110167, China
[3] Dalian University of Technology, Dalian 116081, China
ycguan@sau.edu.cn
[4] Shenyang University of Technology, Shenyang 110801, China

Abstract. The low-altitude economy is empowering various industries, with UAV (Unmanned Aerial Vehicle) serving as the primary technological support. Relevant technical theories present new challenges for engineering talent cultivation in universities. This paper proposes an innovative teaching framework that integrates the PDCA (Plan-Do-Check-Act) cycle with DRL (Deep Reinforcement Learning). This framework continuously optimizes teaching objectives, content, and methods through the PDCA+DRL method, and uses DRL in the evaluation phase to enhance multi-dimensional assessment capabilities. Statistical analysis of UAV teaching practice cases indicates that this model can improve teaching effectiveness and provides a reference for teaching reform for UAV-related courses in low-altitude economy.

Keywords: Low-Altitude Economy · Unmanned Aerial Vehicle · Plan-Do-Check-Act cycle · Deep Reinforcement Learning · Teaching Reform

1 Introduction

As the low-altitude economy emerges as a global strategic emerging industry, it has empowered diverse fields [1], and is profoundly reshaping industry competition and gradually forming new industrial forms, including logistics, air mobility, etc. The forecasts show China's low-altitude economy scale will exceed 1.5 trillion RMB yuan by 2025, creating a demand for millions of interdisciplinary talents. UAV (Unmanned Aerial Vehicle), due to its immense potential in areas like smart logistics, has become a frontier trend in the fields of artificial intelligence and autonomous systems [2].

Universities worldwide are building related courses but commonly face multiple challenges: 1) high technical barriers, related intelligent system technologies

J. Chi et al. (Eds.): CNETCNED 2025, CCIS 2809, pp. 175–182, 2026.
https://doi.org/10.1007/978-981-95-7124-6_14

and theories are required, 2) practice disconnect, experiments are needed for practical operations, 3) evaluation lag, teaching effectiveness assessment is singular, lacking evaluations of the systematic knowledge cultivation and application innovation. Simultaneously, engineering education accreditation emphasizes cultivating the "ability to solve complex engineering problems," necessitating deep innovation in teaching models. How to resolve these pain points and construct an efficient, cutting-edge, and assessable UAV-related courses teaching system has become an urgent teaching reform task [4]. Eddye et al. develop navigations for UAV education [5]. Manfred employs AI to gain competition in PDCA-based management [6]. Chen et al. consider multiple intelligence for teaching evaluation [7]. Lin et al. use DRL (Deep Reinforcement Learning) for optimal management strategies [8]. The above work has not considered PDCA with DRL to optimize strategies in each cycle. This paper integrates the classical PDCA cycle (Plan-Do-Check-Act) [3] with the advanced artificial intelligence technology DRL, attempting to pioneer a new path for teaching reform.

2 Related Technologies

(1) PDCA Cycle: Educational Process Management for Continuous Improvement

Proposed by Deming, the PDCA is a core methodology for pursuing continuous improvement, enables dynamic optimal improvement of teaching quality [3].

Plan: design teaching objectives, content, and establish evaluation criteria.

Do: execute the plan, including theoretical learning, experiments, and project.

Check: Assess student learning results through multi-dimensional areas.

Act: Analyze the causes of deviations, optimize teaching objectives, content, and methods, and enter the next cycle.

(2) DRL: Multi-Dimensional Evaluation and Optimization

DRL combines the associative representation capabilities of deep learning with the iterative optimization capabilities of reinforcement learning [9]. It can rapidly establish a robust evaluation model integrating multi-dimensional indicators through simple iterations based on data and effects, allowing flexible definitions. Multi-dimensional evaluations are used as rewards to express students' multifaceted abilities, different learning stages as the state space, teaching strategies as the action space.

3 The PDCA+DRL Teaching Framework

The PDCA+DRL based teaching framework is shown in Fig. 1. The Plan phase involves objective-oriented decomposition of teaching tasks. The Do phase involves the implementation of the decomposed tasks aligned with objectives. The Check phase involves optimization based on a multi-dimensional evaluation system. The Act phase involves feedback-based spiral optimization for the next cycle.

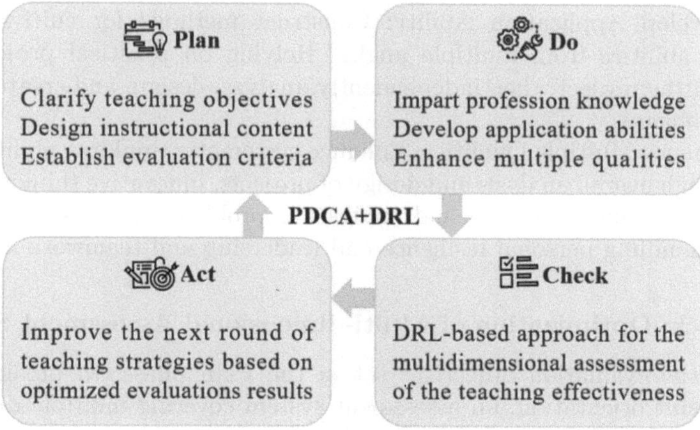

Fig. 1. The PDCA+DRL based teaching framework

3.1 Plan: Objective-Oriented Teaching Task Decomposition

In the planning phase, the teaching process is designed, to clarify teaching objectives, design teaching content, and establish evaluation criteria.

(1) Clarify Teaching Objectives: Cultivate students to master UAV-related technologies and theoretical knowledge oriented towards the low-altitude economy, develop the ability to apply knowledge and experience to solve practical engineering problems, foster systems thinking, innovative awareness, and teamwork spirit.

(2) Design Instructional Content: Foundational UAV-related technologies and theories in the low-altitude economy, specific tools and platforms for UAV practice and application; solutions for applying UAV to solve practical problems; basic scientific research methods and processes for participating in competitions.

(3) Establish Evaluation Criteria: Multi-dimensional evaluation criteria for students, including degree of mastering technical theoretical knowledge, proficiency in using related practical tools, ability to independently analyze, design, and solve practical problems, to independently conduct innovative scientific research [10].

3.2 Do: Implementation of Objective-Aligned Teaching Task Decomposition

The plan is decomposed into knowledge, ability, and literacy aspects, corresponding to specific teaching tasks during student cultivation.

(1) Impart Profession Knowledge: Construct teaching content on UAV-related technologies and theories for the low-altitude economy, including involved foundational knowledge, application platform tools, to establish a systematic course structure to lay a solid foundation for subsequent practical application.

(2) Develop Application Ability: Construct methods for cultivating and expanding abilities from multiple angles. Relying on practical projects: first understand the project, then independently analyze, design, and create projects to solve problems.

(3) Enhance Multiple Qualities: Enhance systematic thinking, ability to conduct thorough overall analysis and design of projects, innovative thinking, ability to have unique understanding and analysis of problems, proposing reasonable solutions, handling personal resilience and leadership and teamwork abilities.

3.3 Check: Optimization of Multi-dimensional Assessment System

Based on the evaluation objectives set in the Plan phase, to break through singular result orientation, an assessment system covering multiple dimensions is established, which employs DRL for evaluation and optimization.

After defining the content objects of the check and the evaluation criteria, DRL is integrated by using the check content as the input for DRL and the evaluation criteria as the reward function for DRL, thereby optimizing the evaluation model. The DRL model used for evaluation is DDPG (Deep Deterministic Policy Gradient) [11]. Figure 2 shows the DDPG-based multi-dimensional teaching effectiveness evaluation method.

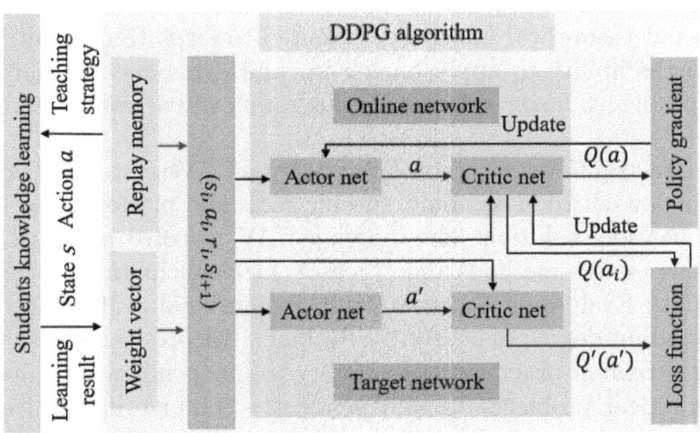

Fig. 2. DDPG-based multi-dimensional teaching effectiveness evaluation method

The executed actions is set as the degree of attention (weight) given to different teaching contents, representing the emphasis during the cultivation process, as shown in Formula (1), where Ei is the evaluation content for the i-th item, Pi is the importance weight for the i-th evaluation point Ci. The learning reward R is set as the weighted sum of student test and assessment results, including degree of mastery of technical theory, project understanding, solving practical problems and project outcomes, conducting scientific research. As shown in Formula (2), Wj is the impact weight for the j-th evaluation result point Gj. The state is the accumulated evaluation results across various dimensions at different stages.

$$E_i = P_i \times C_i\,, \quad \left(\sum_{0 \le i \le n} P_i = 1,\ P_i \in [0,1] \right) \tag{1}$$

$$R = \sum_{0 \le j \le m} W_j \times G_j\,, \quad \left(\sum_{0 \le j \le m} W_j = 1,\ W_j \in [0,1] \right) \tag{2}$$

3.4 Act: Feedback-Based Spiral Optimization for the Next PDCA Cycle

Based on the evaluation results, targeted adjustments is made to related strategies by improving the relevant planning and implementation processes, to improve and optimize evaluation results in the next PDCA cycle iteratively.

According to the calculated evaluation scores, by adjusting the allocated importance weights, the scores derived from the DRL network are made to exceed the current scores by a certain proportion. Changes in importance weights reveal the direction for subsequent adjustments, which are the aspects requiring targeted improvement in the next cycle.

4 Teaching Practice Case: UAV Swarm Navigation Project

4.1 Teaching Task Description

The teaching method is combining theory and applied practice, using specific UAV application cases oriented in the low-altitude economy, to cultivate students' multi-dimensional abilities in related fields. The research scenario is set in an environment with buildings distributed along different streets, trees, and randomly appearing obstacles. UAVs are equipped with GPS navigation, cameras, and LiDAR sensors for positioning and environmental perception. A swarm of 5 UAVs flies in formation from a starting position to a target position. Relevant algorithms for navigation and obstacle avoidance are implemented to achieve the swarm's formation flight, autonomous navigation, and obstacle avoidance capabilities.

4.2 PDCA+DRL Cultivation Process Design

(1) Plan: The teaching content is to master UAV project using the Airsim simulation platform, including overall framework design, UAV-related technologies, theories and algorithms, and simulation implementation to achieve UAV swarm navigation. Finally, a new project task is assigned to enhance students' independent innovation ability. The teaching period is 3 weeks, conducted in groups of 2-3 students per group, culminating in a defense assessment for acceptance.

(2) Do: The knowledge includes UAV flight control, swarm formation methods, sensor data acquisition and processing, machine learning-based path planning and obstacle avoidance algorithms, Airsim simulation platform project implementation, UAV-related scientific research innovation fields and idea.

(3) Check: To obtain evaluation content and assessment results with different weights, stage-based assessment evaluations are conducted for students during the teaching process. Stage-based defense scoring is performed including mastery of technical theoretical knowledge, understanding of algorithms, problem analysis and solution design, specific practical application in the project, and innovation ability. Each item is scored in 5-point, assessed weekly.

(4) Act: Based on the obtained evaluation scores, the improvement is to adjust teaching strategies to obtain higher scores, that is, to determine different allocation weights based on the strategic importance of teaching content. For content with larger weights, focus more on designing subsequent improved teaching content to enhance evaluation effectiveness, thereby influencing the next PDCA cycle.

5 Teaching Effectiveness Evaluation

Based on the teaching practice case, according to the weekly teaching progress, different teaching strategies were set to influence the emphasis on different teaching contents. The evaluation results of different teaching strategies were statistically analyzed to verify the effectiveness of the PDCA+DRL teaching innovation framework.

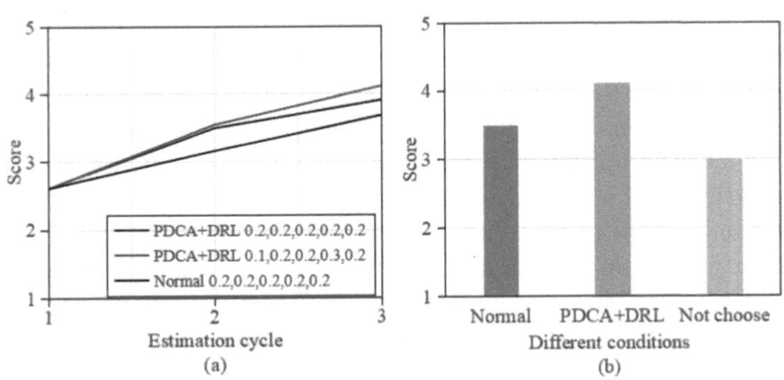

Fig. 3. (a) Scores for PDCA+DRL with different weights and normal teaching methods; (b) Scores for PDCA+DRL, normal and students not choosing this practice course

Figure 3(a) shows the student evaluation scores at different stages across multiple teaching processes for three methods, namely, PDCA+DRL with different weights and normal method without PDCA+DRL. As teaching gradually accumulates, student scores gradually increase, and the PDCA+DRL methods demonstrate more improvement. Therefore, the proposed method gets a positive teaching effect. Figure 3(b) shows the final student evaluation scores for three methods, namely, with and without PDCA+DRL, and students not choosing this practice course. Students choosing the course get higher scores and this means the course contributes to the cultivation for UAV-related course in low-altitude economy. The PDCA+DRL method performing better than others also shows the effectiveness of the proposed method.

6 Conclusion

This paper proposes a PDCA+DRL based teaching framework and applies it to a UAV application practice teaching case for the low-altitude economy. Utilizing the strong association and representation capabilities of DRL, the multi-dimensional evaluation method is further optimized. Within the iterative cycles of PDCA, learning effectiveness was effectively improved, providing a reference for the teaching reform of related courses for the low-altitude economy.

Acknowledgements. This work was supported in part by the Fundamental Research Funds for the Universities of Liaoning Province under Grant LJ212510143015.

References

1. Yang, J., et al.: A case study on the development and application of low-altitude economy in agriculture in china: Based on demand supply-environment perspective. Academic J. Bus. Manage. **6**(9), 168–176 (2024)
2. Xiaoya Z., et al.: UAV swarm-enabled collaborative post-disaster communications in low altitude economy via a two-stage optimization approach. IEEE Trans. Mob. Comput., 1–18 (2025)
3. Jun, H., Chaoju, T.: A developed plan-do-check-act and contextual teaching and learning model. In: 14th International Conference on Quality. Reliability, Risk, Maintenance, and Safety Engineering, pp. 1–4. Harbin, China (2024)
4. Abdelrahman A., et al.: Integrating drones into STEM education at Al Hussein Technical University. In: 22nd International Conference on Research and Education in Mechatronics, 113-118. Amman, Jordan (2024)
5. Eddye V., et al.: Evaluation of YOLOv8n as a suitable tool for UAV navigation. In: 22nd International Conference on Research and Education in Mechatronics, pp. 262–267, Amman, Jordan (2024)
6. Manfred, S.: Artificial-Intelligence-driven management. IEEE Eng. Manage. Rev. **48**(2), 15–19 (2020)
7. Chen W., et al.: Portfolio assessment method: a new model of multiple intelligences theory in the evaluation of undergraduate teaching effectiveness. In: 14th International Conference on Information Technology in Medicine and Education, pp. 832–838, Guiyang, China (2024)
8. Lin, F., et al.: A DDPG algorithm for portfolio management. In: 19th International Symposium on Distributed Computing and Applications for Business Engineering and Science, pp. 222–225, Xuzhou, China (2020)

9. Liu, Y., et al.: Service function chain embedding meets machine learning: deep reinforcement learning approach. IEEE Trans. Netw. Serv. Manage. **21**(3), 3465–3481 (2024)
10. Choi, S.: Industry insights on future convergence education: a survey of key competencies and educational directions. In: 2024 IEEE Global Engineering Education Conference 1-3, Kos Island, Greece (2024)
11. Zhang, L., et al.: A state-decomposition ddpg algorithm for uav autonomous navigation in 3-D complex environments. IEEE Internet Things J. **11**(6), 10778–10790 (2024)

Author Index

J. Chi et al. (Eds.): CNETCNED 2025, CCIS 2809, pp. 183–184, 2026.
https://doi.org/10.1007/978-981-95-7124-6

MIX
Papier aus verantwortungsvollen Quellen
Paper from responsible sources
FSC® C105338

If you have any concerns about our products,
you can contact us on
ProductSafety@springernature.com

In case Publisher is established outside the EU,
the EU authorized representative is:
Springer Nature Customer Service Center GmbH
Europaplatz 3, 69115 Heidelberg, Germany

Printed by Libri Plureos GmbH
in Hamburg, Germany